STATE DEATH

STATE DEATH

THE POLITICS AND GEOGRAPHY
OF CONQUEST, OCCUPATION, AND ANNEXATION

Tanisha M. Fazal

PRINCETON UNIVERSITY PRESS   PRINCETON AND OXFORD

Published by Princeton University Press,
41 William Street, Princeton, New Jersey 08540

In the United Kingdom: Princeton University Press,
3 Market Place, Woodstock, Oxfordshire OX20 1SY

Library of Congress Cataloging-in-Publication Data

Fazal, Tanisha M.
  State death : the politics and geography of conquest, occupation, and annexation /
Tanisha M. Fazal.
     p. cm.
  Includes bibliographical references and index.
  ISBN-13: 978-0-691-12986-0 (hardcover : alk. paper)
  ISBN-10: 0-691-12986-X (hardcover : alk. paper)
  ISBN-13: 978-0-691-13460-4 (paperback : alk. paper)
  ISBN-10: 0-691-13460-X (paperback : alk. paper)
  1. Geopolicitics— History— 20th century.   2. Political geography.   3. Buffer states.
4. Sovereignty—history.   I. Title.
  JC319.F39   2007
  327.11′7— dc22

                                                                                              2006101828

British Library Cataloging-in-Publication Data is available

This book has been composed in Sabon
Printed on acid-free paper. ∞
press.princeton.edu

Printed in the United States of America

10 9 8 7 6 5 4 3 2 1

TO MY GRANDPARENTS:

ALEXANDRINE, MARIAM, PABLO, AND SHAMSHU

Contents

Figures

Tables _____

Acknowledgments

When I decided to research state death, I knew that understanding this phenomenon would require a long, arduous journey. I was right: from late nights in Palo Alto, Cambridge, and New York to dusty archives in Aix, London, and Austin, I have learned more and slept less than I would have ever anticipated. What I did not expect was that the journey would hold such joy for me. I attribute this in part to my good luck in being able to do what I love doing, but mostly to the wonderful people who have helped me through this process. I regret only that I am sure to omit many of them in what follows, and hope that they will accept my apology for doing so.

At Stanford, where I began researching state death for my dissertation, I was extraordinarily lucky to have Scott Sagan and Steve Krasner as cochairs of my dissertation committee. Both gave consistently sage advice, supporting me every step of the way. I am particularly grateful for Scott's thoughtful and caring mentorship—he is the best model I know as both teacher and scholar, and I will be striving to emulate him throughout my career. Jim Fearon, who joined the Stanford faculty after I began research, nonetheless had a remarkable impact on this project, sharpening my thinking about the issues at hand every time we spoke. And Simon Jackman was incredibly patient with my deluge of questions about duration analysis and quantitative methods in general. My cohort at Stanford, especially Anu Kulkarni, Svetlana Tsalik, Sybil Rhodes, Sara Pritchard, Sean Theriault, Ron Hassner, Will Howell, and Dave Lewis, were critical and generous sounding boards throughout my graduate career. By the time my dissertation had begun to take form, I was spending most of my time at Stanford's Center for International Security and Cooperation, which served as a wonderful home for me as I conducted predoctoral research. Conversations with two groups of fellows at CISAC, including Risa Brooks, David Edelstein, Ann Hironaka, Jeremy Suri, and Barry O'Neill, shaped my thinking about state death in critical ways. And Lynn Eden's support and friendship were key bulwarks from the time I first stepped into Galvez House to cleaning out my desk in Encina upon graduation.

During a postdoctoral year at the Olin Institute for Strategic Studies, I was fortunate to continue to receive valuable feedback from Monica Duffy Toft, Steve Rosen, Ajin Choi, Jacques Hymans, and Kevin Narizny, among other colleagues. I am also grateful to participants in seminars and workshops at the University of California San Diego, Yale University, the George Washington University, the University of Chicago, the University of Virginia Law School, Georgetown University, and Duke University.

I completed this book as an assistant professor at Columbia University, where I have found an unparalleled intellectual home. My colleagues at Columbia are tremendous. Dick Betts, Bob Jervis, Jack Snyder, Helen Milner, Erik Gartzke, Vicky Murillo, and Melissa Schwartzberg were extremely generous with their time, reading all or part of the manuscript and offering insightful comments that forced me to rethink many key issues. Page Fortna deserves special thanks (not to mention a lifetime of free hot chocolate) for reading the manuscript twice. I also thank Ingrid Gerstmann and the staff at the Saltzman Institute for helping to make my new intellectual home such a welcoming place. I have been very lucky in my research assistants at Columbia. Brooke Greene, Suzanne Katzenstein, Thania Sanchez, and Jessica Stanton provided valuable and careful help at key moments in the project. Elizabeth Cardente collected data on terrain used in the quantitative analysis, and Bernd Beber used his mastery of GIS to produce the maps in the book.

I have been extremely fortunate in my colleagues and friends outside my home institutions, especially Nora Bensahel, Risa Brooks, David Edelstein, Marty Finnemore, Taylor Fravel, Hein Goemans, Peter Liberman, Mike Tomz, Ben Valentino, and Chris Way. All were very generous with their time and made important contributions to the argument of this book. Beth McFadden provided outstanding editorial assistance, and Natalie Ciccone was most helpful in identifying possible images for the book cover. The anonymous reviewers of the manuscript provided invaluable comments that made this work a much better book. I also thank Chuck Myers, Terri O'Prey, and Will Hively at Princeton University Press for their support and especially their understanding of the challenges of juggling the preproduction and postpartum processes. Chuck deserves special kudos for patiently shepherding this project through to its completion.

For financial support, I thank the Carnegie Corporation, the Center for International Security and Cooperation, Stanford's Social Science History Institute and Institute for International Stucies, Harvard's Olin Institute, the MacArthur Foundation, the Ford Foundation, the Lyndon B. Johnson Presidential Library, Columbia's Earth Institute, the National Science Foundation, and the Lane Foundation. Portions of this book appeared in an earlier form as "State Death in the International System," *International Organization* 58.2 (April 2004): 311–44, published here with the permission of Cambridge University Press.

I am also profoundly grateful for support I have received outside academia. My parents, Maydene and Abul Fazal, have always believed in my ability to achieve my intellectual and professional goals. My sister, Shaena, has consistently buoyed me with wit and enthusiasm. And finally, my husband, Louis Ciccone, has been my rock every step of the way—from the first paper on state death to the final version of this book. He has patiently read and commented on innumerable drafts and pushed and probed me to solve every problem he (and others) raised. He and our son, Tagore, bring more joy and laughter into my life than I could have ever imagined possible.

STATE DEATH

Chapter 1 _____

Introduction

OF ALL THE states on the map of the world in 1816, nearly half no longer exist today. The fate of these states is the subject of this book. Both as the primary form of organization in international politics and as specific actors on the global stage, states have come to be the central pillar of international relations theory and politics. And while scholars and practitioners alike have questioned whether the state as an institution will survive,[1] the survival of particular states is typically assumed and, further, assumed to be desirable. The conventional wisdom appears to be that states do not—and should not—die.

This perception is belied by both recent and distant history. The collapse of the Soviet Union was a defining moment of the late twentieth century, cementing an end to the Cold War. Less than fifty years earlier, World War II witnessed numerous attempts to "kill" other states and ended with the dismemberment of Germany. As any series of historical maps will reveal, international relations is in many ways captured by the emergence and disappearance of states in the international system.

This book addresses three main questions: (1) What is the historical record of state death? (2) Why do some states die while others survive? and (3) What explains the decline of violent state death after 1945? By "state death," I mean the formal loss of control over foreign policy making to another state. This definition distinguishes state death from cases of extreme regime change, internal state collapse, or minor territorial exchanges. Typically, state death occurs when one state takes over another, or when a state breaks up into multiple, new states. For example, the partitioning of Germany after World War II constitutes a state death, but the Cuban Revolution of 1959 does not. The British conquest of Punjab in 1846 led to the death of the Punjabi state, but even though internal collapse left the state of Somalia without clear internal authority structures, Somalia continued to exist as a member of the international system in the 1990s. Although the argument advanced here has important implications for domestic political changes, the focus is on the survival of states in the international system.

The argument of this book is that geography is a key determinant of

---

[1]See for example Strange 1996.

state death and survival—it endangers some states while securing others. Buffer states—states that lie between two other states engaged in rivalry —are particularly likely to die. Indeed, buffer states account for over 40 percent of state deaths. Each rival fears that its opponent will take over the buffer state between them and gain a strategic advantage. While both rivals might prefer to maintain the sovereignty of the buffer state so as to decrease the risk of war, the fear of losing strategic ground, coupled with the rivals' inability to trust each other *not* to encroach on the buffer, generally signal the demise of buffer states.

Under certain conditions, however, the dynamics of rivalry can be mitigated such that a buffer state survives. If the rivals' hands can be metaphorically "tied"—because their resources face serious and simultaneous constraints, because they must jointly meet another threat in a separate theater, or because buffer state sovereignty is guaranteed by even more powerful actors—buffer states can escape the fate of their fellows. But these conditions are likely to be (and historically have been) rare. They may occur with the coming of world wars, with revolution, or with the creation of new world orders. And even when buffers are protected by more powerful actors, the incentives to take them over do not disappear; the form of conquest merely changes. The post-1945 era provides an example of a superpower—the United States—sponsoring a rule against conquest that prevented rivals from taking over the buffers between them. The norm against conquest is an intervening variable that reshapes the way in which states seek to control other states. Thus, the bright-line prohibition against taking over other states has led to a proliferation of interventions to achieve ends formerly sought through conquest.

Relevance

The issue of state survival lies at the heart of international relations theory and practice. International relations scholars typically take state survival to be a minimum, and primary, goal of states, statesmen, and citizens.[2] But international relations (IR) scholarship lacks systematic, rigorous analyses of variation in state death and survival.[3]

The survival assumption is empirically verifiable. States and their citizens *do* seek survival.[4] From Haile Selassie's impassioned plea to the League of Nations in 1936 to the French resistance to German occupa-

---

[2] Adams 2000; Howes 2003; Waltz 1979.

[3] For a recent exception, see Adams 2000.

[4] Although Howes notes some unusual cases where states may prefer to give up at least some of their sovereignty. Howes 2003. Also see Rector 2003.

tion during the Second World War, loyalty to state and homeland appears to be an extremely strong motivator, one to which people have often sacrificed their lives.[5]

This push for survival is justified; state death is more frequent than scholars have believed.[6] Since 1816, 66 of 207 states have died. Fifty of these cases (over 75 percent) are instances of violent state death, which constitutes the narrower focus of this book. Violent state death occurs when one state uses military force to deprive another of its formal control over foreign policy making. Typically, violent state death occurs in the form of conquest or occupation. It is not unusual for state death to be a cause or a consequence of war. For example, the Iraqi annexation of Kuwait was the trigger for the Persian Gulf War, just as the takeover of Poland led Britain and France to join the Second World War. Following World War II, Germany was dismembered for almost five decades.

Recent events have highlighted the import of thinking seriously about state death. While the lack of scholarship on this topic may be attributed to the relative absence of state death—or, at least, violent state death—since 1945, the recent US occupation of Iraq may reverse this trend. Understanding the dynamics that may endanger some states while bolstering others has reemerged as a central problem for policy makers.

The Literature

State death is a touchstone issue for international relations theorists. I test my argument alongside three major hypotheses drawn from the international relations literature: a balancing argument drawn from realism; a social constructivist claim about the relationship between international legitimacy and state survival; and a set of arguments that suggest that states whose populations are likely to resist conquerors are most likely to survive.

State death plays a fundamental, yet underappreciated, role in neorealism. A basic premise of realist arguments is that states will balance against power; when faced with external threats, states should build up their militaries and seek alliances. Kenneth Waltz, in his famous explication of neorealism, works from the assumptions that states seek survival and that anarchy is the governing principle of the international system.[7] The assumption of rationality is also frequently ascribed to Waltz's work, but the rationality of states or state actors is not a neorealist assumption. In-

[5]Goemans 2003.
[6]Waltz 1979; Wendt 1999, 279.
[7]Waltz 1979, chs. 5–6.

stead, neorealists avoid making a strict rationality assumption by making a selection argument: states that "do not help themselves, or who do so less effectively than others, will fail to prosper, will lay themselves open to danger, will suffer."[8] At the same time, neorealists assert that the death rate of states is low.[9] If irrational behavior is punished by death, and the death rate of states is low, neorealists claim, then states must behave as if they were rational. Even if we take the assumptions as empirically correct, the logic behind the deduction is shaky at best. Not all states face equal threats and, further, power and alliances—which are the preferred form of balancing for neorealists—may attract (or indicate) rather than deter threats to survival.[10]

In addition, if selection pressures are as acute as neorealism suggests, the rate of state death should be high, not low.[11] The fact that the rate of state death is higher than previous scholars have assumed does not, however, necessarily support the neorealist balancing argument. I show that the strong relationship between power, alliances, and state survival suggested by this argument does not exist. This finding does not necessarily lead to a conclusive rejection of the balancing argument. Death in the international system could take many forms, from a decline in power to a regime change to state death—I test the application of this argument only to punishment by state death. But my findings do illustrate that balancing behavior does not govern state death and survival.

Unlike realists, constructivists do not assume or conclude that states behave rationally. According to constructivists, states and state actors socially construct their world such that certain actions are permissible and others are forbidden. For example, David Strang and Alexander Wendt have argued that states confer degrees of international legitimacy on other (aspiring) state actors.[12] Some of these actors are designated as being in the "in-group" while others are in the "out-group." This distinction among actors is accompanied by different rules of behavior. To conquer and occupy an illegitimate state is permissible, while conquest of a "legitimate" state is taboo and will be punished. Using a new measure of international legitimacy, and by adding previously ignored states to standard data sets, I find considerable support for this argument. Indeed, the claim that more legitimate states are more likely to survive could be consistent with the argument that a norm against conquest has prevented violent state death after 1945. Particularly if the standards for international

---

[8]Waltz 1979, 118.
[9]Waltz 1979, 138; see also Wendt 1999, 279.
[10]Alastair Smith 1995.
[11]Setear 2004.
[12]Strang 1991; Wendt 1999.

recognition of states have been more liberal in the post-1945 era, the general norm against conquest and the specific norm against conquest of legitimate states may have become congruent.

The issue of state death is also relevant for a third set of arguments from comparative politics and international relations theory—what I will call the "nationalist resistance" argument. Proponents of this argument have suggested that nationalistic societies will generate particularly high costs for states that conquer them.[13] The resistance to conquest inspired in these particularly nationalistic states would make conquest untenable. Would-be conquerors, behaving strategically, thus avoid taking over states whose populations would generate high levels of resistance. The logic of this argument, as Peter Liberman suggests, may be incomplete because nationalism often coexists with industrialization.[14] The infrastructure that characterizes industrialized states may actually make conquest and resource extraction *easier,* and resistance more difficult, than nationalist resistance theorists would suggest. Furthermore, signs of nationalism may generate a reaction opposite from what one would hope for, angering would-be conquerors and accelerating the process of state death.

Method

The primary focus of this book is variation in the incidence of violent state death. Violent state death is the most common form of state death; one could argue that it is also the most pernicious form. Typically, violent state death occurs via conquest or annexation. Nonviolent state deaths, on the other hand, are usually attached to voluntary state unifications or dissolutions. While there is some overlap among these categories—Bavaria and Württemberg, for example, voluntarily acceded to the Prussian Confederation, but only after observing the conquest of nearby states like Hanover and Saxony—by and large, the processes of violent and nonviolent state death appear quite distinct. It would be surprising, for example, if the same causal explanation could account for the British takeover of the Indian princely states *and* the breakup of the Soviet Union.[15] Because these types of events are so different, I have chosen to focus on the group of outcomes that is most common among state deaths.

I employ both quantitative and qualitative methods to test hypotheses derived from my argument as well as alternative hypotheses. Statistical

---

[13]See for example Gellner 1983; Emerson 1967; Kaysen 1990.

[14]Liberman 1996.

[15]While the dissolution of the USSR (and, for that matter, Yugoslavia) was accompanied by violence, the term "violent state death" here refers to violence inflicted by external actors.

analysis permits the uncovering of patterns, or correlations; it allows us to verify or disconfirm initial hunches. It also lends the benefit of systematic testing. At the same time, statistical analysis suffers from at least two weaknesses: first, not all variables are easily quantified and, thus, not all hypotheses can be tested using quantitative analysis; and second, while statistical results can show correlation, they typically do not uncover the causal processes that most intrigue political scientists. Even if I am able to show that buffer states are more likely to die than nonbuffer states, I also need to show that my argument explains these outcomes in particular cases. Mixing methods combines the best of both worlds: rigorous, systematic statistical analysis allows generalization, while case studies permit illustration of causal mechanisms.

Plan of the Book

The remainder of this book is divided into three main sections: "Patterns and Causes," "Buffer State Death and Survival," and "The Norm against Conquest and State Death after 1945." Chapter 2, "Definitions and Patterns," has two tasks. First, I describe in detail the coding criteria and decisions for variables used in this analysis that have not been used frequently in the international relations literature. I explain how and why I generated a new list of states. I also discuss the definition and coding of "state death," going so far as to explain why certain borderline cases were excluded. Second, I present an overview of state death, taking on the questions of who, what, where, when, and how.

The "why" of state death is addressed in chapter 3, which is devoted primarily to presenting and explaining the argument that the dynamics of rivalry and geography determine state death and survival. I argue that geography, by which I mean location, is a prime predictor of state death—buffer states are particularly likely to die because rivals face strategic imperatives to take over the buffers that lie between them and are typically unable to make credible commitments to preserve buffers. At times, however, unusual circumstances may intervene that decrease the probability that rivals will take over buffer states. I lay out three such conditions: "tiring hands," when rivals' resources are simultaneously constrained such that they *cannot* take over the buffer; "diverted rivalry," when the rivals must become temporary allies against a threat in another theater, creating incentives to cease fighting over the buffer so that necessary resources are not sapped; and when a particularly powerful state intervenes to guarantee the sovereignty of the buffer state, creating a situation whereby buffers are secure from conquest because rivals fear the costs of violating dictates issued by more powerful actors in the system. This third condition has characterized much of the post-1945 period. The United States in particular has supported a norm against conquest, altering other states' incentives to take over their neighbors. I trace the evolution of the norm against conquest both in the United States and abroad, in part to understand to what degree it has been internalized and, further, to what degree it may be reversible. Chapter 3 concludes with a review of additional explanations for state death, particularly the balancing argument, the international legitimacy argument, and the nationalist resistance argument.

The heart of the book's quantitative analysis is presented in chapter 4, which begins the section on buffer state death and survival. This chapter focuses on general explanations for state death, using duration analysis to test hypotheses about the role of buffer states, balancing behavior, international recognition, and nationalism with respect to state death. Analyses of variation in buffer state survival are also included.

Chapter 5 presents pre-1945 case studies of eighteenth-century Poland, the Dominican Republic in 1916, the Dominican Republic in 1870, and late nineteenth- and early twentieth-century Persia. The two variables used to select these cases were buffer state status and state death/survival. I sought to maximize variation on both the dependent and independent variables for each set of case studies. For each case, I ask several questions: Was the state a buffer state? Why did it die/survive? Did the state balance? And, to what extent were (would-be) conquerors concerned about the prospects of resistance? The results from these cases are extremely consistent, illustrating the import of the dynamics of rivalry to both state death and state survival, and challenging the notion that balancing behavior or nationalist rebellion could or did stave off conquest.

Eighteenth-century Poland represents a classic case of a prolonged, some would say agonizing, buffer state death. This case aptly illustrates the dynamics of rivalry that led to Poland's demise in 1795. By contrast, Persia in the late nineteenth and early twentieth century is an exception to the rule that buffer states will die. Persia's survival can be explained by extending the logic of the argument that buffer states are particularly likely to be taken over; rare, extenuating circumstances mitigated the Anglo-Russian rivalry that had repeatedly jeopardized the Persian state. In 1870, the United States considered annexing the Dominican Republic, but ultimately rejected this scheme. These events constitute the third case study, and can be explained by the *absence* of a strategic imperative to take over the Dominican Republic. The Dominican Republic survived precisely because it was not a buffer. Finally, forty-five years later, the US occupation of the Dominican Republic in 1916 appears, on the surface, to be a case of a nonbuffer state death. On examination, however, it becomes evident that the US occupation was driven by fear of German adventurism in the Caribbean; like Poland, the Dominican Republic was a victim of the strategic imperatives facing rivals.

While the empirical chapters begin to provide some answers regarding the causes of state death, they also raise important questions. Why is it that violent state death declined dramatically after 1945? Why are some states resurrected? The third section of this book explores these questions in the context of the norm against conquest that emerged in the early twentieth century.

Chapter 6 turns to the question of state resurrection, asking, why are only some state deaths reversed? A series of quantitative analyses applies a number of hypotheses on state death to state resurrection. I test to see whether the probability of resurrection increases in tandem with the strengthening of the norm against conquest. This argument is supported by results of the quantitative tests as well as case studies of the 1919 resurrection of Poland and 1924 resurrection of the Dominican Republic. Interestingly, the nationalist resistance argument also appears to explain state resurrection, even though it does not seem to shed light on state death generally.

Chapter 7 explores the norms argument further, first by testing corollary hypotheses meant to distinguish the norms argument from alternative explanations for the post-1945 decline in violent state death. While a variable for the post-1945 period is included in the primary statistical analysis in chapter 4, this variable on its own is a very blunt instrument, and could capture a number of other phenomena—such as the onset of the Cold War or the development of nuclear weapons—that coincide with this time period. One method to distinguish the predictions of these different arguments is to generate and test corollary hypotheses of each. Among others, extensions of the norms argument suggest: (1) a rise in reversals of violent state deaths in the twentieth century; (2) an increase in interventions to replace regimes and leaders when conquest is prohibited; and (3) an increase in the number of state collapses as leaders exploit state resources knowing that they face little or no risk of conquest. Each of these arguments is tested using quantitative analysis. The results of these tests consistently support the norms argument.

I turn next to four post-1945 cases: Poland and Hungary in 1956; the Dominican Republic in 1965; and Kuwait in 1990. The questions asked in this chapter are slightly different: Why did the state survive, suffer intervention, or die? Were (would-be) interveners concerned about violating the norm against conquest or about the resistance they might encounter? Again, both primary and secondary evidence confirms the notion that the norm against conquest, as opposed to a fear of increased nationalist resistance, constrained states from taking over their neighbors. Documents from Soviet-era archives are used to analyze the first set of cases—Poland and Hungary in 1956. Both states were buffer states during the Cold War, but the USSR intervened only in Hungary in 1956. This difference in outcome is explained by the fact that Hungary was "more" of a buffer state in 1956, making credible threats to defect from the Warsaw Pact. I also show that the probability of resistance was essentially equal in Hungary and Poland at the time. For the next case, the US intervention in the Dominican Republic in 1965, archival sources reveal that, as in 1916, the United States was very concerned about encroaching rivals, and that concerns about violating the norm against conquest prevailed in preventing a complete US takeover of the republic. The final case, that of the Iraqi annexation of Kuwait in 1990, initially appears to contradict both the buffer state and norms arguments. While Kuwait was not a buffer state,[16] this case is the exception that proves the rule that the norm against conquest prevented violent state death after 1945. Simply put, the intent to enforce the norm was not signaled clearly to the Iraqi regime; the norm was violated because it was not clear that violation would be punished.

The final chapter summarizes the main arguments presented here and considers implications for international relations theory and policy. One of the principal theoretical implications of this book is that state death and survival are primarily determined by geography. Geography is a critical, yet often ignored, variable in global politics. Another contribution of this book, then, is to try to "bring geography back in" to international relations scholarship. Several policy implications also follow from this analysis. First, balancing against power does not appear to be an effective option for survival. This implication is especially important for nonbuffer states with limited resources. Second, international recognition does appear to be related to state survival. States like East Timor have done well to acquire it, while states like Taiwan should continue to pursue recognition. Finally, I argue that the norm against conquest that has prevented rivals from taking over buffers since 1945 is by no means a permanent addition to the international system. Indeed, the state that has served as the key proponent of this norm—the United States—is now behaving in ways that directly contradict this norm. A discussion of the 2003 Iraq War and the ensuing occupation suggests that the United States did not intend a long-term occupation of Iraq; nonetheless, the consequences and precedent of this occupation may be particularly fateful for the norm against conquest. Although violent state death has become an extremely rare event in recent years, it may become increasingly common in the future.

[16]Although, insofar as Iraqi-Saudi relations were hostile, one could claim that Kuwait served as a buffer at the time.

Conclusion

The death of a state is a momentous event in the international system. State death forces citizens and cartographers alike to revise their vision of the world. Yet diplomats and scholars have had a poor understanding of this phenomenon, in part because the conventional wisdom assumes that state death almost never occurs. My first goal for this book is to lay out the historical record of state death, showing that this phenomenon has been more frequent than has previously been thought. The next, critical task is to explain variation in state death. Here I also take on the conventional wisdom by arguing that it is the politics of geography—and not a process of selection—that accounts for state death and survival in the international system. My final goal for this book is to explain the shift away from state death after 1945, and to consider how the causes of this shift may bear on future international relations.

PART I

PATTERNS AND CAUSES

Chapter 2 _____

Definitions and Patterns

STUDENTS OF international relations are usually—and rightly—concerned with current events. Putting these events in historical context is critical to understanding patterns of behavior in world politics. This chapter attempts to do just that for the phenomenon of state death. The main goal is to lay out the history of state death over the past two centuries.

Because state death has not previously been considered by international relations scholars, the topic raises important definitional issues that must be addressed before any patterns can be identified. For example: How do we identify states? How do we know when a state has died? This topic also suggests questions that require a survey of state death, such as: Which states have died? When and where has state death occurred? In what way have states tended to die—do they typically give up their sovereignty voluntarily, or fight to the death? My goal in defining heretofore undefined terms is to develop clear, sensible definitions that can be translated into an effective coding scheme. Nonetheless, virtually all the definitions presented here could be contested. I attempt to answer possible challenges to my definitions in my discussion of each term. I have also included discussions of a number of cases that are particularly difficult to code.

The remainder of this chapter proceeds as follows. First, I propose definitions of terms germane to the project: "state" and "state death." I briefly challenge and revise the primary extant list of states in international relations scholarship—the Correlates of War list of members of the interstate system—on grounds of bias and uneven implementation.[1] I also discuss extensively both my definition and my coding of state death, and include a list of state deaths since 1816. Note that the overview of state death extends beyond the primary focus of this book, which is violent state death. The discussion of nonviolent state death is useful for the purposes of contrast as well as opening avenues for future research. Next, I present an overview of state death that addresses questions of who, what, where, when, and how, leaving why for the following chapters. This survey yields several patterns of state death, revealing in particular the relative frequency of violent state death in general, and marked changes in the incidence and manner of state death after 1945.

---

[1]A more extensive discussion of this process and list of revisions made to the Correlates of War can be found in appendix A.

When Is a State a State?

States are conceived of as having some kind of internal hierarchy, ability to wield force, and territorial boundary. They are also defined as institutions that are sovereign over a specified population and territory. In their most pristine form, states do not suffer any incursions of sovereignty. Max Weber defines the state as the unit claiming "a monopoly of the legitimate use of physical force within a given territory."[2] J. P. Nettl defines the state as "a collectivity that summates a set of functions and structures . . . a unit in the field of international relations . . . an autonomous collectivity as well as a summating concept of high social generality. It is thus in a functional sense a distinct *sector* or arena of society . . . a sociocultural phenomenon."[3] Charles Tilly defines states as "coercion-wielding organizations that are distinct from households and kinship groups and exercise clear priority in some respects over all other organizations within substantial territories."[4]

These definitions of statehood refer largely to a state's domestic capabilities. While conceptualizing the state in these terms is useful, the question posed in this book refers to states as part of an international system. Thus, it is also useful to examine how international law conceives of states. For example, the Montevideo Convention on Rights and Duties of States declares: "The State as a person of international law should possess the following qualifications: (a) a permanent population; (b) a defined territory; (c) government; and (d) capacity to enter into relations with other States."

Although the conceptions of statehood presented above are complementary, many of the terms in these definitions are undefined. To effectively analyze cases of state death, a simple coding scheme is needed to identify states. This scheme should comprise rules that are logical and that yield a list of states that overlaps significantly with our intuition about what such a list should look like.

Of course, no such list will satisfy everyone's intuition about the list of states in the world. A natural place to start, however, is with the Correlates of War (COW) list of members of the interstate system.[5] The COW list of members of the interstate system forms the foundation of a number of major data sets—and, consequently, quantitative analyses—in in-

[2]Weber 1946, 78.
[3]Nettl 1968, 562–66.
[4]Tilly 1990, 1.
[5]The Correlates of War project was founded in 1963 by J. David Singer and Melvin Small. Data collected through COW were used to pioneer statistical analysis of international conflict.

ternational relations scholarship. Below, I briefly present the logic behind the criteria underlying the COW list, critique it, and then offer amendments to the list based on sounder coding rules.[6]

The Correlates of War project defines requirements for membership in the interstate system as follows:

(a) prior to 1920, a population of 500,000 or more and establishment of diplomatic missions at or above the rank of chargé d'affaires by Britain and France

(b) after 1920, membership in the League of Nations or United Nations *or* a population of 500,000 or more and establishment of diplomatic missions from any two major powers[7]

The goal of the Correlates of War, and my goal in identifying states, is to identify those states engaging in significant relations with others. Members of the interstate system constitute a subset of all states in the world at a given time. It is possible that states existed in the world that are not included in either the original or the revised version of the Correlates of War list of members of the interstate system. This exclusion is justified by the purpose of the data set: to help scholars analyze international relations. In theory, political units that exhibit the traits associated with statehood but are completely autarkic are not properly members of the interstate system, because they do not interact with other states.

While the general principle of using size and recognition as markers of statehood, or membership in the international system, is sound, the pre-1920 measurement of international recognition used in the Correlates of War project is problematic. Relying solely on the establishment of British and French diplomatic missions generates a list of nineteenth-century states that is incomplete, at best. Further, this list is biased; some European states are omitted, and virtually all Asian and African states are left out.

The purpose of the legitimacy criterion is to distinguish those states "sufficiently unencumbered by legal, military, economic, or political constraints to exercise a fair degree of sovereignty and independence."[8] Both sovereignty and independence have long been considered criteria for statehood. Stephen Krasner defines international legal sovereignty as "the practices associated with mutual recognition, usually between territorial

[6]A number of other scholars also have challenged the COW list of members of the interstate system. See Bennett and Zitomersky 1982; Bremer and Ghosn 2003; Gleditsch and Ward 1999. A more extensive discussion of my revisions to this list can be found in appendix A.

[7]Small and Singer 1982, 39–43.

[8]Small and Singer 1982, 40.

entities that have formal juridical independence."[9] In the international legal sense, independence is defined as "the capacity to enter into relations with other states."[10] Logically, then, it would seem that states that are recognized and have already entered into formal relations with other states have met this standard.

As international legal scholar Ti-Chiang Chen writes, "It is generally agreed that the conclusion of bilateral treaties constitutes recognition."[11] Certainly, the conclusion of treaties testifies to a state's ability to engage in formal international relations. In a number of important cases, the conclusion of a bilateral treaty has been considered to constitute recognition.[12] Lauterpacht refines this claim by arguing that "it is clear that the conclusion of a bilateral treaty is a proper mode of recognition in all cases in which there is no reasonable doubt as to the intention of the parties on the subject. *This would apply in particular to such treaties as a comprehensive treaty of commerce and navigation or a treaty of alliance.*"[13]

It therefore seems advisable to add the conclusion of a treaty of commerce, navigation, or alliance with Britain *or* France to the Correlates of War criteria for membership in the interstate system prior to 1920.[14] From 1800 to 1817, France and Britain signed a combined 496 treaties with 144 separate polities,[15] of which 23 (including Britain and France) received British or French diplomatic missions.[16] Treaties with unrecognized states (according to COW) include the Treaty of Accession of Hanover to the Treaty of Alliance of 25 March 1815 between the Four Powers (1815), a British treaty of alliance with Persia (1814), and a French peace treaty with Tripoli (1801). In cases where Britain or France

---

[9]Krasner 1999, 3.

[10]Brownlie 1998, 71.

[11]Chen 1951, 192.

[12]"Sir William Scott held in *The Helena* (1801) that the Bey of Algiers must be regarded as a sovereign on account of his treaty relations with Great Britain. In 1822, the United States contended that Spain had accorded recognition to her American Colonies by concluding with them 'treaties equivalent to an acknowledgement of independence.' The International Association of the Congo was recognised by the majority of Powers by the conclusion of conventions. The Turkish Republican Government was recognised by the United States by the signing of the treaties of August 6, 1923. The recognition of the Soviet Government by many States was also achieved by means of bilateral convention." Chen 1951, 192–93.

[13]Lauterpacht 1947, 378. Emphasis added.

[14]Although it might seem that Britain and France would have been disinclined to recognize states they were about to take over, the history of colonization indicates that most of the polities colonized by these imperial powers—even those on the scale of villages, rather than states—had previously received some sort of diplomatic recognition from them.

[15]These data have been compiled from Parry et al. 1970 and de Clercq and de Clercq 1864–1917.

[16]See Singer and Small 1991.

concluded an agreement on commerce, navigation, or alliance with another polity, and where that polity's population meets the 500,000 criterion, inclusion in the COW list of states is deserved.

Thus, the alternative criteria for membership in the interstate system from 1816 to 1919 proposed here are

(a) population of 500,000 or more, and

(b) *either* receipt of diplomatic missions from both Britain and France *or* conclusion of a treaty of commerce, alliance, or navigation with Britain or France

This revision to the Correlates of War adds 16 new states to the list of members of the interstate system and revises the entry dates for an additional 22 states (see tables A.1 and A.2 in appendix A for the complete lists). Among the states added to the list are a number with familiar names, such as Afghanistan, Burma, and Madagascar, all of which met the criteria for statehood prior to being colonized by European powers. Among the states whose entry dates are revised are China, which COW codes as entering in 1860 and I code as entering in 1842; Guatemala, which COW codes as entering in 1888 and I code as entering in 1849; and Nepal, which COW does not count as a member of the interstate system until 1920, even though it met the population criterion and had received international recognition prior to 1816.

Having a more historically accurate list of members of the interstate system is essential to understanding state death. If, for example, most of the states that were colonized were left out of the analysis, we might conclude that the degree of recognition a state received was immaterial to its survival prospects. In general, this less Eurocentric list of states allows us to see a much more accurate picture of the historical record of state death and survival.

Defining State Death

I define state death as the formal loss of control over foreign policy to another state. Exit from the interstate system is synonymous with the term "state death" as it is used here. State death could also be defined in a number of other ways. "State death" has referred to internal state collapse or failure, a regime change, conquest, or division. Because international relations theories' claims about state death explicitly shy away from domestic politics, however, I define state death in terms of loss of sovereignty to another state.

This definition of state death is consistent with Weber's definition of a state as having a monopoly on the legitimate use of force within a territory. Once a state gives up, or is forced to give up, to another state its ability to conduct independent international relations, it also concedes its authority to decide to use force to defend its territory. To further illustrate this point, imagine an ideal-typical case where a state loses its ability to conduct its foreign policy but maintains the responsibility and authority to ensure domestic order. This former state may possess a monopoly on the use of force for one specific purpose: maintenance of domestic peace. Protectorates, such as the Trucial States (now the United Arab Emirates) from 1853 to 1971, fall into this category.[17] Protectorates do not, however, possess a monopoly on the use of force within their territory, as they are precluded from independently deciding to use force to defend that territory. Once a state has died, the monopoly on the use of legitimate force within a territory has been lost.

This concept of state death also conforms to the notion that the preservation of sovereignty is intimately associated with state survival. Stephen Krasner defines and categorizes four types of sovereignty: international legal, interdependence, Westphalian, and domestic sovereignty.[18] States that have lost control of their foreign policy to another state have certainly lost their international legal, interdependence, and Westphalian sovereignty, and often lose their domestic sovereignty soon after. Dead or dying states are no longer recognized as having the right to engage in international contracts (international legal sovereignty); they cannot control movement across their borders (interdependence sovereignty); and they have lost authority over the boundaries of their state (Westphalian sovereignty).

Although my definition of state death is consistent with the Weberian characterization of statehood, an important distinction remains to be made. According to another reading of the Weberian definition, one could conceive of state death in terms of a regime change (as in Cuba in 1959) or state collapse (as in Somalia in 1991). In these cases, though, the state has not exited the system but has undergone serious internal changes.

---

[17]Note, however, that the Trucial States are not included in the list of state deaths, because they do not appear to meet the population criterion for statehood. Available estimates suggest that the population of the Trucial States in the early nineteenth century was under 100,000. Zahlan 1978, 2–3; Heard-Bay 1982, 1, 24.

[18]"International legal sovereignty refers to the practices associated with mutual recognition, usually between territorial entities that have formal juridical independence. Westphalian sovereignty refers to political organization based on the exclusion of external actors from authority structures within a given territory. Domestic sovereignty refers to the formal organization of political authority within the state and the ability of public authorities to exercise effective control within the borders of their own polity. Finally, interdependence sovereignty refers to the ability of public authorities to regulate the flow of information, ideas, goods, people, pollutants, or capital across the borders of their state." Krasner 1999, 3–4.

While students of comparative politics frequently label such cases as state death, I exclude these categories from my definition of state death to clarify the domain of my dependent variable. This exclusion hinges on the notion that foreign policy capabilities must be lost to another state for a state death to have occurred. A regime change or state collapse may well compromise interdependence, domestic, or Westphalian sovereignty. It does not, however, necessarily compromise international legal sovereignty. Although some states may revoke recognition based on these changes in domestic politics, it is difficult to conceive of Cuba, for example, as having left the international system after 1959.

While the focus of this book is understanding state death as defined above, the argument of the book may be relevant to alternative forms of state death, such as state failure and regime change. Certainly, the international pressures that lead to state death—and violent state death in particular—could also cause state failure and either internally or externally imposed regime changes. But the assumption here is that these types of events are as, if not more, likely to be caused by domestic rather than international factors. Including state death as conquest, state death as state failure, and state death as regime change under one analytic umbrella would likely generate causal as well as definitional confusion. Narrowing in on one "type" of state death allows a much deeper exploration of a single phenomenon, as opposed to probing more superficially a variety of causes of a very heterogeneous dependent variable.

My definition of state death also can be distinguished by its reference to the *formal* loss of foreign-policy-making powers. Treaties similar to those that accord recognition also can deprive a state of its foreign-policy-making powers. Treaties creating protectorate status, for example, were typical of colonization, and required that the state receiving protection defer to the state offering protection in all future foreign policy decisions. Instruments of surrender are frequently used during wars, and again may transfer foreign-policy-making powers to the victor. Proclamations of occupation serve as another formal expression of state death. When states break up into smaller units, the formal loss of foreign-policy-making power typically occurs as new states are formally recognized and/or one particular state is recognized as the successor to the original "parent" state.[19] The formal loss of foreign-policy-making powers is important in defining state death because it allows for much cleaner codings of state death than would otherwise be the case. Hopefully, explanations for state death as the formal loss of control over foreign policy can also be applied to state death as the generic loss of control over foreign policy.

State death can occur in one of four ways. First, states may die through

[19]Brownlie 1998, 80–83.

conquest. They may be colonized, as were the Indian princely states; or they may be taken over, and sometimes parceled out, as was Poland in World War II. Second, complete, prolonged military occupation is another form of state death, as in the cases of Japan after World War II or the Dominican Republic in 1916. Third, states can die through federation or confederation (or reunification) with other states, as did East Germany in 1990 and Zanzibar in 1964. Finally, state death may occur through dissolution. Cases in point are Czechoslovakia in 1992 and Germany in 1945. Note that while cases of conquest and occupation are always violent, unification and dissolution can also occur violently, as in the Two Sicilies' annexation to Piedmont in 1861.

Sixty-six of 207 states have died since 1816. They are listed in table 2.1.[20]

What About . . . ?

A number of states might seem as if they should be included in (or excluded from) the list of state deaths presented here. Below, several important candidates for addition to or omission from the list are discussed briefly. I focus first on polities not included in the list of states, and second on states not included in the list of state deaths.

STATES NOT INCLUDED AS MEMBERS OF THE INTERSTATE SYSTEM

Tibet

Tibet is not considered a member of the international system, because it did not receive international recognition as a state during the nineteenth and twentieth centuries. To be sure, Tibet is a difficult case to categorize based on foreign-policy-making powers and international recognition. For most of its history, it was dominated either by the Mongols or, principally, by China. Although the British signed a commercial treaty with Tibet in 1904, this treaty was concluded in between numerous recognitions of Chinese suzerainty over Tibet. Two years later, the British signed a new treaty with China that confirmed the 1904 British-Tibetan treaty and recognized Chinese control over Tibetan foreign policy. Five years later, in 1911, Tibet declared itself independent of Chinese rule and, in many ways, was considered an independent state until 1949. During this time, the British concluded two treaties with Tibet, both in 1914. One treaty delimited the Indian-Tibetan border, and the other treaty was a

---

[20]This table, as well as the following analysis, includes a number of states I added to the Correlates of War list of members of the interstate system as a result of my revision of COW's pre-1920 legitimacy criterion.

TABLE 2.1
State Deaths, 1816–2000

State	Violent?	Year
Peshwa (Maratha)	Yes	1817
Indore	Yes	1818
Nagpur	Yes	1818
Algeria (Algiers)	Yes	1830
Bolivia	No	1836
Peru-Bolivia Confederation	Yes	1839
Sind	Yes	1843
Punjab	Yes	1846
Papal States	Yes	1860
Modena	No	1860
Parma	No	1860
Tuscany	No	1860
Two Sicilies	Yes	1861
Hanover	Yes	1866
Hesse Electoral	Yes	1866
Hesse Grand Ducal	No	1867
Saxony	Yes	1867
Mecklenburg Schwerin	No	1867
Baden	No	1870
Württemberg	No	1870
Paraguay	Yes	1870
Bavaria	No	1871
Eastern Turkistan	Yes	1877
Afghanistan (Cabul)	Yes	1879
Peru	Yes	1880
Tunisia	Yes	1881
Egypt	Yes	1882

(*continued*)

TABLE 2.1
Continued

State	Violent?	Year
Annam	Yes	1884
Burma	Yes	1885
Madagascar	Yes	1885
Soudan	Yes	1886
Fouta Toro	Yes	1888
Dahomey	Yes	1895
Korea	Yes	1905
Cuba	Yes	1906
Morocco	Yes	1911
Haiti	Yes	1915
Dominican Republic	Yes	1916
Austria-Hungary	Yes	1918
Ethiopia	Yes	1936
Austria	Yes	1938
Poland	Yes	1939
Czechoslovakia	Yes	1939
Albania	Yes	1939
Netherlands	Yes	1940
Belgium	Yes	1940
Luxembourg	Yes	1940
France	Yes	1940
Estonia	Yes	1940
Latvia	Yes	1940
Lithuania	Yes	1940
Norway	Yes	1940
Denmark	Yes	1940
Yugoslavia	Yes	1941

(*continued*)

TABLE 2.1
Continued

State	Violent?	Year
Greece	Yes	1941
Germany	Yes	1945
Japan	Yes	1945
Syria[a]	No	1958
Zanzibar	No	1964
Republic of Vietnam	Yes	1975
Kuwait	Yes	1990
German Democratic Republic	No	1990
Yemen Arab Republic	No	1990
Yemen People's Republic	No	1990
Soviet Union	No	1991
Yugoslavia	No	1992

[a]Note that the Correlates of War codes Syria as acceding to Egypt/ United Arab Republic (UAR) in 1958. Although the UAR dissolved and Syria returned to the international system in 1961, Egypt is coded as the successor state to the UAR; therefore, this case is not one of state death of the UAR.

trade agreement. While one could certainly argue that the trade agreement constituted recognition, the original negotiations with Tibet included the Chinese, again in the understanding that Tibet was under Chinese suzerainty. The ambiguity surrounding recognition is compounded by the fact that the Chinese eventually left the negotiating table. Because this case is particularly unclear—and because we lack proof of treaty negotiations begun with British treatment of an independent Tibet—I do not code Tibet as a new state.

Texas

In 1836, the Republic of Texas was created and independence from Mexico declared. Ten years later, Texas was voluntarily annexed by the United States. Was Texas a member of the international system from 1836 to 1846?

Both Britain and France signed treaties that qualify as treaties of recognition with Texas during this time.[21] However, the 1840 census of the Republic of Texas counts approximately 10,500 taxpayers (white men over the age of twenty-one) and 12,317 slaves.[22] We would have to assume that, for each taxpayer and slave counted, there were an additional twenty-one people (i.e., women and children or tax evaders) for Texas to reach the population requirement of 500,000 and be considered a member of the interstate system. Given the implausibility of this assumption, Texas is not included in the list of states added to COW.

CASES NOT CODED AS STATE DEATHS

Finland

In 1948, Finland signed a pact with the Soviet Union for mutual defense that also prohibited Finland "from participating in any alliances directed against" the Soviet Union. Did this agreement sufficiently constrain Finnish foreign policy to mean that Finland had exited the international system? Clearly, Finland did not have complete control over its foreign policy. Although Finland may have been more constrained than most states in that the terms of its alliance treaty with the USSR precluded joining NATO, Finland retained formal control over its foreign policy. This control is demonstrated in part by the fact that Finland signed numerous treaties on issues as varied as overflight rights, passport controls, and commerce with non–Soviet satellite states—such as Britain—during the Cold War. Thus, Finland is not considered to have exited the system in 1948.

Soviet Bloc Countries

The foreign policies of Soviet bloc states were clearly constrained during the Cold War. The Warsaw Pact, for example, included provisions for the maintenance of Soviet troops on satellite soil. Nonetheless, I contend that the Warsaw Pact states do not represent cases of violent state death. Although their foreign policies were highly constrained by the Soviet Union, they did not formally lose control over them.[23]

In fact, a number of examples suggest that the Soviet bloc countries retained some control over their foreign policies. Albania withdrew from the Warsaw Pact following the USSR's invasion of Czechoslovakia in 1968. While Nagy's attempt to withdraw from the Warsaw Pact led to Soviet intervention in Hungary, the attempt exhibits greater foreign policy

---

[21]Hertslet and Hertslet 1840–1925, 6:807; de Clercq and de Clercq 1864–1917, 4:502.
[22]White 1966.
[23]For a discussion of the degree of foreign policy control held by these states, see Stone 1995.

capabilities than one would expect of a "dead" state. Independent Yugoslav policies also led to complete withdrawal from the bloc. These states also continued to engage in formal relations with other, non–Warsaw Pact members.[24] The Soviet satellite states represent cases very close to the borderline of state death. They do not, however, cross the line.

Belgium during World War I

In August of 1914, the Germans overran Belgian defenses and occupied most of that country during the course of the war. At the same time, though, the Belgian king retreated to unoccupied Belgium and continued to exercise his powers as commander in chief from there. Thus, Belgium's foreign policy powers were not successfully—or formally—captured by the Germans.

Ottoman Empire

In 1807, the boundaries of the Ottoman Empire stretched from Bessarabia to Kuwait; only by 1924 was it reduced to its principal successor state of modern-day Turkey. Because the change was so gradual (the death of the Ottoman Empire occurred over a century), I do not code the Ottoman Empire as a state death, and instead consider Turkey as a continuous successor to the empire.

Surveying State Death

With definitions and codings in hand, we can begin to uncover patterns in state death. The first pattern of note is that, historically, state death has been a global phenomenon. A map illustrating the geographic reach of state death (fig. 2.1) raises several interesting issues. First, this map suggests that two regions—North America and Australia—appear to be immune to state death. The apparent absence of state death in North America and Australia is a function of how states are defined and of when the data set starts. If Native American or Aboriginal tribes were defined as states, we would observe a much higher incidence of state death in these regions. Moreover, for most of the time period covered by this book, North America and Australia have been populated by very few states. The fact that state death has been rare in North America and Australia, however, raises a fascinating question: to what extent are the relatively isolated geographies of these regions related to the likelihood of state death?

A second, important piece of information that we can glean from this

---

[24]For example Romania, Bulgaria, Hungary, and Poland concluded numerous treaties with Britain during the Cold War.

Figure 2.1. All State Deaths, 1816–2000

map is that there appears to have been a concentration of state death in Europe. Why would this be so? The frequency of state death in Europe is probably due at least in part to the fact that the state as an institution was most dominant in Europe in the early nineteenth century. In addition, nineteenth- and twentieth-century Europe boasted more states per square mile than any other region.[25]

Third, the geography of state death appears to be quite varied. Both interior states such as Bolivia and coastal states such as Algeria have died. At the same time, most states that die—about three-quarters—have coastlines (as do most states in the international system). Very large states, like the Soviet Union, join very small counterparts, like Hanover, in their demise. The average size of states that die is about 243,000 square kilometers; the size of states that die ranges from about 1,000 square kilometers to over 8 million square kilometers. Although state death has been concentrated in Europe and rare (even absent) in North America and Australia, it has been distributed fairly evenly among South America, Africa, and Asia.

Table 2.1 suggests a temporal pattern in state death. All but eleven of the sixty-six state deaths occurred prior to 1945. Figure 2.2 demonstrates this trend graphically, focusing on historical trends in violent state death in particular. As this graph shows, violent state death has declined dramatically since 1945. Although there have been a number of post–World War II nonviolent state deaths, one of the major questions suggested by the data is, how can we account for the lack of violent state death after 1945?

In addition to the general post-1945 decline in violent state death, there appear to be spikes in the incidence of state death, some of which track major historical events. German and Italian unification, as well as the scramble for Africa, account for the late-nineteenth-century cluster of state deaths. World War II also makes an appearance on this graph. Although certain key events—such as World War I—do not appear to be associated with elevated levels of state death, this graph does suggest that states may die in waves.[26]

How states die—violently or nonviolently—appears to vary much less than when and where they have died. This finding may be unsurprising in that we might expect that states will always fight for survival. Temporal patterns of state death become even more clearly delineated when different types of state death are distinguished. Of the sixty-six states that have

[25]At the same time, it is important to recall that some of these observations are artifacts of timing and coding; going back as far as the Chinese warring states period, for example, could certainly increase the number of state deaths in East Asia. Hui 2005.

[26]This observation raises additional questions: Why is it that World War II produced so many state deaths but not World War I? If states die in waves, are they also born in waves?

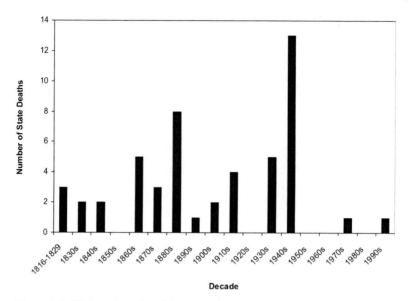

Figure 2.2. Violent State Death by Decade, 1816–2000

died, fifty—the clear majority—have died violently. By "violent state death," I mean state death that occurs via the use of military force. Military occupation and conquest are typical examples of violent state death. State dissolution *can* occur violently, as in the case of Germany in 1945, or peacefully, as in the death of Czechoslovakia. When dissolution occurs violently primarily as the result of civil (as opposed to international) war, however, I do not code the state death as violent, because I am focusing on the *international* relations that may produce state death.

Figure 2.3 illustrates that most state deaths have been violent. According to this map, the major exceptions to the rule that states die violently are cases like the dissolution of the Soviet Union, which are dramatically different from most cases of state death.[27] While fascinating, cases of voluntary state "suicide" are relatively few. The question of why it is that some states die violently and others peacefully is not addressed in this book. This intentional omission is predicated on the assumption that violent and nonviolent state death may have very different causes. Intuitively, it seems eminently plausible that the same model is unlikely to explain the colonization of Egypt and the fall of the Soviet Union. At the same time, it is important to acknowledge that the distinctions drawn here present some drawbacks. Limiting the analysis in this way assumes that

[27]Toft 2003; Hale 2004.

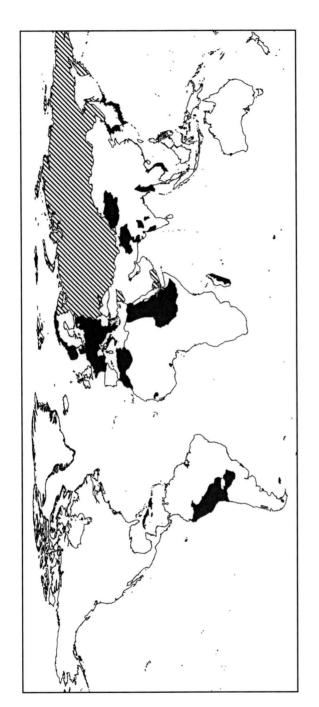

Figure 2.3. Violent State Deaths, 1816–2000

▨ Non-violent State Deaths   ■ Violent State Deaths

state death as a result of civil war or even a peaceful decision to cede sovereignty to another state is *not* caused by international pressures. But we can certainly conceive of cases where surrounding powers sought to foment civil war, or where states about to be conquered decide to surrender rather than fight a costly war. Although the argument of this book might help explain these types of cases, by focusing first on instances of violent state death we can gain leverage in understanding variation in the means of additional types of state death.

State Resurrection

Table 2.2 reveals that a large number of states that have exited the system have reentered. Many of the states that reenter the system do so almost (or entirely) in their original form. This tendency is particularly true for ultimately short-lived wartime occupations or for cases where geography clearly delimits national boundaries. All such cases are coded as state resurrections.

Somewhat problematic are cases where, after a state death, a new state enters the system that contains some, although not all, of the territory belonging to the original state. Nonetheless, it seems clear that while North and South Korea both contain parts of Korea, they do not represent the resurrection of the Korean state. But other cases—such as the independence of the Indian state in 1947 (containing Punjab, Peshwa, Indore, and Nagpur) and of North and South Vietnam in 1954 (both containing parts of Annam)—might suggest resurrection in a slightly adjusted form.

In this study, states that are reborn as parts of new states are not considered resurrected states. Clearly, these states never reenter the international system as independent actors; as subnational units, they do not have control over their foreign policy. Thus, for a state to be resurrected, it must reenter the system in a form exactly like or very close to its original one.

Resurrection typically occurs as a result of one of five (potentially overlapping) processes: decolonization, state dissolution, peaceful reunification, termination of an occupation, or concession of a conquest. The means by which states reenter the international system can vary depending on the events preceding resurrection. Decolonization was—and is—often a gradual process, typically characterized by stages of transfer of government and concluding with the lowering of the imperial flag and acceptance of the newly independent state into the United Nations. States that reenter the system as the result of dissolution of a larger state (for example, the Baltic states) typically issue a declaration of independence that is soon after recognized by other states in the international system and, in

TABLE 2.2
State Deaths and Resurrections, 1816–2000

State	Year of death	Resurrected?
Peshwa (Maratha)	1817	No
Indore	1818	No
Nagpur	1818	No
Algeria (Algiers)	1830	Yes
Bolivia	1836	Yes
Peru-Bolivia Confederation	1839	No
Sind	1843	No
Punjab	1846	No
Papal States	1860	No
Modena	1860	No
Parma	1860	No
Tuscany	1860	No
Two Sicilies	1861	No
Hanover	1866	No
Hesse Electoral	1866	No
Hesse Grand Ducal	1867	No
Saxony	1867	No
Mecklenburg Schwerin	1867	No
Baden	1870	No
Württemberg	1870	No
Paraguay	1870	Yes
Bavaria	1871	No
Eastern Turkistan	1877	No
Afghanistan (Cabul)	1879	Yes
Peru	1880	Yes
Tunisia	1881	Yes
Egypt	1882	Yes

(continued)

TABLE 2.2
Continued

State	Year of death	Resurrected?
Annam	1884	No
Burma	1885	Yes
Madagascar	1885	Yes
Soudan	1886	Yes
Fouta Toro	1888	No
Dahomey	1895	Yes
Korea	1905	No
Cuba	1906	Yes
Morocco	1911	Yes
Haiti	1915	Yes
Dominican Republic	1916	Yes
Austria-Hungary	1918	No
Ethiopia	1936	Yes
Austria	1938	Yes
Poland	1939	Yes
Czechoslovakia	1939	Yes
Albania	1939	Yes
Netherlands	1940	Yes
Belgium	1940	Yes
Luxembourg	1940	Yes
France	1940	Yes
Estonia	1940	Yes
Latvia	1940	Yes
Lithuania	1940	Yes
Norway	1940	Yes
Denmark	1940	Yes
Yugoslavia	1941	Yes

(*continued*)

TABLE 2.2
Continued

State	Year of death	Resurrected?
Greece	1941	Yes
Germany	1945	Yes
Japan	1945	Yes
Syria	1958	Yes
Zanzibar	1964	No
Republic of Vietnam	1975	No
Kuwait	1990	Yes
German Democratic Republic	1990	No
Yemen Arab Republic	1990	No
Yemen People's Republic	1990	No
Soviet Union	1991	No
Yugoslavia	1992	No

particular, by the "parent," dissolving state (although recognition from the parent state is often quite delayed).[28]

Peaceful reunification usually occurs by treaty, as in Germany in 1990.[29] Terminations of occupations, where sovereignty is transferred back to the occupied state, also constitute resurrections. The US occupation of Japan was concluded when the 1951 peace treaty went into force in 1952. Interestingly, the more recent US occupation of Iraq also was concluded in a formal ceremony, but not with a peace treaty, perhaps because the United States and Iraq were not officially in a state of war.[30] Concessions of conquests can often be most difficult to code as resurrections, as the conquering state may be unwilling to sign a formal renunciation of its claims. Instruments of surrender and/or peace treaties are often one mechanism to formalize concessions of conquests. As the use of peace treaties

[28]For an illustration of the process of recognizing new states, see Fabry 2005.

[29]North and South Yemen also signed a treaty of unification in 1990, although the unification of Yemen is not coded as a resurrection, because a prior independent Yemeni state does not appear in the data set.

[30]Filkins 2004.

in interstate war has declined, however,[31] this mechanism is less likely to be available. International organizations are likely to step into the breach, such as when the UN Security Council passed a resolution delimiting the Iraqi-Kuwait border in April 1991. Although the process of reentry into the international system varies, as described above, reentries are dated according to the same criteria used to code membership in the international system (population + recognition *or* membership in the League or United Nations).

As with state death, and particularly violent state death, resurrection exhibits a clear temporal trend. In particular, states that died violently after World War I seem particularly likely to have been resurrected. Non-violent state dissolutions, on the other hand, appear unlikely to be reversed. Among states that have been resurrected, the duration of exit from the international system varies widely; Syria, for example, exited the system for only three years, while Germany was divided for forty-five years prior to reunification.

As Figure 2.4 illustrates, the incidence of resurrection is as highly geographically varied as the incidence of state death.[32] Indeed, the geography of state resurrection varies much more than the timing of resurrection. These patterns, as well as causes of state resurrection, are discussed in greater detail in chapter 6.

Conclusion

Defining states and state death is a crucial first step in understanding the causes and consequences of these very varied phenomena. As this chapter has shown, state death has been much more common than the conventional wisdom of international relations would suggest. It has also shown that state death has been geographically varied, mostly violent, and often reversed. Another clear pattern that emerges from this very broad survey is that state death in general, and violent state death in particular, have declined in frequency since 1945. The apparent absence of state death

---

[31]Fortna 2004; Fazal 2006.

[32]At the same time that figure 2.4 shows the varied geography of state resurrection, it may also overstate the frequency of state resurrection. Because some state deaths and resurrections overlap, a quick glance at the map might imply, for example, that all the German city-states that died in the process of nineteenth-century German unification were resurrected. As we know, these states have not been resurrected; instead, Germany itself was resurrected after being divided in 1945. Similarly, the shading of Peru and Bolivia might suggest resurrection of the short-lived Peru-Bolivia confederation when, in fact, the shading represents the separate resurrections of Bolivia (following the collapse of the confederation) and Peru (following the War of the Pacific).

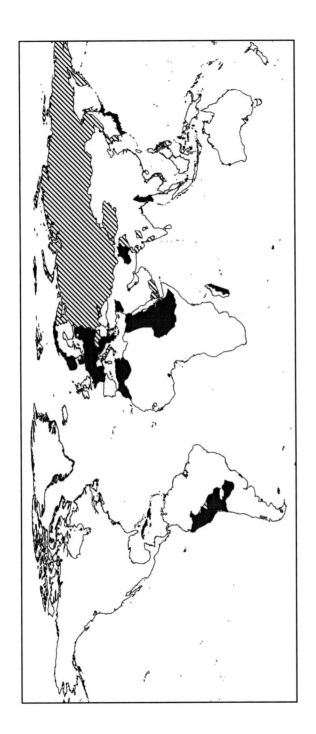

Figure 2.4. State Resurrection, 1816–2000

▨ Non-reversed State Deaths   ■ Reversed State Deaths

during the same time that "modern" international relations scholarship developed may account for the conventional wisdom that states do not die.

To ensure that the analysis that follows is as representative as possible, I have tried to correct biases in existing lists of states in the international system, on the understanding that a study of state death that focused only on Europe might be vulnerable to the criticism of nongeneralizability. More important, a study based on a biased data set could miss—or over-state—key causes of state death. The following chapters address the causes of the trends observed thus far. They offer a general explanation for state death, suggesting causes for resurrection, as well as answers to why violent state death became such a rare event after 1945.

Chapter 3

Location, Location, and Timing

PRITHVINARAYAN SHAH, the founding king of Nepal, is said to have described his country in 1762 as "a yam sandwiched between two stones."[1] These words suggest a focus on geography that is key to understanding the conditions under which states die violently.[2] States caught between two others engaged in an enduring rivalry—buffer states—are particularly likely to die. Buffer state survival is possible, though, if the rivals' relationship and circumstances are altered such that rivals' ability or incentives to take over buffers become highly circumscribed, or if the costs of taking over buffers are driven up sharply. Three mechanisms likely to generate these outcomes are discussed below, the most important being a post-1945 norm against conquest that was sponsored by the United States—the most powerful state in the system. Because the post-1945 period is coincident with a number of major changes in the international system, I derive corollary hypotheses of the norms argument so that its effects can be distinguished empirically from the predictions of alternative hypotheses.

The broader international relations literature offers a range of additional explanations for state death. Neorealists have claimed that a failure to balance against power can be punished by state death. Constructivists attribute state survival to greater international legitimacy. Other scholars have argued that survival is a function of nationalism, or the level of opposition to conquest, within a state. While distinct from my own argument about the role that geography plays in state death, these claims should be taken as complementary, rather than competing, arguments. For example, it could well be that buffer states that receive less international recognition are more likely to die than buffers that receive more international legitimacy. A number of these claims about state death have been frequently asserted but virtually never tested. Below, I examine the logics of these claims and derive specific, testable hypotheses from them.

The remainder of this chapter proceeds as follows. I first lay out my

---

[1] Quoted in Fineman 1989.

[2] I am not advocating an argument in support of geographic determinism, à la Halford Mackinder or Jared Diamond. In other words, I do not claim that the rivalries that create buffer states are inevitable. Mackinder 1962; Diamond 1997.

own theory of state death, beginning with an explanation for why buffer states are particularly likely to die. This account is followed by an examination of a series of unusual circumstances that can intervene to abate or condition rivalries such that buffers become less likely to die. Among these circumstances, the most important is a norm against conquest that has greatly increased the costs of taking over buffer states after 1945. A fair amount of space is spent outlining my conception of international norms, the history of this particular norm, and, critically, additional observable implications of the norm.

The latter half of the chapter is devoted to alternative explanations for state death and survival. Following the discussion of the post-1945 norm against conquest, I turn first to competing explanations for the decline in violent state death observed in chapter 2. I then discuss more general (and less time-bound) explanations for state death derived from the broader international relations literature. This chapter concludes with a summary of hypotheses derived from my own argument as well as from competing accounts of state death.

The Geography of Death

States engaged in enduring rivalries have strong incentives to take over the buffer states that lie between themselves and their opponents. The security dilemma that typically arises around buffer states falls into the family of commitment problems that are common in international relations. Well-known solutions to these problems[3] can sometimes also be applied here. One of the innovations of this study is presenting a prohibitive norm, as enforced by a great power, as a solution to the commitment problem that typically leads to buffer state death.

Stuck in the Middle: Buffer States and the Dynamics of Rivalry

Conventional wisdom suggests that buffer states should enjoy a privileged position in terms of their prospects for survival. Neighboring powers have a stake in preserving buffer states that mitigate the effects of rivalry and, potentially, reduce or delay the effects of war.[4] In fact, however, buffer states are in a particularly bad position. Although rivals have a clear interest in maintaining the presence of buffer states, they are more often tempted to acquire territory that their competitors desire, even when such behavior places them next to an enduring rival.[5]

---

[3]Such as tying hands and having a third party guarantor. Fearon 1997; Walter 2001.

[4]Paul Schroeder provides an excellent discussion of the historical value—and the survival prospects—of buffer states, or intermediary bodies. Schroeder 1994.

[5]Gary Goertz and Paul Diehl identify enduring rivalries along three dimensions: compet-

| Rival A | Buffer State B | Rival C |

Figure 3.1. The Geography of Rivalry

Buffer states are particularly vulnerable because they are potential battlegrounds for surrounding rivals; more important, they are a source of a potential advantage for one or both rivals. Buffer states can be created as such, or can become buffers over time. Belgium, for instance, was established in 1830 as a neutral state. The Polish state, in contrast, existed as early as the fourteenth century, but Poland became a buffer state only centuries later in life and closer to death.

To explain why it is that buffer states are likely to die, I propose a rivalry game with three actors: two mutual rivals and a buffer state that lies between them (fig. 3.1). The first assumption of this game is that, all else equal, it is always cheaper to rule indirectly than it is to rule directly.[6] Direct rule typically requires a significant troop and administrative presence, while indirect rule can be exercised with fewer such personnel, foreign aid, or both. The second assumption is that each rival is concerned about its opponent taking over the buffer area, thus gaining an unacceptable advantage in terms of its ability to win a war or to extract concessions.

The components of this simple model generate a Prisoners' Dilemma between the two rivals, with respect to the buffer area. The outcome of this dilemma is a familiar one. In equilibrium, the buffer area will be eliminated. The certainty of direct influence, while costly, trumps the less costly—but also more risky—policy of indirect influence. Thus, precisely because of their geography, buffer states are likely to die.[7] If we assume that the two rivals would prefer not to go to war, then it is in their interest to maintain the sovereignty of the buffer state—the buffer will be functional for them, serving as a sort of barrier to war. This outcome, how-

---

itiveness over scarce goods; extended conflict; and a dyadic relationship between competitors. Specifically, they code "enduring rivalries [as] any of those rivalries that involve six disputes or more *and* last for at least 20 years." Diehl and Goertz 2000, 44.

[6]Indirect rule refers to a situation where influence is wielded by one state over another—for example, through aid disbursements—without the influential state explicitly governing the state being influenced. In situations of direct rule, by contrast, one state has absorbed, conquered, or formally taken over the decision-making powers of another. Note that state death occurs under conditions of direct, rather than indirect, rule. For a discussion of the relative costs and benefits of direct and indirect rule, see D. A. Lake 1999.

[7]Spykman and Rollins provide an earlier version of this logic with particular reference to buffer states. Robert Jervis provides the general intuition governing the dynamics of security dilemmas, and even refers to a particular security dilemma over a buffer zone. Jervis 1978; Spykman and Rollins 1939.

ever, is unlikely to occur if the two rivals do not trust each other. Lack of trust emanates from the security dilemma produced by the condition of rivalry. Even if each rival knows that its opponent would prefer to avoid war, neither can be certain that this preference will dominate the strategic imperatives facing the rivals. Gaining control of the buffer state would translate into a significant strategic advantage, one that cannot be passed up on the chance that one or both rivals will exercise restraint with respect to the buffer. Both rivals know that they would be better off if they could exercise mutual restraint with respect to the buffer area. But they both also want to avoid the worst-case outcome of being "suckered"; neither rival wants to exercise restraint while its opponent takes over the buffer area.[8]

One potential problem with this analysis is that, while it relies on the basic logic of the Prisoners' Dilemma, we know that cooperation can be a stable equilibrium in an iterated Prisoners' Dilemma.[9] Long-standing rivals would certainly seem to be engaged in this type of repeated game. Why, then, are they unable to cooperate to preserve the buffer state?

There are at least four possible responses to this question. First, as discussed below, the question is sometimes moot; rivals can *appear* to cooperate to preserve the integrity of a buffer state when they are mutually constrained from taking over that buffer state. Second, rivals often *do* cooperate—to carve up buffer states. The partitions of Poland discussed in chapter 5, for instance, serve as telling examples of cooperation among rivals that nonetheless led to the decimation of a buffer. Third, even when iteration leads to short-term cooperation, it is essential to remember that the international system is extremely kinetic and, as such, vulnerable to exogenous shocks that can upset cooperative equilibria. These exogenous shocks often take the form of a misstep by one rival that is interpreted as threatening by the other (the appearance, for example, of no longer playing "tit for tat"). Finally, as Fearon points out, a long shadow of the future may hinder cooperation when the stakes are particularly high, as states bargain so hard that they are unable to come to an agreement.[10] Thus, iteration is not a sufficient condition for cooperation.

---

[8]To what extent is the offense-defense balance helpful in clarifying this model? Issues of operationalization aside, predictions based on the offense-defense balance would be indeterminate. If the offense were dominant—in other words, in cases where it is easier to attack than to defend—it would be easier to take over the buffer state, but the rivals also might be more reluctant to become direct neighbors, as the probability of war might be particularly high. Conversely, the rivals might fear contiguity less when the defense is dominant, but defense dominance also makes it more difficult to take over the buffer state. On the offense-defense balance, and particularly on measurement issues, see Jervis 1978; Glaser and Kaufmann 1998; Biddle 1999; Adams 2003/4; Van Evera 1999; J. S. Levy 1984; Biddle 2004.

[9]Axelrod 1984; Axelrod and Keohane 1993.

[10]Fearon 1998. In fact, Fearon uses the Russo-Japanese dispute over the Kurile Islands—

Buffer states are therefore in a very dangerous situation. Nineteenth-century Paraguay (as well as Uruguay), for example, was caught between the nascent Argentine-Brazilian rivalry. According to a Brazilian diplomat at the time, the preservation of both Paraguayan and Uruguayan sovereignty were essential to maintaining the balance of power between Brazil and Argentina. "The annexation of Paraguay to the [Argentine] Confederation would give to the latter, in addition to pride of conquest, an increase of territory and forces such that the equilibrium would cease to exist."[11] When Paraguay and Uruguay attempted to balance with each other against the surrounding powers, Brazilian attacks on Uruguay were not deterred. In response to Brazilian actions, Paraguay declared war on Brazil. A Paraguayan request for permission to cross Argentine territory was rebuffed, and Argentina soon joined the fray, ostensibly in protest of the violation of its territory, but quite possibly also to prevent Brazil from having the buffers to itself.[12] The Triple Alliance—an agreement between Brazil and Argentina and, nominally, Uruguay—secretly agreed to dismember Paraguay.[13] The lengthy occupation following the war meant that Paraguay did not return to the international system until 1876.[14]

Why, though, are buffer states more likely to die than nonbuffer states? Let us consider an expanded geography (fig. 3.2). Once again, we have Rivals A and C and Buffer State B. In addition, however, there is (Small) State D,[15] located on the other side of Rival A. Buffer State B is more likely to die than (Small) State D. The reason for this difference in outcomes is

---

which is not dissimilar from two rivals competing over a buffer (although the Kuriles do not qualify as a state)—as an illustration of his argument.

[11]Quoted in Burr 1955, 47. Argentina had attempted to annex Uruguay in the mid–nineteenth century.

[12]Burr 1955, 49. Also see Abente 1987.

[13]Burr 1955, 50.

[14]Paraguay represents a fairly standard instance of a buffer state, one contiguous with each of two rivals. While a relatively strict definition of buffer states is employed in the core of this book, the dynamics of rivalry are observable around a broader set of cases. Rivals are often separated by great distances. For example, buffer states may exist between empires far beyond the homelands of dueling imperial powers. When the British threatened to encroach on French trading posts in West Africa, these posts were fortified and naval stations were built. In such cases, it can be difficult to predict where and around which states competition will become most intense. But where competition does arise, it plays out very similarly to that around more conventional buffers. Certainly, the height of Franco-British rivalry in Africa coincided with the scramble for Africa that marked the transition from indirect to direct rule in the region. Successful trade and resource extraction had long preceded formal colonization in both Africa and Asia. The shift to formal imperialism was driven by the need to secure profits against the coming of imperial rivals. Newbury and Kanya-Forstner 1969, esp. 253, 268, 274.

[15]Recall that power—or the lack thereof—is not part of the definition of a buffer state. While it is useful to illustrate this argument assuming a typical distribution of power between rivals and buffers—and, by comparison, between rivals and nonbuffers—it is not necessary to the argument that D (or B) is a weak state.

Figure 3.2. Buffer States and Nonbuffer States

primarily due to the fact that Rival A is not concerned about an opponent taking over (Small) State D. Furthermore, because (by assumption) it is cheaper for A to rule D indirectly rather than directly, A (and C) are more likely to take over B than to take over D. Again, precisely because of where it is located, Buffer State B is more likely to die than nonbuffer State D. Returning to the South American example from above, Venezuela was not threatened by Brazilian power in the same way that Paraguay was.

"Solving" the Commitment Problem

The same general logic that predicts buffer state death can be extended to predict variation in buffer state death. Buffer states are particularly likely to die because they are surrounded by rivals unable to make credible commitments to preserve the sovereignty of the buffer. If, however, the nature of the rivalry and/or the ability of rivals to take over the buffer changed, so would the survival prospects of the buffer state change. But if rivals are able to reduce the level of competition within their rivalry such that the sovereignty of the buffer is preserved in some situations, why don't they seek the same outcome in all situations? Why make credible commitments in only *some* cases? Why abate the rivalry in only *some* instances?

Although rivals would generally prefer to be able to avoid taking over the buffer state, the conditions that allow for buffer state survival are often outside their control. Intentionally tying hands and sinking costs[16] may be ineffective in cases where the level of trust between rivals is virtually nonexistent and every move is regarded with suspicion. But rivals may encounter situations that effectively tie—or tire—their hands for them. For example, if both of the rivals' resources are simultaneously and unavoidably committed elsewhere (such as in another theater of conflict), drained, or constrained (because of, for example, domestic political crises), circumstances create space for a new equilibrium—the rivals will not take over the buffer state because they *cannot* do so.[17] Here, the rivals themselves do not engage in the design of institutions that generate credible commitments, but the effects are the same—buffers sur-

---

[16]Fearon 1997.

[17]Taylor Fravel and Jeremi Suri make related arguments, suggesting that crises at home can lead to peace abroad. Fravel 2004; Suri 2003.

vive because circumstances intervene to mitigate the rivals' commitment problem.

During the early twentieth century, for example, at a time when Mongolia would have been fairly easy to annex, both the Soviet Union and China were undergoing severe domestic crises. The Soviets were consolidating their rule following the Russian Revolution while the Chinese were riven by factionalism and at the beginning of their own revolution. Problems at home meant that significant resources had to be committed to quell domestic unrest, leaving less time and fewer resources for one-upmanship in the region. Russia and China were aware of each other's crises; each power knew that the other's hands were tied.[18] Thus, Mongolia survived through World War II, after which the norm against conquest could serve as a credible commitment mechanism for surrounding rivals. Given the condition of simultaneity, it is unlikely, but still possible, that rivals may find themselves willing but unable to take over a buffer state because their resources are simultaneously constrained.

Similarly, if situations arise whereby the rivalry abates, or is temporarily put on hold, the buffer state may be safe from conquest, at least for the time being. The most obvious type of situation that could lead to this outcome is a conflict in another theater that requires the rivals to become allies, again at least on a temporary basis. Rivals that become allies against a superior force would seek to bolster their rival-ally, and one way to accomplish this end is to call a temporary truce with respect to any buffer states so as not to divert resources necessary for a separate (and perhaps more important) task. The Anglo-Russian alliance during World War I, for example, led to the suspension of hostilities over imperial buffers in central Asia. As with the case of both rivals being unable to take over the buffer owing to exogenous circumstances, the likelihood of rivals becoming allies in this way—even on a temporary basis—seems low, although still greater than zero.

A third logic that could explain buffer state survival speaks to the duration of rivalries. If, for instance, a rivalry ends before the buffer can be taken over, we can take the conclusion of the rivalry as the explanation for the survival of the buffer. This reasoning builds on the argument that the nature of the rivalry must somehow be altered for a buffer state to survive the rivalry that surrounds it. If, though, the buffer state outlives the rivalry, its chances for survival increase dramatically. While the dynamics underlying rivalry emergence and duration are not well understood,[19] it

---

[18]The only conflict between the USSR and China during this time was the 1929 Sino-Soviet War, which was in many ways an extension of each regime's attempt to consolidate control domestically.

[19]For analyses of rivalry commencement and termination, see Bennett 1996, 1998; Cioffi-Revilla and Sommer 1996; Diehl and Goertz 2000; Goertz and Diehl 1993, 1995.

is not difficult to see how the timing of the rivalry itself could affect the survivability of any buffer states associated with the rivalry. Indeed, the buffers would cease to be buffer states at the conclusion of the rivalry.[20] The end of the Cold War provides an interesting illustration of this phenomenon; not only did the Soviet satellites cease to serve any function as buffer states, but states that the USSR had previously absorbed regained their independence.[21]

Finally, the nature of the rivalry could be affected directly by a more powerful state. If such a state were to guarantee the sovereignty of buffers, that guarantee could tie the rivals' hands. They would refrain from taking over buffer states because the cost of being punished would exceed the expected cost of being suckered. An example of this type of phenomenon is evident in the post-1945 era, with the emergence and strengthening of US support for a norm against conquest.

The Tie That Binds: A Post-1945 Norm against Conquest

Arguments based on the impact of norms run the risk of tautology. For example, one could argue that "we know a prohibitive norm exists because the behavior prohibited by the norm does not occur, or occurs only rarely." Or, "we know a norm is declining in strength because violations of the norm are becoming more frequent." The problem with both of these claims, of course, is that they lack any *ex ante* foundations regarding the emergence and robustness of norms.

Martha Finnemore and Kathryn Sikkink define a norm as "a standard of appropriate behavior for actors with a given identity."[22] The notion of a "logic of appropriateness" embedded in Finnemore and Sikkink's definition is critical because it suggests that norms serve to inform actors how they *ought* to behave. At the same time, it is important to recognize that the dichotomy that is often set up between "logics of appropriateness" and "logics of consequences" can sometimes be a false one. Although many studies of international norms have focused on seemingly irrational behaviors—those that might conform to a logic of appropriateness but appear to contradict a logic of consequences—this trend in scholarship on international norms was surely dictated at least in part by the fact that

---

[20]Interestingly, the cessation of buffer status can create serious domestic problems for (former) buffer states. Arturo Sotomayor argues that, following the Argentine-Brazilian rapprochement of the early 1990s, the Uruguayan military faced a serious identity crisis in the absence of the primary reason for its traditional role. Sotomayor 2004, 161.

[21]It is important to note, however, that buffer states remain relevant after the Cold War. Taras 1997.

[22]Finnemore and Sikkink 1998, 891.

such cases facilitated the study of international norms when they were a relatively new topic of investigation.

Most international norms combine logics of appropriateness and consequences in their emergence, if not in their sustenance. Norms about how prisoners of war should be treated, for example, were inspired as much by concerns about reciprocity as by humanitarian concerns.[23] Similarly, the norm against political assassination grew out of political leaders' mutual desire for self-preservation.[24] The norm against conquest likewise gained prominence because it served the interests of powerful actors in the international system. For the United States in particular (and, possibly, for the Soviet Union as well), a norm against conquest was useful after World War II as a means to prevent future war and promote the maintenance of the status quo.

Powerful actors can be key to norm emergence, by imposing their normative preferences on other actors and threatening to punish behavior that does not accord with those preferences.[25] This route of norm emergence is similar to the concept of "normative entrepreneurship."[26] It is also similar to Keohane's analysis of the emergence and sustenance of cooperation in a hegemonic world.[27] An important means for norm emergence is for a powerful actor to endorse and support a norm, thereby granting it prominence in the system.

Norms can be followed for many reasons. Sometimes actors adhere to norms because they fear punishment in the event of a norm violation. There are also cases where a norm becomes so embedded for an actor that it is followed virtually without thought. As John Mueller notes, the norm against dueling as a method of conflict resolution is so well entrenched in Western civilization that settling matters of honor through dueling has virtually exited our behavioral repertoire.[28] The notion that norms can be adhered to for different reasons, and that they may become increasingly embedded over time, is captured in Wendt's description of the three degrees of norm internalization. According to Wendt, the first degree of internalization is characterized by adherence to a norm for fear of being punished for any violations. The second degree of norm internalization has been reached when actors follow a norm because they view adherence to be in their self-interest. Finally, the third degree of norm internalization describes a situation where the norm is so deeply embedded into actors'

---

[23] Morrow 2001.

[24] Thomas 2000.

[25] Axelrod 1986.

[26] Florini 1996. Note, though, that Florini makes the point that normative entrepreneurs need not be powerful actors.

[27] Keohane 1984; Florini 1996.

[28] Zell Miller notwithstanding. *Hardball with Chris Matthews* 2004; Mueller 1988.

subconscious that they believe it is the "right" thing to do; it does not occur to them that they could not—or should not—follow the norm.[29]

Wendt argues that norm internalization is a linear, although not necessarily inevitable, process. A key question that emerges from his analysis of norm internalization is, how do actors transition from one stage of norm internalization to another? The best answer provided by the literature thus far is time. The longer the tenure of a norm, the greater the likelihood that it will become more deeply internalized. This answer, however, lacks a clear causal mechanism.

I submit that repetition could serve as the missing causal link in the process of norm internalization. The more a behavior is repeated, the more actors may believe that that behavior is right and correct. This logic is supported by psychological studies, specifically in the fields of moral development and organizational psychology. Habit formation, the evolution of tradition, and the sometimes apparently inexplicable behavior of organizations are often explained by repetition. Similarly, repeating a moral lesson to a child can assist in the internalization of the moral rule.[30] Incorporating the idea of repetitive behavior into theories of norm internalization provides microfoundations for the claim that time has an important effect on norm internalization.

At least as important as understanding how the process of norm internalization works is acknowledging that it may vary by actor. It seems intuitive that, for any given norm, different actors may be at different degrees of internalization. But why might this be so? Once again, combining the logic of appropriateness and the logic of consequences generates telling conclusions. The degree to which the enforcement of a norm affects actors' material interests will vary greatly. For some actors, the norm will accord perfectly with their interests, or will be irrelevant to those interests. For other actors, the norm may directly oppose *ex ante* material interests.

We should expect the process of norm internalization to vary with the relationship between the norm and actors' prior interests. Using the norm against conquest as an example, states that either have no interest in conquest or whose interests dictate an opposition to conquest are more likely to internalize the norm deeply and quickly than states that would like to conquer other states. Where the norm against conquest runs contrary to a state's material interests, the threat of punishment is critical to adherence. Assuming that the threat of punishment is an effective one, behavioral differences between actors in the first and third degrees of internalization may be difficult to observe. But those who would still prefer to

---

[29]Wendt 1999, esp. ch. 6.
[30]For a useful summary, see Oulette and Wood 1998. Also see Casey and Burton 1982.

conquer might pursue their interests in another way or, in the absence of a credible threat, actually engage in the prohibited behavior.

This explanation for norm internalization lays the groundwork for understanding how the norm against conquest operates in the international system. This norm was sponsored by a powerful actor in the international system in large part because it was viewed as being in that actor's interest. We should expect that other states adhere to the norm for various reasons. The combination of a logic of appropriateness and a logic of consequences in explaining the origins and maintenance of the norm against conquest provides a nuanced view of norm emergence and internalization. While some states may follow the norm because they fear punishment, others believe that conquest is a moral wrong.

ORIGINS OF THE NORM AGAINST CONQUEST

The norm against conquest emerged and became consequential because it was sponsored by the most powerful state in the system. Specifically, the norm was espoused by two US wartime presidents—Woodrow Wilson and Franklin Delano Roosevelt—in different forms and to different degrees. Their ideological commitment to the norm against conquest dovetailed with the United States' position as a rising and actual superpower. During its first century, conquest was seen as very much in the United States' interest; certainly, expansion and acquisition characterized much of US foreign policy both on the continent and beyond. By the time of the world wars, the United States had consolidated its gains and, importantly, sought to keep them. Outlawing territorial aggression met these ends because it was viewed as a way to preserve the status quo. While it is difficult to separate the origins of Wilson and FDR's commitment to the norm against conquest from US interests at the time, their ideology plus US interests created a potent combination that undergirded one of the key principles of the post-1945 era.

Respect for states' territorial sovereignty was at the top of Wilson's international agenda during World War I. Wilson saw the outlawing of territorial aggression as a means to prevent future wars, and convinced the US voting public that his plan for peace, which was based on this principle, was a workable one.[31] War wariness certainly contributed to widespread US popular support for the League of Nations during and immediately after World War I.[32] Because most wars had been fought

---

[31]This point agrees with Mark Zacher's argument that a desire to avoid war in the future was one of the motivations behind the widespread establishment of the territorial integrity norm.

[32]Knock 1992.

over territory, removing territory—in the form of states—as a legitimate source of conflict was seen as a way to prevent war.[33]

But Wilson's allegiance to a norm against conquest was complicated by his concomitant support of the principle of self-determination of peoples. Wilson's extremely public and clear devotion to the right of self-determination led to unintended consequences, particularly with respect to the preservation of borders. The exposition of this principle was meant to apply to such peoples as the Poles, who had clearly constituted an independent state in the past, and who had managed to preserve their national unity in the face of multiple territorial partitions. But the publicity afforded Wilson's pronouncements led to demands for sovereignty from much smaller nationalities. As Wilson later ruefully noted, "When I gave utterance to those words ('that all nations had a right to self-determination') I said them without the knowledge that nationalities existed which are coming to us day after day."[34]

Thus, a paradox of Wilson's vision of postwar order was exposed. Two of the foundational principles of this order—the preservation of territorial integrity and the right to self-determination—were, unexpectedly, in tension. Although Wilson originally conceived of these ideas as complementary principles—territorial aggression could hardly be consistent with self-determination—states' territorial sovereignty could be threatened from within as well as from without.

One method Wilson used to contain the threat of general instability and constant questioning of state borders was to reaffirm the commitment to the right of self-determination while, concomitantly, drawing a "bright line" with respect to the territorial sovereignty principle. This bright line was the prohibition of the conquest of states. Wilson wanted some flexibility built into the territorial integrity norm, but not so much that all claims to nationhood, no matter how small the nation and how destabilizing the claim, would be honored.[35] In Wilson's own words, he desired "that all well-defined national aspirations shall be accorded the utmost satisfaction that can be accorded them without introducing new or perpetuating old elements of discord and antagonism that would be likely in time to break up the peace of Europe and consequently of the world."[36]

In the Wilsonian era, then, the principle of self-determination preceded and, in some respects led to, the emergence of the norm against conquest.[37] The examples of territorial aggression witnessed during the Great

---

[33]Knock 1992.

[34]Quoted in Temperley, Institute of International Affairs, and Royal Institute of International Affairs 1920, 4:429.

[35]Cobban 1969, 75–84.

[36]"An Address to a Joint Session of Congress," Feb. 11, 1918. Link 1966, 46:323.

[37]The concept of self-determination goes back as least as far as the French Revolution, and Wilson focused on this principle prior to coming to support the norm against conquest.

War were violations of the right to self-determination. One way to prevent such aggression in the future—and, by extension, to prevent war—was to enshrine the principle of territorial sovereignty. This process was led by a normative entrepreneur with great power, Woodrow Wilson. Wilson insisted that both self-determination and territorial sovereignty were necessary to a future peace, but when he saw the two principles in conflict, he opted to support the principle of order over the principle of justice.

This principle is codified in Article 10 of the Covenant of the League of Nations, which states: "The Members of the League undertake to respect and preserve as against external aggression the territorial integrity and existing political independence of all Members of the League." Wilson's critical role in the formation of the League and its Covenant have been well documented; indeed, it is probably not going too far to say that Wilson was necessary to their creation. In insisting on tying the general peace settlement to the formation of the League, Wilson ensured the participation of the European (and other) powers in the League and its formation.[38] The death of Teddy Roosevelt (the likely 1920 Republican presidential nominee) just prior to the start of the peace negotiations heightened Wilson's stature abroad. Roosevelt's vision of the postwar world had been more traditional than Wilson's; but without Roosevelt "waiting in the wings," other conference participants believed that bargaining space over the League had shrunk.[39] As president of the committee assigned to draft the Covenant, Wilson wielded significant power. Specifically, he was the key author of Article 10, drafting and insisting on the clause protecting the "territorial integrity and existing political independence" of League members.[40]

That the norm against conquest was a principal tenet of the Wilson administration is clear; that Wilson and his successors in the interwar period were unable to pursue a foreign policy based on this principle is equally clear. Controversy over the norm against conquest certainly helped dampen its effects following Versailles. In addition to US partisan conflict, which led to the defeat of the League in Congress, key leaders sincerely questioned the utility of the norm. Senator Henry Cabot Lodge, for example, viewed conquest as a potentially useful tool in the search for peace and justice, and one that should not be abandoned so easily as Wilson wished.[41] Lord Cecil, the British representative to the League Commission, also opposed the commitment to preserve states' territorial integrity and political independence as placing too heavy a burden on League members.[42] Most important, the US retreat into isolation after World War I immensely limited the power of the norm against conquest.

[38]Walters 1952, 31.
[39]J. Cooper 2001, 44.
[40]J. Cooper 2001, 11, 28, 48.
[41]J. Cooper 2001, 22.
[42]J. Cooper 2001, 51.

Years later, reaction to the severity of the Second World War created an ideational shift in US public opinion that led to stepped-up support for the protection of states' territorial sovereignty after the war. At the conclusion of World War II, isolationism was seen as a failed policy; learning from this perceived failure dramatically increased support for "internationalism" in the United States.[43]

The return of the United States to the world stage was in large part engineered, and certainly shaped, by the next wartime president, Franklin Delano Roosevelt. The United States reemerged as a normative entrepreneur during FDR's presidency. FDR inherited many of Wilson's ideological commitments, although his behavior was governed as much by pragmatism as by idealism. For example, Roosevelt was outraged by the Italian invasion of Ethiopia, publicly opposed the notion of a US right to intervene in Latin America, and refused to intervene in the Spanish Civil War on the grounds of US nonintervention policy.[44] Indeed, Roosevelt was willing to delay an alliance with the Soviet Union by refusing to honor Stalin's request to recognize Soviet annexation of the Baltics.[45] While Roosevelt shared Wilson's conviction that violations of the norm against conquest would and could lead to war, his conviction was not absolute. For example, he refrained from publicly denouncing the German annexation of Austria during the Munich conference, in the slim hope that British and French appeasement of Germany might work.[46]

While it is unclear how Roosevelt might have further shaped US foreign policy had he lived longer, FDR's commitment to the norm against conquest was accepted by Truman in word if not in spirit. When a much less experienced Harry Truman took over the presidency upon FDR's death, he inherited many of Roosevelt's chief foreign policy advisers. At the close of World War II, US fears of growing Soviet power were on the rise. Truman's advisers—and Truman himself—wanted to restrict Soviet expansion.[47] In the norm against territorial aggression in particular, Truman saw a rhetorical device that would allow him to pursue a containment policy toward the Soviet Union. The norm against conquest thus continued to be a clearly articulated principle of US foreign policy through the end of World War II.

Like Wilson, FDR—and Truman after him—sought to propagate key norms of international politics through new international institutions. The norm against conquest was no exception. It was enshrined in Article 2.4 of the UN Charter, which states: "All Members shall refrain in their

[43]Legro 2000.
[44]Dallek 1995, 106, 110, 116, 123, 131, 156.
[45]Feis 1967, 58–64.
[46]Dallek 1995, 158.
[47]Leffler 1992, 17, 21, 45, 52.

international relations from the threat or use of force against the territorial integrity or political independence of any state."

US primacy in shaping the UN Charter, as well as the institution itself, is a point of consensus among historians.[48] Importantly, domestic consensus around the need for an institution like the United Nations to prevent future aggression also existed at the close of (indeed, during) World War II.[49] From the Newfoundland coast, where the Atlantic Charter was signed,[50] to Big Three (and sometimes Four)[51] meetings in Moscow, Tehran, Dumbarton Oaks, Yalta, and, of course, San Francisco, the United States was the persistent agenda setter. It was almost always the case that the US delegation arrived with the most complete set of proposals, which then formed the basis for discussion; the final product of each meeting very much resembled the original US proposal.[52] One point of disagreement among the Big Three was whether the key international institution(s) governing the postwar era should be regional as opposed to global in nature. The US negotiators felt strongly that a global organization would be more effective in maintaining the peace, and won the day.[53] Certainly, an institution with global scope would serve better to propagate a global norm than would several regional organizations.

Thus, the norm against conquest was adopted and promoted by the United States for material as well as idealistic reasons; it conformed with FDR's Four Freedoms and a general view that halting territorial aggression was key to the future peace. Both Roosevelt and Truman used the emerging UN system to propagate this norm. But if the norm against conquest was seen as such an effective tool, why wasn't it deployed earlier? Keep in mind that this norm challenged not only the interests of a number of powerful states but also a long-standing tradition of territorial indemnification following wars.[54] Upsetting both these interests and this tradition would have been no easy task. But the postwar era had suffi-

---

[48]See for example Russell 1958, 1; Luard 1982, ch. 2; Hoopes and Brinkley 1997, ch. 4.

[49]Numerous congressional proposals underline this point, especially the "B2H2" proposal. Further, while executive bureaucracies, such as the State Department and the War Department, disagreed on relatively minor points, all involved endorsed the basic principles of the United Nations and its charter. See Hoopes and Brinkley 1997, ch. 5; Russell 1958, 126.

[50]For an analysis of the role of FDR and the United States in using the Atlantic Charter and subsequent meetings and documents to propagate global norms, see Borgwardt 2005.

[51]The United States, USSR, and United Kingdom constituted the "Big Three." FDR's fourth "policeman" was China.

[52]For example, at the Moscow meeting, the US delegation arrived with a full agenda, while the Soviets wanted to focus on only one point. In general, the USSR and China in particular tended to react to US proposals, rather than make proposals themselves. Russell 1958, 128; Luard 1982, 24 and ch. 2.

[53]Luard 1982, ch. 2.

[54]Korman 1996; Schroeder 1994.

ciently weakened other states vis-à-vis the United States such that the United States was able to set the normative agenda. This rare confluence of circumstances and superpower preferences created an unusual opportunity for norm emergence.

ADHERENCE

The explanation for adherence to the norm against conquest rests on a combination of US normative entrepreneurship and US power; the United States had the will and the means to enforce this norm, although US commitment to the norm may have been governed more by pragmatism than by idealism. States that preferred or were indifferent to the norm did not have to be convinced to follow it. While it is always difficult to determine beliefs, it is reasonable to conjecture that Denmark today believes firmly in the norm against conquest, despite its long history of Viking pillages (and perhaps because of being subject to German domination during World War II). Most states that might have preferred to engage in conquest adhered to the norm because they feared punishment. China, for example, has clearly desired to reunite Taiwan with the mainland since 1949 but has also known that aggression against Taiwan would be punished with US military might.

While the United States might have been able to impose its will on most states—where the gap in power was so large as to seem insurmountable—the Soviet Union did not face the same set of incentives to behave according to US rules. The USSR did, however, have other incentives to observe the norm against conquest. First, like the United States, the Soviet Union may have had a status quo bias that was served by the norm against conquest. Second, the USSR also may have had reputational reasons to adhere to the norm. The Soviet Union was engaged in a heavily ideological foreign policy, at least in terms of its rhetoric. By annexing other states in the way it had done with the Baltics, it would have damaged its ability to recruit additional states to its camp. Indeed, these problems were anticipated in the Cold War Kremlin.[55] And further, although the Soviet Union may (or may not) have had less to fear from US power than most other states, US retaliation for Soviet violations of territorial sovereignty was not something to be sought.

Similarly, for the United States, there were reputational costs to violating this norm. Insofar as the norm against conquest assisted the US position in the world by contributing to stable international relations, violation of this norm also would have led to negative international reper-

[55]Jones 1990.

cussions for the United States. Would-be conquerors might have taken their cues from American aggression, and would-be victims of conquest might have become increasingly wary in their relations with the United States.

ADDITIONAL EFFECTS OF THE NORM AGAINST CONQUEST

The norm against conquest is quite specific in its prohibition of conquest and annexation; these behaviors are clearly criminalized. But the norm is more ambiguous with respect to less blatant violations of the rights to territorial sovereignty and self-determination.

What are the various behaviors that might be prohibited by this norm? The clearest behavior, once again, is the takeover of states by coercive means. Another behavior might be limited territorial incursions: the conquest or annexation of parts, but not the entirety, of states. Taking limited amounts of territory, though, is not as clearly proscribed as taking over an entire state; therefore, we should expect the decrease in the conquest or annexation of states to be greater than the decrease in forcible territorial change.

Prohibiting state conquest also may have generated unintended effects. If state borders become sacrosanct, or even near-sacrosanct, the frequency of state failure also may increase. At least two, complementary logics support this claim. First, previous state failures may have been preempted by invasion and conquest. If states saw neighbors (or, even more threatening, buffer states) on the verge of collapse in the past, they may have intervened to prevent the spread of disruption. Second, leaders of states at risk of failure today might succumb to moral hazard: knowing that border incursions will not be tolerated due to the presence of the norm against conquest, individual leaders can exploit the state in ways that are likely to lead to failure without risk of being taken over by another state.[56]

US isolationism during the interwar period greatly limited levels of adherence to the norm against conquest. Nonetheless, the presence of the norm in the system as well as the reemergence of support for this norm on the part of the World War II Allies suggests that we should see limited adherence to this norm early in its tenure in the international system. For example, while support for the norm might not have been strong enough to prevent state conquest and annexation in the interwar period, it might have been sufficiently strong to prevent these state deaths from being permanent. Another prediction of the argument, then, is that states that died

[56]I thank Avner Greif for suggesting this second logic of how the norm against conquest may lead to state collapse. For similar arguments, see Herbst 1989, 1990; Jackson 1990; Clapham 1996.

violently after World War I should have been more likely to be "resurrected" than states that died violently before World War I. A related prediction is that all states suffering violent deaths should have been more likely to be resurrected after World War I than before.

Another early effect of the norm against conquest—one that would also be seen in the early part of the twentieth century, particularly in the interwar period—refers to the changing nature of state death. Whereas outright annexation was accepted state practice in the nineteenth century and before, as the norm against conquest gained strength in the international system, we might expect to see states "relabeling" annexations as occupations, or even being more likely to engage in occupation as opposed to annexation.

A final set of behavioral implications of the norm against conquest refers to alternative means that states might seek to achieve the same ends. Faced with strong normative constraints against conquest and annexation, would-be conquering states should seek other methods to satisfy the goals previously achieved through conquest and annexation. One such alternative is the replacement of regimes or leaders of would-be conquered states. Thus, as the bright line prohibiting conquest and annexation hardens, predatory states should alter their behavior; as conquest and annexation decrease, external replacement of regimes and leaders should increase.[57] Wilson himself implicitly suggested this course of action by distinguishing limited intervention from territorial conquest: "I understand that article [Article 10 of the League Covenant] to mean that no nation is at liberty to invade the territorial integrity of another. Its territorial integrity is not destroyed by armed intervention; it is destroyed by the retention of territory, by taking territory away from it."[58]

If the claim that a norm against conquest accounts for the dramatic decline in violent state death after 1945 is correct, then we also should see a smaller decline in coercive territorial change beyond state death, a rise in state resurrections, a temporally bounded surge in occupations as opposed to annexations, an increase of state failures, *and* more interventions to replace regimes and leaders. Developing and testing these corollary hypotheses helps set out the conditions under which the argument that a norm against conquest accounts for the post-1945 trend could be falsified.

[57]On historical changes in intervention, see Finnemore 2003.

[58]"A Conversation with Members of the Senate Foreign Relations Committee," Aug. 19, 1919. Link 1966, 62:392. Note, however, that a shift from territorial conquest to interventions to replace regimes and leaders does not necessarily bear a unique relationship to the norm against conquest. Indeed, many of the possible alternative causes of the decline of conquest also could lead to a replacement of violent state death by such interventions.

Alternative Explanations for the Post-1945 Decline in Conquest

The argument that a norm against conquest works to prevent violent state death is a difficult one both to develop and to prove. While normative arguments are generally challenging, in this case the situation is complicated by the fact that the post-1945 period is rife with a number of unique or unusual historical phenomena.

At least five alternative hypotheses could potentially predict a decrease in the incidence of violent state death after 1945. The first alternative explanation refers to the bipolar nature of the Cold War world. Neorealists in particular have suggested that bipolar systems are associated with lower rates of war and greater system stability. This hypothesis has not been supported by available evidence beyond the Cold War. While bipolarity has been historically rare, comparisons to past eras of bipolarity suggest relatively unstable systems.[59]

The unipolar system that has characterized the post–Cold War era has been as rare as bipolarity. As William Wohlforth notes, neorealists expect that unipolar systems will be similar to multipolar systems in their instability.[60] For neorealists, then, the shift from multipolarity to unipolarity should presage a return to conquest. But the past fifteen years of history do not provide evidence for an increase in the number of violent state deaths.

Wohlforth's own view is that the preponderance of power and the status quo bias held by the United States today will make for a stable, durable unipolarity.[61] The persistence of the norm against conquest—and the continued absence of violent state death—in the current unipolar system is certainly consistent with this logic, especially given that the key sponsor of the norm is the single remaining superpower. In a unipolar world, the survival of the norm against conquest will be contingent on the power and preferences of the United States.

A second alternative explanation for this trend looks to the potential restraining power of nuclear weapons on state behavior.[62] Like bipolarity, nuclear weapons entered the international scene very close to 1945. Unlike bipolarity, nuclear weapons continue to exist today. The logic behind the argument that nuclear weapons might prevent violent state death

---

[59]Copeland 1996; Hopf 1991. Copeland as well as Bueno de Mesquita have also challenged this claim on deductive grounds. Copeland 2000; Bueno de Mesquita 1978.

[60]Wohlforth 1991, 5.

[61]Wohlforth 1991.

[62]Adams (2000, 2003/4) makes the general argument that technological changes—and particularly the emergence of nuclear weapons—have important effects on state death and survival.

suggests that states with nuclear weapons will engage in limited wars with similarly armed opponents because they do not want to reach the nuclear brink. It is important to remember, however, that most states do not have nuclear weapons. Of the nuclear-age buffer states, for example, four to seven were buffers between nonnuclear powers, ten to eighteen were buffers between one nuclear and one nonnuclear power, and eight to sixteen were buffers between two nuclear powers.[63] Given the distribution of buffer states and nuclear weapons states, the logic of mutually assured destruction would not enter into the calculations of most post-1945 rivals surrounding buffers. Were nuclear weapons more widely proliferated, my assessment of their effect on the probability of state death might be different.

Third, a number of scholars have hailed the post-1945 era as one of unprecedented interdependence leading to unprecedented peace. The logic of this argument is that, among states that share high levels of trade with each other, the potential benefits of war are no longer worth the costs. The benefits of war, the argument goes, can now be captured via trade; further, any additional benefits are not worth the opportunity costs of lost trade.[64] Because levels of economic interdependence have increased substantially since World War II, the incidence of war—and, by extension, conquest—should decrease.

I raise two general objections to this argument. First, this logic can be convincing as an explanation of the post-1945 trend away from conquest only if it applies to other time periods as well. Increased interdependence should generally be correlated with a decrease in conquest. It is not clear that this prediction is borne out empirically. For example, as Stephen Krasner notes, the years from 1820 to 1870 saw very high levels of trade openness.[65] These same years, however, are correlated with very high levels of violent (and nonviolent) conquest, in the form of German and Italian unification. Second, the argument that increased levels of interdependence can explain decreased levels of conquest after 1945 assumes that the effects of interdependence will be entirely positive *and* that the quest for economic resources is a (if not the) primary motive for conquest. As recent scholarship has shown, however, the relationship between economic interdependence and international conflict may not be so clear-cut. Indeed, increased levels of interdependence may be related to increased

[63]Ranges of number are offered above to address cases where nuclear proliferation was ambiguous (as in the Israeli case) or had not occurred until later in the rivalry.

[64]See, for example, Brooks 1999; Oneal and Russett 1997; Brooks 2005.

[65]Krasner 1976. NB: Oneal and Russett's 1997 analysis is exclusive to the Cold War period, examining only the years 1950–1985, while Barbieri's analysis (mentioned below) includes at least part of the nineteenth and early twentieth centuries as well. For a recent critique of Barbieri's analysis and subsequent responses, see Gartzke and Li 2003b; Barbieri and Peters 2003; Oneal 2003; Gartzke and Li 2003a.

levels of conflict.[66] In addition, as argued above, motives for conquest are by no means always economic.[67]

A fourth potential explanation for the post-1945 change in violent state death engages the democratic peace research program. If democracies tend not to fight each other, and if there are more democracies in the international system after 1945 than before, perhaps this "empirical regularity"[68] accounts for the observed pattern in the data. This argument predicts stepwise decreases in the rate of violent state death that occur in tandem with "waves" of democratization. The post-1945 decrease in violent state death does not, however, occur in stages; there is instead a very sharp break after 1945 that does not appear to be consistent with this version of the democratic peace proposition.

A more sophisticated version of this general argument, however, might be more promising in its potential to explain the change in violent state death. Bruce Bueno de Mesquita et al. suggest that democracies are less likely to engage in territorial wars than are autocracies because democratic leaders have incentives to provide public goods to their supporters, while autocratic leaders face an opposing set of incentives.[69] Because violent state death usually takes the form of conquest or occupation, if there are more democracies in the international system, perhaps rates of conquest and occupation decline because democracies have fewer incentives to engage in conquest.

The relevant set of cases to consider in evaluating this argument is the set of states engaged in rivalries after 1945. If most rivalries are democratic-democratic (a phenomenon that should not occur, according to democratic peace theorists), the argument suggests that the rivals will be less likely to take over the buffers between them. If most rivalries are autocratic-autocratic after 1945, then the argument does not suggest a shift in patterns of violent state death. In fact, most post-1945 rivalries are mixed, with one rival a democracy (or close to a democracy) and the other an autocracy (or close to an autocracy).

[66]Barbieri 2002; Beck, Katz, and Tucker 1998. For a reply, see Oneal and Russett 2001 (although the impact of interdependence in the fixed effects model in this article may be ambiguous—see table 1, 473). Further, Oneal and Russett appear to confine their dependent variable to militarized interstate disputes (MIDs), while Barbieri finds that the positive relationship between interdependence and interstate conflict is stronger for wars than for MIDs.

[67]MacDonald (2006) provides a useful analysis of Britain's economic motives for imperialism, ultimately finding that economic motives cannot account for the pattern of British colonization in Africa and Asia. See especially MacDonald's ch. 3.

[68]J. Levy 1989a, 270.

[69]Bueno de Mesquita et al. 1999. For additional analyses of the relationship between regime type, leader tenure, and international conflict, see Chiozza and Goemans 2004; Goemans 2000.

What behavior should we expect from "mixed" rivalries with respect to buffer states? If autocratic states believe that their democratic rivals are unlikely to absorb buffer states, they might be more reassured about the potential consequences of exercising restraint with respect to the buffer area. On the other hand, a fundamental part of the argument is that autocratic leaders have very strong incentives to take over territory that can then be distributed among their supporters. Autocracies facing democratic rivals might then be *more* likely to take over buffer states than autocracies facing autocratic rivals, because they would expect less competition over territory from their rival.

Another important argument that falls under the umbrella of the democratic peace literature is that democracies are more competent war fighters than nondemocracies.[70] Autocracies facing democratic rivals might then be less likely to take over buffer states, because they fear war with their rivals. At the same time, an additional proposition derived from this argument is that autocratic leaders are less concerned about losing wars than are democratic leaders.[71] Given the strong incentives for territorial expansion faced by autocratic leaders combined with their relative willingness to lose wars, the logic of this argument does not lead to a prediction of fewer cases of conquest and occupation after 1945, when most rivalries are mixed, as opposed to before.

Finally, the decline in violent state death might be due to a decline in rivalries and/or buffer states after 1945. Both the number of buffer states and the number of rivalries, however, increase after 1945.[72] The dynamics of rivalry that govern buffer state survival remain relevant, but are highly constrained, after the Second World War.

When probed, alternative explanations for the post-1945 shift away from violent state death seem unable to account for this change in state behavior. But the argument that a norm against conquest does account for this change should not be accepted because of a process of elimination. Here, the corollary hypotheses generated by the norm are key. Of all the possible explanations for the post-1945 decline in violent state death, only the norms argument and the claim that territory has declined in value might also predict that reversals of violent state death will increase over time, that interventions to replace regimes and leaders will begin to substitute for conquest of states, *and* that forcible territorial change will de-

---

[70]Lake 1992; Schultz and Weingast 1996; Reiter and Stam 2002.

[71]For a separate analysis of the relationship between regime type and war termination, see Goemans 2000.

[72]The number of rivalries increases from 29 to 44. The number of buffer states increases from 32 to 37. The greater increase in the number of rivalries is due to the fact that a high percentage of post-1945 rivalries are between contiguous states; these rivalries do not produce buffer states.

cline generally. But a fundamental tenet of the claim that the value of territory has declined over time is that, in the past, territory was taken because it was, at that time, valuable for imperialists and conquerors. Many of these territories were in fact not particularly valuable for their conquerors, or at least any value that resided in the territory could be extracted via indirect, as opposed to direct, rule.[73] Further, it is not clear that the argument that territory has declined in value predicts an increase in state failure, which the norms argument does predict. Similarly, it is difficult to connect a decrease in the value of territory to the transition from annexation to occupation to intervention predicted by the norm against conquest. Comparing the norms argument and its corollaries with alternative explanations for the post-1945 shift away from violent state death therefore suggests that empirical support for the corollary hypotheses should translate into accepting the claim that a norm against conquest has prevented violent state death after 1945.

THE NORM AGAINST CONQUEST AS AN INTERVENING VARIABLE

The buffer state and normative arguments presented here may seem contradictory, especially because the buffer state argument has its origins in classical realism, while the normative claim is closer to a constructivist perspective. Taking a step back from the major paradigms of international relations theory is important to understanding how these arguments fit together.

A basic rationalist perspective reconciles the buffer state and norms arguments. The norm against conquest—and in particular, the role of the United States as a sponsor of the norm—serves as a commitment mechanism that prevents rivals from taking over their buffer states. If both sides are confident that the norm will be enforced, the buffer state can survive. In this sense, the norm serves as an intervening variable in the general argument as well as in the world. The norm does not remove incentives for conquest, but it does alter the manner in which control can be exerted over buffer states. As figures 3.3 and 3.4 illustrate, the norm against conquest intervenes in the dynamics of rivalry by restricting the behavior of rivals. Prior to the emergence of the norm, states were unconstrained in acting on their desire to take over buffer states. After 1945, the drive toward conquest must be expressed differently—specifically, in external interventions to replace regimes and leaders. Before 1945, buffer states should be vulnerable to conquest; after 1945, it is the *leaders* of buffer states who should fear political demise.

---

[73]MacDonald 2006, ch. 3.

Rivals ⟶ Buffer State ⟶ PD ⟶ Buffer Death

Figure 3.3. The Dynamics of Rivalry before 1945 (Note. PD = Prisoners' Dilemma)

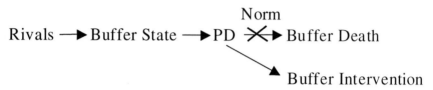

Figure 3.4. The Norm against Conquest as an Intervening Variable

Additional Explanations for State Death

Any book on state death would be remiss without a discussion of the multitude of possible explanations for state death that emerge out of the rich literature in international relations. This book presents an opportunity to consider these claims theoretically and empirically, putting a number of conventional wisdoms to the test. Below, three main alternative arguments that could predict state death generally are considered: that states that balance against power are most likely to survive; that states that receive greater levels of international recognition are most likely to survive; and that states that are likely to generate high levels of nationalist resistance if conquered are most likely to survive.

Balancing

Neorealists argue that states that fail to behave rationally will be selected out of the system. In realist terms, rationality refers to balancing—the internal buildup of military power and the external formation of alliances. The definition of "selection" for neorealists is less clear; one could conceive of punishments ranging from a decline in great-power status to the actual demise of a state. The focus here is on the possible relationship between balancing behavior and state death, but it is important to recognize that the neorealist claim could predict a range of consequences of a failure to balance.

It is clear that on issues ranging from the construction and influence of international institutions to evaluations of the shape of various trade policies, realists consider power a central explanatory variable for international relations outcomes.[74] More to the point, Waltz writes: "Power provides the means of maintaining one's autonomy in the face of force that others wield."[75] Thus, one hypothesis derived from this argument is that powerful states should be more likely to survive than weak states.

Neorealists also expect a central role for external balancing. The formation of alliances is considered to be in a state's interest whenever it perceives a major threat, and critical to success in deterrence and/or war whenever internal resources are insufficient to the task.[76] Allying with other states when alliances are required for successful balancing is rational behavior in the neorealist lexicon. Certainly, if a state faces threats to its survival, neorealists expect that it will find and form an alliance to counter those threats and, further, that states that fail to form alliances in similar situations will face a much higher risk of extinction. Thus, a second realist hypothesis drawn from this argument is that states that form alliances are more likely to survive than states that do not form alliances.

One could refine the claim about alliances by considering the likelihood that threatened states may be the most likely to form alliances; thus, a selection effect precedes the constitution of alliances. Taking this logic even further, one could also argue that, given the high threats faced by states seeking allies, those states may be unable to find alliance partners. Thus, it may well be that the effect of alliances on state survival will be indeterminate.

Also with regard to alliance formation, we can distinguish between balancing and bandwagoning. States that balance seek to counter powerful states; states that bandwagon ally with the most powerful state. While both types of alliance offer advantages, proponents of the balancing argument might suspect that states that engage in balancing alliances are behaving more rationally than states that bandwagon.[77] Recent scholarship supports the idea that alliance behavior is related to the type of alliance in which states are engaged. Specifically, Leeds et al. have shown that states engaged in defensive alliances are most likely to meet their alliance commitments.[78] This finding suggests the hypothesis that states in defensive alliances are most likely to survive, as their alliance partners will be most likely to come to their aid, while states in ententes or neutrality pacts are less likely to survive than states in defensive alliances.

More generally, it could be that only states in threatening situations are at risk of death—thus, irrational behavior by these states is punished par-

---

[74]Mearsheimer 1994.
[75]Waltz 1979, 194.
[76]Walt 1987.
[77]Walt 1987.
[78]Leeds 2003; Leeds, Long, and Mitchell 2000.

ticularly severely. To test this claim, it is important to examine the degree
of power held by buffer states vis-à-vis surrounding rivals as well as to
compare alliance status *among* buffers. This test would use an a priori
measure of threat, comparing the consequences of (not) balancing for
states in similarly threatening situations.

The anarchy that defines the realist world means that states must be
ever vigilant, because attacks can happen without warning, and because
states seek survival at the least and world conquest at the most.[79] In this
very dangerous world, a failure to balance is severely punishable, even by
death. Note that while neorealism is typically taken to be a theory of
great-power behavior, Waltz, in explicating his argument, specifically
makes the point that, despite many differences, weak and powerful states
are functionally similar. Following this point, he argues that "international politics consists of like units duplicating one another's activities."[80]
Thus, neorealist claims about balancing and state death should apply to
all states. Weak, unallied states should face dim prospects for survival, especially when they face grave threats to their existence.

Legitimacy

Unlike realists, constructivists do not view the environment in which
states operate as a strictly, or necessarily, competitive one. Instead, the international system can be socially constructed to be more or less benign
and, thus, generate more or fewer threats to states. Furthermore, because
the international system is socially constructed, membership in the system
is not objectively determined; there may be rules that include or exclude
states as "legitimate" based on religion, region, or political system.

David Strang has elaborated one constructivist claim by arguing that
states that are "unrecognized" have a lesser chance of retaining their independence than states that are officially recognized. Strang, one of the
few social scientists to have addressed the question of state death, examines "transitions of status." He shows that transitions to "unrecognized"
or "dependent" status are much less stable than transitions to "sovereign"
status. Independent unrecognized political units that become dependent
(e.g., through colonization) will tend to have an unstable status; they may
easily become recognized as sovereign or return to an independent, but
unrecognized, condition. Once a political unit has been recognized as sovereign, however, transition to unrecognized or dependent status is unlikely. Strang attributes the few cases he identifies of such transition to the
young age of these states.[81] Essentially, Strang is arguing that states per-

[79]Waltz 1979.
[80]Waltz 1979, 94–96.
[81]Strang 1991.

ceived as less legitimate are more likely to die. Following Strang, Wendt suggests that even relatively stable state systems are governed by norms that do not apply to "nonmembers" or less legitimate states. "Indeed, placing the fate of these unrecognized states next to that of recognized ones provides some of the strongest evidence for a structural difference between Lockean and Hobbesian anarchies."[82] This logic generates the important hypothesis that less legitimate states are more likely to die than more legitimate states.

Nationalist Resistance

The notion that some states are more likely to resist conquest than others, and that the anticipated costs of resistance will forestall conquest, has been frequently asserted but rarely tested well. While scholars of nationalism might disagree on the extent to which nationalism is an ancient or a modern phenomenon, consensus emerges on the point that nationalism is an especially potent force in the modern era, one that harnesses the passions and resources of citizens seeking to defend their homeland.[83] International relations scholars have applied this logic to explain a decrease in the number of territorial wars in the twentieth century,[84] the decline of colonialism,[85] and the so-called obsolescence of major war.[86]

The logic of the nationalist resistance argument is as follows. Centralization of education, the establishment of mass armies, and increased urbanization in the nineteenth century redirected citizens' loyalty away from local interests and toward the nation.[87] With the advent of nationalism, publics were more easily mobilized—particularly when their nations were threatened. Thus, states that were advanced (industrialized) economically had sufficiently loyal populations to generate high levels of resistance to conquest.

A parallel logic also predicts high levels of nationalist resistance in the modern era. Liberal norms of self-determination that developed in Western Europe were diffused to colonial Africa and Asia, generating resistance to imperial powers both abroad and at home.[88] Colonial revolts born of nationalism increased governance costs beyond acceptable bounds and led to decolonization.

Notable among the few existing studies of the nationalist resistance argument is Peter Liberman's reframing of this proposition as a cost-

---

[82]Wendt 1999, 284.
[83]A. Smith 1988; Gellner 1983; Emerson 1967.
[84]Rosecrance 1986, 32–38.
[85]Gilpin 1981, 140.
[86]Kaysen 1990.
[87]See for example Posen 1993.
[88]Crawford 1993.

benefit analysis.[89] Liberman challenges the conventional wisdom by pointing out that, just as industrialization may increase nationalism and therefore the costs of occupation, it may also increase the benefits of occupation and the costs of resistance. In studies of mostly European world war cases, he finds that highly economically developed societies can be effectively repressed and their resources extracted efficiently at small cost to the conqueror. Thus, even if the relationship between industrialization and nationalism holds, it does not necessarily translate into a net loss for a potential invader.[90]

While most of these arguments have referred to existing states' ability to fend off potential conquerors, they may also be suited to states that have already exited the system. Conquerors may not know the probability of resistance prior to an occupation. Because resistance may occur only after conquest, it may have a greater effect on the duration of conquest than on the probability of conquest. Tests of the nationalist resistance argument will therefore be conducted on two dependent variables: violent state death and reversals of violent state deaths.

The arguments about state death that have emerged from international relations theory suggest that the international system will punish (1) failures to balance, (2) illegitimacy, and (3) a lack of nationalism. The argument I propose focuses more on the incentives facing states that might take over other states. Although the two types of argument are quite different, they can be combined. For example, neorealists might respond to my argument by suggesting that, for states in very threatening situations, failures to balance will lead to particularly drastic consequences. To the degree that neorealists believe buffer states are threatened by virtue of their position, then balancing against power will be essential to survival for buffer states. Those buffer states that fail to balance are most likely to be selected out of the system. Tests of these hypotheses will therefore control for buffer state status; if the state attributes suggested by previous international relations scholars explain a significant amount of variation in survival among buffer states, then their claims need only be modified.

Similarly, among these alternative explanations for state death, the legitimacy and nationalist resistance arguments in particular may well be compatible with the claim that a norm against conquest has prevented violent state death after 1945. If, for example, the international legitimacy accorded to states was relatively stratified pre-1945 as opposed to after,

---

[89]Liberman 1996.

[90]Stephen Brooks challenges Liberman's analysis with respect to the post–World War II world by arguing that the globalization of production has reduced the benefits of conquest after 1945. Brooks 1999.

and a general norm against taking over legitimate states has historically governed the international system, then these two logics could combine to predict a decline in violent state death as more states gain full legitimacy in the international system. Similarly, if nationalism has increased over time—and particularly if a rise in nationalism is causally related to the principle of self-determination (from which the principle of territorial integrity is derived)—we would expect to see the effects of nationalism and the norm against conquest operating in tandem.

Summary of Hypotheses

THE DYNAMICS OF RIVALRY

1. Buffer states will be more likely to die than nonbuffer states.
   1a. When rivals' resources are mutually, simultaneously constrained, the buffer state(s) between them will be more likely to survive.
   1b. When rivals put aside their competition in order to meet a threat in another theater, the buffer state(s) between them will be more likely to survive.
2. A norm against conquest will prevent violent state death after 1945.
   2a. Reversals of violent state deaths will be more likely after the norm against conquest enters the international system as opposed to before. More specifically, resurrection of states that have suffered violent death after 1920 will be more likely than resurrection of states that have suffered violent state death before 1920.
   2b. All violent state deaths will be more likely to be reversed after 1920.
   2c. Occupation will become more frequent in the early twentieth century, particularly in the interwar period, as opposed to the nineteenth century and post-1945 era.
   2d. The decline in violent state death will be accompanied by a rise in external interventions to replace regimes and leaders, particularly in buffer states.
   2e. The decline in violent state death will be accompanied by a decline in forcible territorial change generally.
   2f. The decline in violent state death will be accompanied by a rise in state failures.

HYPOTHESES FROM THE INTERNATIONAL RELATIONS LITERATURE

1. States that balance against power will be more likely to survive than states that fail to balance.
   1a. More powerful states will be more likely to survive than weaker states.

      1b. Allied states will be more likely to survive than unallied states.

      1c. Unallied states will be more likely to survive than allied states.

      1d. The effect of alliance on state survival will be indeterminate.

      1e. States engaged in defensive alliances will be more likely to survive than states in neutrality pacts or ententes.

   2. States that receive greater diplomatic recognition will be more likely to survive than states that receive less recognition.

   3. More nationalistic states will be more likely to survive than less nationalistic states.

      3a. More nationalistic states will be more likely to be resurrected than less nationalistic states.

Conclusion

Geography is a key explanatory variable in international relations, but one that is often overlooked in scholarship. Geography—specifically, buffer state status—plays a major role in endangering or securing states. In general, surrounding rivals are unable to credibly commit to a policy of restraint, whereby they would preserve the sovereignty of the buffer states that lie between them. Thus, buffer states are particularly likely to die.

Under rare conditions, rivals' ability and incentives to take over buffer states can shift dramatically downward, and when these circumstances emerge, buffer states are more likely to survive. When rivals' resources are mutually and simultaneously drained, they do not attack buffer states, because they cannot attack. When rivals face a mutual threat in another theater, buffers are more likely to survive because each rival has an incentive to preserve the other's resources. And finally, when a third party imposes a policy that prohibits conquest and is willing to impose costs on violators such that the costs of violation exceed the strategic advantage of conquest, rivals' hands are also effectively tied from taking over buffer states. This last condition emerged after 1945, with US sponsorship of a norm against conquest. But the survivability of this norm would itself be in question should there be a change in US power or preferences.

PART II

BUFFER STATE DEATH AND SURVIVAL

Chapter 4 _____

Quantitative Analysis of State Death

THE FINDINGS presented in this chapter indicate that the politics of geography exert the strongest effects on the probability of violent state death. Buffer states are born to lose. Among the major alternative explanations for state death, the legitimacy argument is the only one that also seems to bear on the probability of state death and survival. As it is measured in this chapter, nationalism is unrelated to state death. Perhaps most surprisingly, however, balancing behavior also seems to be unrelated to state death.

In addition to the finding that buffer status is highly predictive of state death and survival, the data analyses below reveal the very important effect of survival to (and/or existence after) 1945 in predicting violent state death. Along with other variables, exclusion of a control for the post-1945 period impairs the goodness of fit of the statistical models presented in this chapter. The fact that survival to 1945 greatly enhances a state's prospects for survival is consistent with a number of different explanations, as discussed in chapter 3. Given the importance and complexity of this finding, part III of this book is devoted to explaining state death after 1945. For the purpose of this chapter, however, I will note but not attempt to explain the significance of survival to 1945; instead, controlling for time periods, this chapter's purpose is to explore a variety of additional hypotheses regarding violent state death.

The remainder of this chapter is divided into four sections. First, coding of key independent variables is discussed. In the second section, general claims that predict violent state death are tested. Third, a series of robustness checks that address possible coding challenges is conducted. I first focus on potential objections to the list of buffer states and specifically to the possibility that buffer states are undercounted during the Cold War. I then turn to tests of robustness where the dependent variable is altered to exclude state deaths associated with World War II, and to include the Soviet satellite states as state deaths. These robustness checks are not meant to signal a change in the coding rules discussed and implemented in chapter 2. But because many of these codings could be challenged, it is important to know how sensitive the results might be to such challenges. This chapter concludes with a more extensive empirical analysis of variation in buffer state survival. I test for a number of factors that could explain variation in buffer state survival, including: whether more mountainous buffer states are more likely to survive; whether the timing and likelihood of buffer state death can be predicted by the balance of power between surrounding rivals; and whether the power held by buffers vis-à-vis rivals accounts for variation in buffer state death.

Independent Variables

Buffer States

I define a buffer state as a state geographically located between two other states engaged in a rivalry, unless the rivals are separated by an ocean.[1] This definition is generally considered a minimum criterion for buffer state status.[2] Buffer areas or systems, constituted by more than one state, often exist between rivals. For example, a number of small states separated nineteenth-century France and Prussia, two long-term rivals well before German unification. More than ten states were physically located between France and Prussia during the course of the rivalry; some bordered France, some Prussia, and others were in between their fellow small states. And yet, none of these states bordered *both* France and Prussia. Because all these states lay between the two rivals, all were vulnerable to victimization as a result of the dynamics of rivalry. For this reason, I require only that a state lie in between two rivals, not that it border one or both of them, to be considered a buffer state.

Two additional issues must be addressed in defining buffer states. First, under certain conditions, we might consider some states buffers even if they do not meet the strict geographical criterion of lying between two rivals. For example, strong arguments can be made for considering states geographically located between two imperial powers as buffers. Indeed, the term "buffer state" was first used to describe Afghanistan, caught between the British and Russian empires, in the late nineteenth century.[3] Because a number of the (buffer) states in question are states that I have added to the COW list of members of the interstate system, the primary measure of buffer states used here encompasses both continental and imperial buffer states.

---

[1] Given the challenges of projecting power over water, it would be difficult to classify the states lying between two such rivals as buffer states. The exception regarding oceans affects only the coding for the US-Soviet and US-Chinese rivalries. The other sets of rivals separated by bodies of water are China-Japan, Japan-Russia, and those involving the United Kingdom and European or Asian powers. In none of these cases are the rivals separated by an ocean.

[2] Partem 1983, 4.

[3] About a century earlier, Britain viewed Afghanistan as a buffer between the French and British empires. See Ross 1986, 16; and Jenkins 1986, 174.

Second, one could argue that coding buffer states from preexisting, enduring rivalries biases the data in favor of the buffer state argument made here. Alternative codings of buffer states, however, would yield largely overlapping results. For example, a list of all states that lay between major powers not separated by oceans would essentially be a subset of the list of buffers presented in tables B.1 and B.2 in appendix B.[4] On a similar note, it would be interesting to compare actual buffer states to potential buffer states—that is, states that lie between two other states that could be, but are not, rivals. The first step in constructing such a list of "unrealized" buffers is to determine which dyads could produce these would-be buffer states. An obvious choice is to examine states that lie between two nonrival major powers. This strategy, again, generates a list that overlaps substantially with the lists of buffer states below. For example, the Correlates of War codes both France and Italy as major powers from 1860 to 1940, but the two states are never coded as rivals. Switzerland, then, is an unrealized buffer in the unrealized Franco-Italian rivalry. During this same period, though, Switzerland is a buffer state between France and Germany, the United Kingdom and Turkey, and France and Turkey, as well as additional rivalries. In addition to the fact that alternative codings would generate very similar lists, it is important to note that, because of the relatively strict coding rules employed here, buffer states are most likely undercounted in the analysis below.

Before constructing a list of buffer states, it is necessary to have a list of rivals. Fortunately, a large body of literature already exists on the causes, consequences, and nature of enduring rivalries. Paul Diehl and Gary Goertz identify enduring rivalries along three dimensions: competitiveness over scarce goods, extended conflict, and a dyadic relationship between competitors. Specifically, they code "enduring rivalries [as] any of those rivalries that involve six disputes or more *and* last for at least 20 years."[5] D. Scott Bennett operationalizes enduring rivalries according to slightly different criteria:

- At least five reciprocated militarized interstate disputes (MIDs) lasting at least thirty days each occur between the two states.
- At least twenty-five years occur between outbreak of the first dispute and termination of last dispute.
- If the gap between any two MIDs exceeds ten years, the rivalry continues

---

[4]This list would be a subset of the list in these tables because nonmajor powers also can be involved in rivalries, thus expanding the potential list of buffer states.

[5]Note that Goertz and Diehl's definition of rivalry limits the problems of the potential stochastic properties of enduring rivalries exposed by Erik Gartzke and Michael Simon. See Diehl and Goertz 2000, 44, 145; and Gartzke and Simon 1999.

only if the territorial domain and issues remain unresolved and there is at least one MID within a period of twenty-five years
- The issues at stake in dyad must be connected over the life of the rivalry.
- Once identified, rivalry continues until these issues are settled.[6]

Once a rivalry is identified by the above rules, the first MID concerning the relevant issues (which is not necessarily the first qualifying MID) is the start date of the rivalry.

Using Diehl and Goertz's and Bennett's lists of enduring rivalries, contemporary and historical maps, and the Correlates of War list of members of the interstate system, I generated two lists of buffer states by identifying those states geographically located between two rivals for the duration of the rivalry. For example, in identifying buffer states in the Franco-Prussian rivalry, I drew lines from Mulhouse in France to southern Silesia in Prussia, and from Calais in France to Stralsund in Prussia (see figure 4.1). These lines defined the boundaries of the buffer area—they captured the states that lay between France and Prussia at the time. Any state within such a buffer area was considered to be a buffer state unless an ocean divided the rivals. Tables B.1 and B.2 in appendix B list buffer states generated by the Diehl and Goertz and the Bennett list of enduring rivalries, respectively.

These measures of buffer states, however, do still present a problem, because both lists of enduring rivalries are based on the COW list of members of the interstate system, thereby excluding the precolonial African and Asian states discussed in chapter 2 and appendix A. Thus, no buffer states are identified in the revised or added country-years. This is misleading because many of these precolonial states were caught in the middle of intense rivalries, specifically the imperial rivalries—such as between France and Britain—that governed much of extra-European international politics.

To address this problem, two key imperial rivalries (UK-Russia and UK-France) were identified, and the coding scheme for "continental" buffer states was replicated for states between these empires. Any states between British India and Imperial Russia were coded as imperial buffer states for the duration of the Anglo-Russian imperial rivalry (or for the duration of the states); similarly, states between French Indochinese and British Indian rivals were coded as buffer states. Note that this change is consistent with standard interpretations of history,[7] and suggests that a general redefinition of rivalry may be in order. Table B.3 in appendix B lists imperial buffer states. Three operationalizations of the buffer state variable are

---

[6]Bennett 1996, 170–71.
[7]See for example chapters in Gifford and Louis 1971.

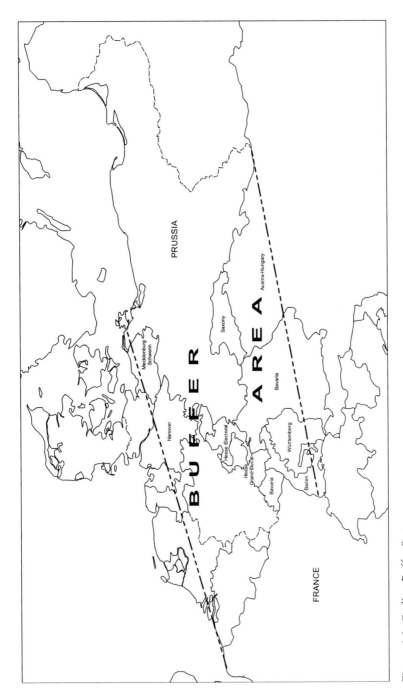

Figure 4.1. Coding Buffer States

therefore used in this chapter: Goertz and Diehl buffer states, Bennett buffer states, and all (Goertz and Diehl + imperial) buffer states.

Capabilities and Alliances

The capability variable, which is based on data from the Correlates of War National Material Capabilities Index,[8] has six components: military expenditure, military personnel, iron and steel production, energy consumption, urban population, and total population. The measure itself is calculated by determining what proportion of global resources a state holds, in a given year, on each dimension. The proportions are then averaged to obtain the state's capability score for that year.[9]

For country-years added to the Correlates of War, secondary sources were used to collect data on the components of capability. For states whose entry dates were backdated, observations on energy consumption and iron and steel production were imputed where later data were available in COW. For all country-years added to COW, total population and urban population were interpolated for missing years. When these efforts were not sufficient, values from similar, contemporaneous states were used.[10] Where possible, the same sources used by COW in the construction of the original data set were used to collect these additional data.[11]

Alliances were also measured in the standard manner. The Formal Interstate Alliance Data Set was used for states already in the Correlates of War.[12] Included in this data set is a measure of the "type" of alliance: defensive agreements, neutrality pacts, or ententes. This measure was used to test hypotheses on the general relationship between alliance type and state survival as well as the specific relationship between neutrality and buffer state survival. The alliance variable was recoded such that states with no alliance received a 0; states in ententes received a 1; states in neutrality pacts received a 2; and states in defensive alliances, considered to be the strongest among the three types, received a 3.

---

[8]Singer and Small 1993.

[9]This method is described in Singer, Bremer, and Stuckey 1972. I obtained capability scores as well as data on alliance patterns from D. Scott Bennett and Alan Stam's Expected Utility Generator, which includes data to 2000. Bennett and Stam 2000.

[10]The strategy of using contemporaneous states to interpolate data was employed in only two cases. First, because population data for Peshwa were suspect, I used neighboring Indore's data as Peshwa's data, on the principle that the states were of similar size and were similarly organized (if anything, Peshwa would have had a larger population than Indore). Somewhat similarly, I used COW's 1825 data for Tunisia's population and Africa's continental growth rate at the time to interpolate Tunisia's population back in time.

[11]For example, Chandler 1987 and Mitchell 1982, 1993, 1998.

[12]Gibler and Sarkees 2004.

The alliance data set was constructed using alliance treaties.[13] Thus, for states added to or amended in the Correlates of War, the treaties used to amend the list were also used to determine whether these states had formed alliances. Note that these data are incomplete in that I was not able to determine the full scope of these states' alliance patterns, only whether they were allied with Britain or France. Since alliances for added states in particular may be undercounted, the results may be biased by overstating the effect of alliances on state survival.

Legitimacy

Just as the domestic legitimacy of a regime can theoretically be measured by the level of internal support it enjoys, the international legitimacy of a state can be measured by the level of external recognition it receives. Recall from the discussion of membership in the interstate system that a new measure of recognition was used to expand the original Correlates of War list of members of the system. While states that concluded treaties with one of the system's legitimizers were included in the system, states that received diplomatic missions (or were members of major international organizations) enjoyed a higher level of recognition, or legitimacy.

The legitimacy variable can be coded dichotomously or trichotomously. For dichotomous coding ("legitimacy indicator"), in any given country-year, a state that is recognized only by treaty is coded as 0 on the legitimacy variable, while states that received diplomatic missions or were members of the League or United Nations are coded as 1. For trichotomous coding ("level of recognition"), in any given country-year, a state that is only recognized by *one* legitimizer is coded as 0 on the recognition variable; country-years where states are recognized by both legitimizers (i.e., have concluded appropriate treaties with Britain and France) receive a 1, while states that meet the COW criteria for recognition receive a 2.[14]

At first blush, it might seem that the inclusion of this operationalization of legitimacy will bias the results, since many of the states that receive a 0 die. It is important to remember, though, that states in this data set can be separated into four types: those that only ever sign treaties with one legitimizer; those that only ever sign treaties with two legitimizers; those that only ever receive missions or join international organizations; *and* those that conclude treaties prior to receiving diplomatic missions or joining international organizations. Thus, not all states that receive a 0 die,

---

[13]Singer and Small 1966; Small and Singer 1969.

[14]The legitimacy variable could be refined further by distinguishing states with one versus two missions. Unfortunately, the COW diplomatic missions data set does not make these distinctions.

and not all states that die receive a 0. In other words, receiving a 0 on the legitimacy variable does not perfectly predict state death, because a state's legitimacy score can vary over time. Nonetheless, it is important to remember that if the construction of this variable were to bias the results, it would lead to an overstatement of the effect of state legitimacy on state survival.

Another potential problem with the legitimacy variable is that it may serve as a proxy for power. To some extent, this is a conceptual problem with the variable, and not with the specific operationalization used here. I return to this issue in my discussion of the effect of legitimacy on state death, below.

Nationalism

Measuring nationalism is no easy task. In order for the nationalist resistance argument to be testable, however, it is necessary to identify measures of nationalism, which is expected to be the primary determinant of nationalist resistance. Because nationalism is difficult to measure directly, more indirect variables that should predict nationalism are used. These include a state's levels of economic development and democracy.

As suggested by Gellner,[15] among others, more industrialized or developed states are likely to have nationalistic populations. The measure for economic development used here is obtained from the Correlates of War National Material Capabilities Index.[16] This index is composed of six variables on three dimensions (military, economic, and demographic). The two economic variables—iron and steel production and energy consumption—are used here as proxies for economic development. The absolute (rather than relative calculations, as are used to determine relative capability) measures of these variables are used here to test the argument that levels of industrialization impact state survival and death. Iron and steel production is measured in thousands of tons, while energy consumption is measured in thousands of coal-ton equivalents.

Democratic states may also be particularly nationalistic. Because populations in more democratic states presumably have more ownership of their government and are more used to self-government, they may also be more resistant to potential conquerors. Standard measures of democracy, taken from the Polity IV project, are used here.[17] Democracy is measured on a scale from −10 (most autocratic) to 10 (most democratic). For country-years added to COW, however, I was unable to collect the

[15]Gellner 1983.
[16]Singer and Small 1993.
[17]Jaggers and Gurr 1995.

finer-grained data needed for the -10 to 10 scale. For this reason, I follow Goemans and trichotomize democracy, distinguishing nondemocratic states from states with mixed regimes and from democracies.[18] Where democracy scores were missing owing to a political transition, the previous year's democracy score was used.

Measures of nationalism in the case studies differ from measures used in the quantitative analysis. The most important qualitative measure of nationalism is the frequency and size of nationalist revolts. Nationalist rhetoric, as espoused by state (or national) leaders, citizens, and soldiers, also may be considered an indicator of nationalism, as may the presence of a mass army and high levels of ethnic homogeneity.

Additional Control Variables

Three control variables are included in the data analysis: an indicator variable for the post-1945 period; a measure of how mountainous a state is; and a measure for the number of great powers in the system in any given year. The argument that a post-1945 norm against conquest prevents violent state death after World War II is discussed in the previous chapter, and more extensively in the next section (part III) of the book. Even more so than nationalism, norms defy quantitative analysis. For the purpose of testing general explanations of state death, however, it is important to include the post-1945 period, in part to see whether there is an independent effect of the post–World War II era once other variables are controlled.

The second control variable—state mountainousness—is used to test the intuition that it will be difficult to conquer states that are particularly mountainous. States with rugged terrain—such as Switzerland and Afghanistan—are thought to be especially safe because their terrain serves as a barrier to potential conquerors. States that are very mountainous or that contain jungles or swamps are, by this logic, expected to be more likely to survive than flat, unprotected states.

The data on mountainousness used here were collected using ArcGIS (Geographic Information Systems) software. "Mountainousness" describes not only elevation but elevation relative to surrounding areas. Four types of areas were coded as mountainous: areas with an elevation above 2,500 meters; areas with an elevation above 1,500 meters and a slope greater than 2 degrees; elevated areas with a slope greater than 5 degrees that were more than 300 meters higher than surrounding areas; and plateaus and

---

[18]States that receive a 6 or above in Polity IV are coded as democracies; states that receive from -4 to 5 are coded as mixed; states that receive below -4 are coded as nondemocracies. Goemans 2000, 56.

valleys within mountainous areas.[19] This variable measures the percentage of a state that meets the criteria for mountainousness, as described above.

The final control variable—the number of great powers in the international system in a given year—is consistent with the intuition that conquest is more likely when the number of states with the ability to conquer increases. Note that this variable also may be correlated with the number of states that have buffer status, in that a rise in the number of great powers may generate a rise in the number of enduring rivalries that then produce buffer states.

Method

Frequently used to analyze phenomena like marriage duration, human survival, and failure times for mechanical equipment, duration analysis is particularly well suited for analysis of state death.[20] Duration analysis allows the modeler to use the state as the unit of analysis but also to include time-varying covariates.[21] The measure of a state's relative power, for example, can change annually in the data set. The model recognizes the United States in 1816 and 1817 as the same state and aggregates the observations relevant to that state. As before, the data used here constitute an amended version of the Correlates of War list of members of the interstate system, and have been formatted for duration analysis by including multiple observations for each case.[22] My dependent variable is the

[19]I thank Marc Levy at Columbia's Earth Institute for providing this definition and coding scheme, and Elizabeth Cardente for collecting the data.

[20]Kazuo Yamaguchi, and Box-Steffensmeier and Jones, offer useful discussions of duration analysis. Box-Steffensmeier and Jones 2004; Yamaguchi 1991.

[21]Importantly, duration analysis also does not impose a normality assumption on the distribution of errors, but instead offers the modeler a choice of several distributions or, in the case of the Cox proportional hazard model, does not require the modeler to make any assumptions about the distribution of the errors.

[22]Note: one problem in formatting these data for duration analysis was determining the time of origin for each state. Two separate variables could qualify as time of origin: the time the state was "born" (i.e., when it formed a cohesive and independent entity) or the time the state entered the international system (i.e., when the state became sufficiently powerful to enter the system and was recognized as a state by other states). I chose the date of entry into the system as the time of origin because violent state death is a nonissue for states that are not members of the international system. In choosing the date of entry into the system, I am imposing an assumption onto the analysis to make the analysis more feasible. Thirty-five states were already members of the system in 1816, when the data set begins. To determine precisely when each of these states entered the system would not only be difficult in terms of an expenditure of resources but also would require extending the data set back to the date of the first (of the thirty-five) state's entry into the system. Thus, I am assuming that the system begins in 1816; another way of thinking about this assumption is that I am dealing with

hazard rate for states, that is, the probability that a state will die violently in a given year, conditional on it not having died already.[23]

Before turning to a discussion of the results, it is important to note that five waves of state death—German unification, Italian unification, World War II, British colonization, and French colonization—stand out in table 2.1. Because the observations in these waves are not independent, observations in these waves are clustered in the analyses that follow.

Results

My primary expectation is that buffer states will be in a higher "risk group" for violent state death. That is, buffer states are more likely to experience violent state death than are other states. Thus, buffer status will have a positive effect on the probability of violent state death. In the vocabulary of duration analysis, we would say that buffer status will increase the hazard ratio for states. Because hazard ratios are interpreted in relation to one, these hypotheses predict that the hazard ratio for buffer states will be greater than one (see table 4.1). If a variable has a hazard ratio greater than one, then an increase in that variable increases the risk of failure (state death). Conversely, variables with a hazard ratio less than one decrease the risk of failure. My prediction is that the indicator variable for the post-1945 era will generate a hazard ratio of less than one, as the norm against conquest allows would-be conquerors to generate a credible commitment to preserve buffer states.

The balancing argument suggests that power and alliances will have a negative effect on the probability of violent state death. The state legitimacy variable is also hypothesized to have a hazard ratio less than one; power, alliances, and legitimacy are expected to have an inverse effect on the probability of violent state death. Similarly, the nationalist resistance argument predicts a state's level of economic development and democracy will improve a state's ability to survive; thus, the hazard ratios for democracy and economic development also should be less than one.

---

left truncation by assuming that all states in the system in 1816 entered the system in 1816, even though we know that many of these states entered the system much earlier. Analyses of the data that omit the thirty-five states "entering" in 1816 yield stable results.

[23] Beck, Katz, and Tucker have proposed an alternative method to analyze time-series cross-sectional data with time-varying covariates that is closer to the better-known logistic regression model. King and Zeng have proposed an additional alternative, relogit, for rare-events time-series data analysis. While state death is a relatively rare event, it is not so rare as to justify use of relogit. Results of logistic regressions using panel-corrected standard errors as per Beck, Katz, and Tucker are stable. Beck, Katz, and Tucker 1998; King and Zeng 2001b.

TABLE 4.1
Expected Effects of Variables

Variable	Hazard ratio should be
Buffer state	Greater than 1
Power × alliance	Less than 1
Power	Less than 1
Alliances	Less than 1
Legitimacy	Less than 1
Level of democracy	Less than 1
Economic development	Less than 1
Post-1945	Less than 1
Mountainousness	Less than 1
Number of great powers	Greater than 1

Table 4.2 reports results of a Cox proportional hazards model of violent state death. It includes variables from the buffer state, balancing, legitimacy, and nationalism hypotheses in various configurations, as well as the control variables discussed above. The goodness of fit of all the models included is very high, exceeding the .001 level of statistical significance. It is necessary to include the buffer state and control variables to achieve a well-fitting model. A comparison of the Nelson-Aalen cumulative hazard function against Cox-Snell residuals also indicates that the model fits well.

The results presented in table 4.2 should be interpreted as follows. In the first column of results, the hazard ratio for the post-1945 period is .08. This result means that a state in the post-1945 period is 92 percent more likely to survive than a state in the pre-1945 period, given that the state has not already died. In the same model, the hazard ratios for the log of power and the alliance indicator suggest that power and alliances are unrelated to state survival; we cannot be certain that the coefficients on the log of power or the alliance indicator are not zero ($p = .595$ and $p = .152$, respectively). The probability that a buffer state will die violently (given that it has not died already) in a particular year is 134 percent higher than for nonbuffer states. Clearly, the effect of the buffer state variable is an extremely large one, as is the effect of being in the post-1945 period. In the second and third columns, results are reported using the list of buffer states generated by Goertz and Diehl's and then Bennett's cod-

TABLE 4.2
Cox Models of Violent State Death

	1	2	3	4	5	6
Buffer status						
All buffers (including imperial)	2.34**			2.32**	2.41***	2.45***
Goertz & Diehl buffers		2.28**				
Bennett buffers			2.01**			
Balancing						
Capabilities (logged)	1.06	1.05	1.03	1.05		
Alliance indicator	1.43	1.39	1.44			
Alliance type				1.14		
Balancing (alliance indicator × logged capabilities)					0.95	0.95
Legitimacy						
Legitimacy indicator	0.22**	0.19**	0.19**	0.22**	0.23**	
Level of recognition						0.46***
Nationalism						
Energy consumption	1.00	1.00	1.00	1.00	1.00	1.00
Iron & steel	1.00	1.00	1.00	1.00	1.00	1.00
Democracy	0.98	0.95	0.99	0.97	0.95	0.94
Controls						
Post-1945	0.08***	0.08***	0.08***	0.08***	0.07***	0.07***
Mountainousness	0.69***	0.70***	0.70***	0.69***	0.69***	0.69***
Number of great powers	1.69***	1.68***	1.71***	1.69***	1.63***	1.61***
Number of subjects	252	252	252	252	252	252
Number of failures	50	50	50	50	50	50
Prob > χ^2	0.00	0.00	0.00	0.00	0.00	0.00

Notes: Dependent variable is the hazard rate: the probability that a state will die in a given year, conditional on its not having died already. Hazard ratios, rather than coefficients, are presented here; the hazard ratio is the exponentiated form of the coefficient. All tests are two-tailed.
  **Significant at the .05 level
  ***Significant at the .005 level

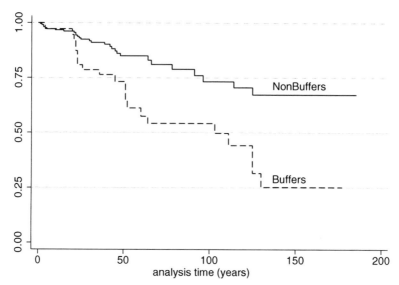

Figure 4.2. Kaplan-Meier Survival Estimates for Buffer States

ings of enduring rivalries (which do not code any states I added to COW as buffer states). The results using these different lists of buffer states consistently indicate that buffer state status and survival to the post-1945 period both generate significantly strong (although in opposite directions) effects on state death and survival.

These results are highlighted in figures 4.2 and 4.3. The Kaplan-Meier survival estimates presented in figure 4.2 distinguish the estimated probability of surviving beyond any given time for buffer and nonbuffer states. Figure 4.3 graphs the hazard rates for Poland (a buffer state) versus Spain (a nonbuffer state) during the interwar period. In addition to being one of the very few western European states that was not a buffer state during the interwar period, Spain was very similar to Poland on scores of capability, alliance, legitimacy, and economic development during that time.

As these graphs illustrate, the probability that a buffer state will survive is much lower than the probability that a nonbuffer state will survive. Inversely, Poland's hazard rate during the interwar period is much greater than Spain's, owing to Poland's status as a buffer state. In all, buffer states account for twenty-one (about 40 percent of) violent state deaths; similarly, about 40 percent of buffer states die, as illustrated in figure 4.4.

Figure 4.5 demonstrates the strong effect of the post-1945 period on state death, illustrating graphically the notion that states are much more likely to survive after 1945 as opposed to before.

Figure 4.3. Polish and Spanish Hazard Rates

The claim that states that balance against power are more likely to survive than those that fail to balance fares poorly in this analysis. Power is never a significant predictor of state survival. This result is driven at least in part by the fact that several powerful states die, while most weak states survive. Similarly, there appears to be no relationship between alliance status and state survival. Even a finer-grained measure of alliance, one that distinguishes between defensive alliances, neutrality pacts, and ententes, fails to generate a significant effect.

The indeterminacy of alliance status on state survival is not entirely surprising given the dynamics that may drive alliance formation. If threatened states are most likely to seek allies, but least likely to be effective in forging alliances, we might expect the impact of alliance formation on state survival to be a wash. In general, though, balancing behavior seems to be unrelated to state survival. Even when we interact power and alliance status, given the possibility that a state must balance both internally *and* externally in order to survive, there is no relationship between balancing and survival.

By contrast, it appears that the more recognition a state receives, the more likely it is to survive. The legitimacy variable is highly significant, and its effects are as predicted. "More" legitimate states are about 80 percent more likely to survive than "less" legitimate states. Figure 4.6 shows contrasting survivor functions for states with and without British and French diplomatic missions. Interestingly, it appears that legitimacy can matter on a finer scale as well; the hazard ratio for "recognition," a tri-

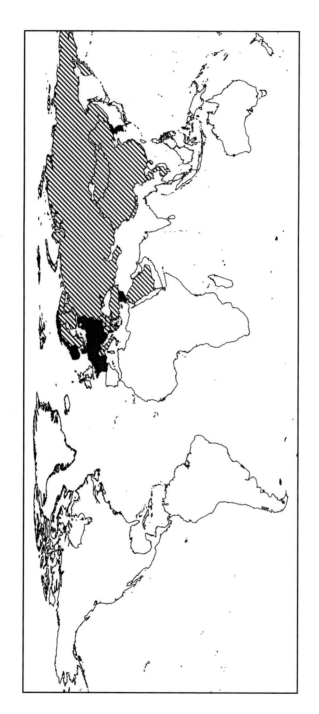

Buffer States that Survived ▨   Buffer State Deaths ■

Figure 4.4. Buffer States That Died, 1816–2000

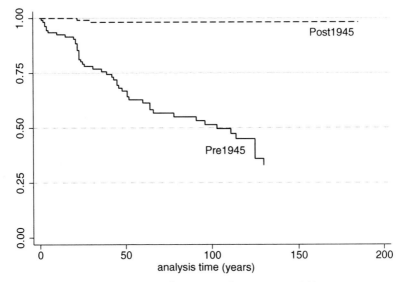

Figure 4.5. Kaplan-Meier Survival Estimates for Pre/Post-1945

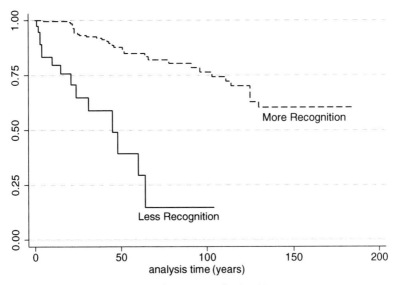

Figure 4.6. Kaplan-Meier Survival Estimates for Legitimacy

chotomous variable measuring three degrees of legitimacy, is significant but does not indicate as large a substantive effect as the dichotomous legitimacy variable.

The legitimacy variable is significantly correlated with power, although the correlation is not substantively large (.02). While legitimacy may be capturing power to a certain degree, it does appear to wield an independent, substantive effect on state survival. This result suggests that states fearing for their survival should seek greater levels of international recognition. But whether that recognition is granted may well depend on the intentions of the major powers of the day—certainly, international recognition of specific regimes has recently been used strategically as a tool of public diplomacy.

Interestingly, the coding rules for membership in the interstate system employed here mean that, after 1945, there is no variation on the legitimacy variable, just as there is an extremely low incidence of violent state death. This fact suggests that there may be a relationship between legitimacy and the cause of the decline of violent state death after 1945. For example, if a norm against conquest prevents violent state death in the post-1945 era, the norms and legitimacy argument might serve as two sides of the same coin in that a norm against conquest might also apply in the pre-1945 era, but only to the most "legitimate" states in the international system.

These results also indicate that the variables suggested by the nationalist resistance argument do not predict state death. None of these variables is significant in any model specification; further, the coefficients on these variables are essentially equal to zero.[24]

To be fair, however, nationalism is a particularly difficult concept to measure quantitatively. These results therefore should not be overstated; although they may cast doubt on the nationalist resistance hypothesis, they do not disconfirm it. Because nationalism can be better measured qualitatively than quantitatively, it is important to defer judgment on this hypothesis to the case studies presented later in this book.

Two additional variables included in the analysis also appear to bear a strong relationship to state death, although not as substantively significant as the effect of either buffer status or survival to 1945. Intuitively, more mountainous states are more likely to survive. Also unsurprising is the result that the likelihood of violent state death increases with the number of great powers, the category of states most likely to engage in conquest and, indeed, to produce buffer states.

---

[24]As a reminder, hazard ratios (not coefficients) are reported in table 4.2 because they are easier to interpret. A hazard ratio of 1 translates to a coefficient of 0.

Tests for Robustness

These results may be sensitive to a number of changes. Among the most important is the expansion of the dependent variable to include all state deaths. The decision to focus only on violent state death was based on the desire to give each hypothesis a fair chance. It seems likely that the balancing and legitimacy hypotheses are more directly applicable to typical cases of conquest and occupation as opposed to those of unification or dissolution. Restricting the dependent variable to only violent state deaths also seemed reasonable because most state deaths (75 percent) are, in fact, violent. Nonetheless, there are good reasons to think that the buffer state hypothesis in particular may also be applicable to some (although not all) nonviolent state deaths. Buffer states may recognize their vulnerability and thus negotiate themselves out of existence rather than subject themselves to an unwinnable war. For example, Bavaria and Württemberg, two nineteenth-century German city-states very reluctant to join the Prussian-dominated German protostate, anticipated on the eve of the Franco-Prussian War that if they did not fulfill their alliance commitments to Prussia and negotiate entry into the German state, they would be coerced out of existence. In the face of insurmountable odds, they joined the German confederation and avoided a war of conquest.[25]

The results for models in which all state deaths are included (see table 4.3) generate a stronger effect for buffer status and, not surprisingly, a smaller effect for the post-1945 indicator variable. The latter change is due to the rise in voluntary state dissolutions (such as Czechoslovakia in 1992) as well as unifications (such as in Germany in 1990) since 1945. Overall, though, the effect of these variables on state death appears stable; both the buffer state and the post-1945 variables continue to be statistically significant and, further, to have large substantive effects on the probability of state death.

Balancing behavior, on the other hand, does not appear to be related to this broader category of state death. Legitimacy is still related to state death, but the size of the effect of legitimacy on state death decreases. This result is not surprising, because greater levels of international legitimacy should be more effective in forestalling conquest than in preventing secession or unification. If there is a norm against taking over "legitimate" states, this norm would not necessarily apply to those states choosing to dissolve or give up their sovereignty to another state. Where legitimacy enters the equation in these cases is in the decision by other states to accord (or not) recognition to these new states in the system.

[25]Carr 1991, 207; Ziblatt 2004.

TABLE 4.3
Cox Models of All (Violent + Nonviolent) State Deaths

	1	2	3	4	5	6
Buffer status						
All buffers (including imperial)	3.18***			3.13***	3.09***	3.14***
Goertz & Diehl buffers		3.56***				
Bennett buffers			3.08***			
Balancing						
Capabilities (logged)	0.93	0.92	0.90	0.92		
Alliance indicator	1.32	1.24	1.31			
Alliance type				1.12		
Balancing (alliance indicator × logged capabilities)					0.95	0.96
Legitimacy						
Legitimacy indicator	0.32*	0.24**	0.23**	0.32*	0.30*	
Level of recognition						0.51**
Nationalism						
Energy consumption	1.00**	1.00**	1.00**	1.00**	1.00**	1.00**
Iron & steel	1.00	1.00	1.00	1.00	1.00	1.00
Democracy	1.01	0.97	1.00	1.01	1.02	1.02
Controls						
Post-1945	0.19***	0.20***	0.21***	0.19***	0.20***	0.20***
Mountainousness	0.70***	0.71***	0.72***	0.70***	0.71***	0.71***
Number of great powers	1.36**	1.36**	1.38**	1.36**	1.39**	1.38**
Number of subjects	252	252	252	252	252	252
Number of failures	66	66	66	66	66	66
Prob > χ^2	0.00	0.00	0.00	0.00	0.00	0.00

Notes: Dependent variable is the hazard rate: the probability that a state will die in a given year, conditional on its not having died already. Hazard ratios, rather than coefficients, are presented here; the hazard ratio is the exponentiated form of the coefficient. All tests are two-tailed.
  *Significant at the .1 level
  **Significant at the .05 level
  ***Significant at the .005 level

Variables related to the nationalism argument remain stable in statistical and substantive insignificance, with one exception. Energy consumption appears to be related to the likelihood of state death generally, although this variable was not significant in the analysis of violent state deaths. The hazard ratio for energy (1.000002) indicates a slightly positive coefficient, suggesting that more economically developed states are more likely to die. That this (very weak) result appears to contradict the logic of the nationalist resistance argument is less important than the fact that it is driven by an outlier: the Soviet Union. Including Soviet energy consumption in the mean of energy consumption (at the year of demise) for all state deaths quadruples the mean of this variable; the state with the next highest level of energy consumption produces a value that is an order of magnitude smaller than the Soviet value. Even if this result were not driven by an outlier, the coefficient on this variable is essentially equal to zero.

A second issue to test for refers to the fact that buffer states may be undercounted, particularly during the Cold War. As stated above, the buffer state variable was constructed by identifying those states geographically located between two rivals. In my coding of buffer states, I did not count any buffers if the rivals were separated by an ocean. Thus, the US-Soviet rivalry did not produce buffer states. The difficulty in coding buffer states for the Cold War is, of course, that the entire world could be considered a buffer state for this period. This problem was addressed in part by conducting an additional analysis where all European states were coded as buffers for the Cold War period; the results of the analysis show that all variables retained their relative statistical and substantive significance (see table 4.4). Note that the difficulty of distinguishing buffer states attached to the US-Soviet rivalry does not mean that buffer states cease to be meaningful after the onset of the Cold War; a number of other rivalries and buffer states continue and/or develop during this time.

Alterations to the list of state deaths from the international system also could affect the results presented here. It is important to ask, for example, to what degree these results are sensitive to changes in codings of the large number of state deaths that occurred during World War II. An additional analysis that excludes the World War II–associated state deaths yields stable results.

Finally, just as one could argue that the list presented here overcounts state deaths by including occupations during the Second World War, arguments also could be made that state deaths are undercounted because Cold War Eastern European states are not included. An analysis that includes Soviet satellite states as state deaths for the Cold War period, however, also yields stable results. The quantitative results presented above are therefore robust against a number of changes in, and potential objections to, coding decisions justified in this book.

TABLE 4.4
Tests for Robustness: Cox Models on All State Deaths

	Cold War buffers	Excluding WWII deaths	Including Soviet satellites
Buffer status			
All buffers (including imperial)	3.73***	2.50**	3.90***
Balancing			
Capabilities (logged)	0.94	0.95	0.92
Alliance indicator	1.19	1.01	1.28
Legitimacy			
Legitimacy indicator	0.27**	0.25*	0.27**
Nationalism			
Energy consumption	1.00**	1.00*	1.00*
Iron & steel	1.00	1.00	1.00
Democracy	0.97	1.01	0.93
Controls			
Post-1945	0.19***	0.28**	0.18***
Mountainousness	0.71***	0.72***	0.71***
Number of great powers	1.35**	1.17	1.34**
Number of subjects	252	252	251
Number of failures	66	51	65
Prob > χ^2	0.00	0.00	0.00

Notes: These tests were conducted on all state deaths because the revisions necessary to conduct these tests reduce the number of violent state deaths dramatically, undermining the model's estimation ability. The significance of the energy variable is due to the fact that the USSR is coded as a state death (see previous table). Tests including alternate specifications of each variable (e.g., alternative codings of buffer states, alliance, balancing, and legitimacy) yielded stable results.

Dependent variable is the hazard rate: the probability that a state will die in a given year, conditional on it not having died already. Hazard ratios, rather than coefficients, are presented here; the hazard ratio is the exponentiated form of the coefficient. All tests are two-tailed.

*Significant at the .1 level
**Significant at the .05 level
***Significant at the .005 level

These robustness tests underline the strength of the buffer state argument. Defining the dependent variable in terms of all state deaths (versus only violent state deaths) lends further support to the claim that buffer states are particularly likely to die. If we increase the number of buffer states during the Cold War, decrease the number of deaths as a result of World War II, or code the Soviet satellite states as state deaths, the predictive power of buffer status remains. Legitimacy also continues to be an important predictor of state death, but nationalism and balancing behaviors are never statistically significant.

Explaining Variation in Buffer State Survival

Based on the preceding analysis, we can say with confidence that buffer states constitute a threatened group of states. Even among buffer states, however, some die while others survive. How can we explain variation in the survival of buffer states?

Addressing this question may be particularly important in conducting a fair test of the balancing hypothesis. A refined version of this hypothesis suggests that balancing will be most likely—and most necessary—when the level of threat is high. In addition to examining any possible relationship between buffer status and alliance patterns, it is important to assess the role of power held by buffer states vis-à-vis surrounding rivals as a measure of balancing. The variable "Buffers' power (logged)" was constructed by determining how much power a buffer state held with respect to its rivals. Recall that weakness is not a definitional prerequisite for buffer status. The data set includes a number of powerful buffer states that also form alliances—in other words, the data include buffers that appear to balance against surrounding rivals. The balancing argument predicts that these states will be more likely to survive than buffers that fail to balance.

On the other hand, another logic suggests that a weak buffer state is a survivable buffer state. If the advantage conferred by the buffer state is negligible, surrounding rivals should be less likely to fight over it. Given the typical intensity of rivalry, however, it is possible that even very small and weak buffer states will seem valuable to surrounding rivals; also, symbolic victories may be as important as material ones.

A related argument suggests that symmetries of power increase the probability of war. For example, A.F.K. Organski and Jacek Kugler argue that power symmetries between great powers can lead to war for two reasons. First, the challenger state may see war as a means to speed up the process of surpassing the established hegemon; and second, the established state may wish to prevent the rising state from catching up.[26] Similarly, arguments suggesting that war is at least in part an information problem are consistent with the notion that certainty about outcomes is lower when symmetry between rivals is greater.[27] This logic suggests that buffer states will be particularly likely to die when surrounding rivals are relatively equal in power.

With respect to alliances, it is important to assess possible selection effects in the relationship between alliance formation and state survival. This requires first examining the relationship between a group of states that we know is threatened—buffer states—and alliance formation. The correlation between buffers and alliance formation, while significant, is very low (.10). It is not clear that threatened states tend to form alliances or that, among threatened states, those that do form alliances are more likely to survive.

A very small literature on buffer states suggests additional variables that may influence buffer state survivability. A number of scholars have looked to neutrality as a key to survival for buffer states. Chay and Ross argue that "unless a certain degree of neutrality is maintained by a state it cannot effectively operate as a buffer."[28] Joseph Malia agrees: "Unless the buffer succeeds in remaining neutral, its sovereignty is threatened and at times its very existence is placed in jeopardy."[29] Michael Partem also chimes in on this point, stating that "for a buffer, a policy of neutrality is a way to avoid incurring the wrath of the larger neighbors."[30]

The logic behind the argument linking neutrality to buffer state survival is that a neutral buffer state removes itself from the core of the security dilemma played by its neighboring rivals. If a buffer state declares itself to be neutral, the surrounding rivals need not fear that their opponent will take over the buffer state at their expense. Neutrality, it is argued, neutralizes the effects of the rivalry on the buffer state.

There are at least two important problems with this argument. The first difficulty is that states that sign neutrality pacts, or even declare neutrality in their constitutions, may do so as a result of dire straits.[31] Therefore, we might expect that neutrality would have a negative effect on buffer state survival. A second problem with this argument is that it assumes that

[26]Organski and Kugler 1980, ch. 1; Bueno de Mesquita and Lalman 1992.

[27]Blainey 1988; Fearon 1995.

[28]Chay and Ross 1986, 5.

[29]Malia 1986, 30.

[30]Partem 1983, 14. Also see Taras 1997.

[31]This logic is consistent with logic suggesting that alliances may be ineffective deterrents because very determined aggressors would issue their threats regardless of the alliance status of the object of their threat, as well as with results from Huth and Russett and from Signorino and Tarar. Huth and Russett 1984, 1988; Signorino and Tarar 2006; Fearon 1994.

buffer states, which tend to be much weaker than surrounding rivals, can hold stronger states at bay by declaring their neutrality. The nature of the typical distribution of power between buffers and their neighbors, however, suggests that the fate of buffer states is tied more to the behavior of rivals than to that of buffers. Neutrality can be an effective policy tool only when it is convincing. The typical power disparity between surrounding rivals and buffer states in the middle undermines the credibility of any buffer state declaration of neutrality. Even if the buffer state firmly intends to maintain its neutrality, its policies are too vulnerable to the desires and actions of nearby powers to be stable simply because the buffer state has clear intentions.

Finally, an analysis of buffer state survival presents an opportunity to test the claims that rivals whose resources are simultaneously constrained and/or who are forced to become allies in a war in a second theater are less likely to take over the buffers that lie between them. By constructing a variable that codes for whether a buffer's rivals' resources are so constrained *or* whether the rivals are engaged on the same side of a war, we can take a first step in evaluating the hypotheses that tiring hands and diverted rivalries offer buffers a reprieve and, further, predict the timing of buffer state death.

The results presented in table 4.5 are consistent with the analysis on the entire data set (in tables 4.2–4.4). Variables associated with the balancing and nationalism hypotheses do not appear to be related to buffer state survival—it does not appear that these arguments fare better when applied to a set of threatened states, as opposed to the entire population of states. Even more specific measures associated with the balancing hypothesis—such as the relative power held by buffer states with respect to surrounding rivals—are not related to the probability of buffer state death and survival. Further, when the logged capabilities of the buffer state are interacted with the buffer's alliance status, the results are stable—balancing appears unrelated to buffer state death. This result in particular continues to challenge the balancing hypothesis, suggesting that a focus on increasing one's military power may be fruitless for buffer states.

Interestingly, mountainousness also appears unrelated to buffer state survival. This result is surprising in part because we tend to think of buffer states—like Switzerland—as having rough terrain. In fact, the correlation between buffer status and mountainousness is neither statistically nor substantively significant. In part this is because most modern buffer states are not consciously created; rather, they are victims of geography in the sense of being in the wrong place at the wrong time. While mountainous states are generally more likely to survive, the strategic imperative to take over buffer states appears to overwhelm the challenge faced by difficult terrain. Further, one could imagine that inhospitable terrain might make

TABLE 4.5
Cox Models of Buffer State Survival, 1816–1945

	Full	Balancing	Nationalism	Neutrality	Rivals' balance	Buffer power
Balancing						
Capabilities (logged)	0.75	0.83		0.75		
Buffers' power (logged)						0.78
Alliance indicator	1.11	1.03				
Neutrality				0.89		
Legitimacy						
Legitimacy indicator	0.08***	0.06***	0.05***	0.08**	0.04***	0.06***
Nationalism						
Energy consumption	1.00		1.00	1.00		
Iron & steel	1.00		1.00	1.00		
Democracy	1.10		1.11	1.09		
Rivalry						
Rivals' asymmetry					0.71	
Controls						
Mountainousness	0.13	0.15	0.13	0.12	0.15	0.16
Number of great powers	2.11**	2.50***	2.05**	2.09*	2.41***	2.55***
Number of subjects	50	50	50	50	42	49
Number of failures	21	21	21	21	21	21
Prob > χ^2	0.00	0.00	0.00	0.02	0.00	0.00

Notes: These regressions are limited to the pre-1945 era because no buffer states died violently after 1945.

Dependent variable is the hazard rate: the probability that a state will die in a given year, conditional on its not having died already. Hazard ratios, rather than coefficients, are presented here; the hazard ratio is the exponentiated form of the coefficient. All tests are two-tailed.

**Significant at the .05 level
***Significant at the .005 level

buffer states *more* likely to be conquered, as surrounding rivals might wish to internalize these barriers.

Although not reported in table 4.5, rivals' participation in separate, simultaneous wars or on the same side of another war in a separate theater appeared to exert a very strong statistical and substantive effect on the probability of buffer state survival. Indeed, this variable was a perfect predictor of buffer state survival,[32] lending some initial support to the claim that rivals whose hands are "tired" or whose contest is "diverted" are in fact less likely to take over their buffer states. These hypotheses will be explored further in the case studies in following chapters.

Conclusion

Buffer states are born to lose. Balancing, on the other hand, is not very consequential for state survival or death. Even among the most threatened states, relative power and alliance formation are unrelated to state survival. This result—one of the most robust across the series of statistical tests conducted in this chapter—casts serious doubt on the claim that states that balance against power will be the most likely to survive.

The hypothesis that more legitimate states will be more likely to survive receives more positive support. This is good news for constructivists, who argue for the importance of social relations in international politics. An interesting extension of this test would be to compare the survival rates of states in various lists of members of the interstate system;[33] equally interesting would be to study legitimacy as a dependent variable, which would afford an opportunity to address the potential endogeneity problem that recognition might be most likely to be offered to those states that the recognizers have no intention of conquering.[34]

One argument that I have not been able to test well, given available data, is the nationalist resistance argument. The prediction that states with nationalistic populations will generate high costs for would-be conquerors is difficult to assess; although I have used indicators of nationalism suggested by proponents of this argument, these indicators are weak at best. One direct indicator of nationalism would be nationalist revolt; comprehensive data on nationalist revolts would, at the least, allow stronger tests of the hypothesis that nationalistic occupied states are more likely to be resurrected than societies that are less nationalistic. The pres-

[32]The reason this variable was not included in the table is precisely because it perfectly predicted buffer state survival.

[33]See for example Gleditsch and Ward 1999; Bennett and Zitomersky 1982; Adams 2000; Lemke 2006.

[34]Fabry 2005.

ence of mass armies and high levels of ethnic homogeneity also may figure into the probability of resistance. Relying on a much smaller number
of cases, I examine exactly this kind of data in the following case studies
of Poland, Persia, and the Dominican Republic.

In my exploration of the survivability of buffer states in particular, hypotheses regarding the role of neutrality, the power of the buffer relative
to surrounding rivals, the balance of power between rivals, and the role
of rough terrain in promoting buffer state survival are not supported by
the evidence. Involvement of rivals in simultaneous but separate wars, or
on the same side of a war in another theater, on the other hand, perfectly
predict buffer state survival. These hypotheses—that rivals whose resources are constrained by conflict in another theater will refrain from
taking over buffer states—also will be further explored in the following
chapter.

The results of extensive testing of the conditions under which states are
likely to die are clear. The fates of states are determined primarily by geography and timing. The claims tested in this chapter are further analyzed
below in a series of case studies of buffer and nonbuffer state death and
survival.

Chapter 5 ⎯⎯⎯⎯⎯⎯⎯⎯⎯⎯⎯⎯⎯⎯⎯⎯⎯⎯

Buffer State Death and Survival Prior to 1945

As THE quantitative analysis presented in the previous chapter demonstrates, buffer states are particularly likely to die. This chapter begins to take the empirical analysis further, by showing *why* buffer states are endangered in specific cases. The case studies presented in this chapter are also used to continue to evaluate the nationalist resistance and balancing arguments. The evidence from these cases shows that the dynamics of rivalry overwhelm the effects of nationalist resistance as well as attempts to balance. While buffer states might try to generate resistance, build up their militaries, or form alliances, surrounding rivals conspire to keep them weak. Thus, the balancing and nationalist resistance prescriptions are least effective in the cases where they should be most important: buffer states.

Case Selection

Because the probability, and the nature, of state death changed dramatically after 1945, this chapter focuses on pre-1945 cases of state death and survival. Specifically, four cases are examined: the Polish partitions of the late eighteenth century; Persia in the late nineteenth and early twentieth centuries; the United States' near annexation of the Dominican Republic in 1870; and the US occupation of the Dominican Republic in 1916. The cases were selected along two dimensions: whether they involved buffer states and whether the states died.

The first case, late eighteenth-century Poland, is a classic illustration of buffer state death, with Austrian, Prussian, and Russian rivals slowly carving up the Polish state. This case serves as an easy test of the argument advanced here. A particularly interesting feature of the Polish case is the relative fall from power experienced by the Poles. Unlike Belgium, which was created for the purpose of buffering European powers, Poland was previously a powerful central European state. The long history of the Polish state makes it more likely that the nationalist resistance argument will carry some weight, and also makes it easier to distinguish arguments about power and balancing from arguments about geography and strategy.

The second case, that of Persia/Iran in the late nineteenth/early twentieth centuries, is another case of a classic buffer state, but one caught between two empires. Examining the Correlates of War–based list of nineteenth-century buffer states that survived yields only five cases: Italy, Romania, Russia, Sweden, and Switzerland. Although coded as a buffer state, the Russian "buffer" produced by the French-Chinese rivalry is unlikely to yield a useful analysis. Similarly, Italy was not central to the Franco-German rivalry that accorded it buffer status; Switzerland is closer to a classic buffer state, but here Switzerland's very unusual topography also makes it a fairly uninteresting case. The two remaining cases—Romania and Sweden—are both generated by the British-Russian rivalry of the nineteenth century. One could make the argument, however, that that rivalry was actually more acute between the British and Russian empires (beyond Europe) than it was on the continent. Using the revised list of members of the international system allows us to adjust for this fact and include a number of additional buffer states. To the extent that the Anglo-Russian rivalry was expressed primarily in Asia, examining the case of an associated Asian buffer state will be more useful in comprehending the dynamics of rivalry. Thus, although not a continental buffer, Persia is an important case to consider here; indeed, it is a case that appears to contradict my argument because Persia is a buffer state that survived (see table B.3 in appendix B). Thus, Persia is a harder test of the argument of this book.

Third, a case of a nonbuffer state that survived is presented; the United States almost annexed the Dominican Republic in 1870 but refrained from doing so, in part because the Senate could not be convinced that there existed a strategic imperative behind the annexation scheme. This case serves as an easy test of the claim that nonbuffer states should survive. Finally, I examine a case of nonbuffer state death: the US occupation of the Dominican Republic in 1916. Here, the list of state deaths presented in chapter 2 is helpful in the selection of cases of nonbuffer state death. Nine of these states are not buffers for either the Diehl and Goertz or the Bennett list of rivals.[1] Of the remaining states, the African states can be eliminated as possible imperial buffer states. This leaves five Latin American and Caribbean states. Working from the notion that island states are inherently unattractive as buffers suggests a focus on the Cuban, Haitian, and Dominican cases. Given that one of the Hispaniolan states would probably offer considerable analytic leverage in explaining the death of its neighbor, the second case discussed here is the US occupation of the Dominican Republic in 1916. On its face the case of the Dominican Re-

[1] Paraguay, Peru, Tunisia, Egypt, Cuba, Morocco, Haiti, Dominican Republic, Ethiopia. Because Poland, France, Yugoslavia, and Greece as buffers within ten years of their death, and because the Two Sicilies was very nearly a buffer state in the Austro-Hungarian rivalry, they were excluded from the list of nonbuffer states that survived (although they were of course included in my quantitative analysis).

TABLE 5.1
Case Selection for Pre-1945 Cases

	Buffer	Nonbuffer
Death	Poland, 1772–1795	Dominican Republic, 1916
Survival	Persia, late 19th/early 20th c.	Dominican Republic, 1870

public in 1916 is a hard case for my argument because the Dominican Republic does not fit the conventional definition of a buffer state. In the end, however, US-German rivalry in Latin America and the Caribbean in the early twentieth century explains the Dominican loss of sovereignty. Comparing the 1870 case to that of 1916 and, in the next chapter, to the US intervention of 1965 offers the additional advantage of controlling for a number of variables (as both the buffer and would-be conquering state are held constant) in all three cases.

Case selection for this chapter is summarized in table 5.1.

Variable Measurement

For each case, I ask three questions. First, why did state death occur (or not occur)? My expectation is that both deaths and survivals can be attributed to the dynamics of rivalry. In exploring the causes of invasion, then, it is important to look for evidence of rivalry prior to invasion. In addition to the indicators of rivalry used for the quantitative analysis (i.e., a history of violent conflict between two states), statements of heads of state and their advisers are examined for evidence of rivalry. For example, if territorial or other gains by one potential rival were observed by another potential rival, attempts to match these gains would be taken as suggestive of a rivalry. Similarly, if such gains were perceived by policy makers to reduce the security of their own state, statements to this effect should be taken as indicative of a security dilemma. Discussions of trust and the availability of institutions to enforce any commitments made to preserve the sovereignty of a buffer state are also important here. If it is clear that one or both rivals did not trust each other, and/or if there existed no clear institutions, circumstances, or opportunities through which commitments could be enforced, it would be unlikely that any existing security dilemma would be resolved such that the buffer state could survive. If, on the other hand, rivals were able to tie hands or sink costs, or if external circumstances intervened that effected these outcomes for the rivals, we should expect that the likelihood of buffer survival would increase.

The second question I ask in each case is, did the would-be conquerors anticipate costly nationalist resistance in taking over the relevant state?

This question speaks directly to the nationalist resistance argument, which is an important alternative to my explanation for state death. Although the nationalist resistance argument is not supported by the quantitative analysis in the previous chapter, limits on available data make compelling statistical tests of this claim difficult. Therefore, a fair amount of time will be spent exploring this argument in this and the following chapters.

The nationalist resistance argument makes both general and specific predictions. The general prediction is that, over time, nationalism should increase and, in response, would-be conquerors should be less inclined to take over other states. This trend, however, is also consistent with my argument that a norm against conquest has prevented violent state death after 1945. One way to better assess the explanatory power of the nationalist resistance argument is to look closely at particular periods of history. Specifically, the nationalist resistance argument would predict that, if strong signs of nationalism preceded decision making about invasion, invasion would be deterred.

Four indicators could lead to the assessment (or not) of nationalism: revolt in anticipation of conquest, the presence of a mass army, high levels of industrialization, and ethnic homogeneity. Cases where nationalist revolts occurred in anticipation of invasion should constitute easy tests for the nationalist resistance argument. This is not to say, however, that the absence of such revolts should be taken to mean that the state at risk did not have a nationalistic population; it may well be that nationalist revolt is more likely *after* conquest, as opposed to in anticipation of conquest. This possibility is explored in further depth in the following chapter, which examines state resurrection.

The third question I ask in each case is, did the state at risk attempt to balance in order to increase its survival prospects? Like the nationalist resistance argument, the balancing argument is not supported by the quantitative analysis in the previous chapter. More powerful states, as well as those that form alliances, are not particularly likely to survive—this result from the quantitative analysis holds for the general population of states as well as for the more threatened group of buffer states. Another exploration of the balancing argument is presented here. For each case, evidence of military buildups and attempts to form alliances in the face of threats from surrounding great powers will be sought. If the state failed to follow these prescriptions in cases where the state died, the balancing argument will find some support. If however, the state died despite having balanced, this outcome should be taken as further evidence that a strategy of balancing does not necessarily lead to state survival, and that a failure to balance does not necessarily lead to state death.

The timing of these cases means that they will serve better as illustrations of the dynamics of rivalry preceding state death than as illustrations of the claim that a norm against conquest has prevented violent state death after 1945. I use these cases to trace the processes by which the buffer state, nationalist resistance, and balancing arguments might operate. Note that, because the primary purpose of this chapter is to probe further into the buffer state, balancing, and nationalist resistance arguments, the cases were not selected to examine the claim that more legitimate states are likely to survive. A brief discussion of the role of international recognition is, however, included at the end of this chapter.

The Partitions of Poland

In 1764, Stanislas Augustus Poniatowski, the last king of Poland, acceded to a throne stripped of much of its former glory. Once one of the primary powers in central Europe, Poland had become a buffer state between Russia, Austria, and Prussia. Indeed, by 1717 Poland was considered by many to be an unofficial Russian protectorate. By 1795, Poland would completely disappear from the European map following a series of partitions by Russia, Austria, and Prussia.

This turn of events was surprising in that, compared to many other European states, Poland appeared to be in a strong position. "The historical Poland, in 1770, was a vast country, extending from the Baltic almost to the Black Sea, and lying between Russia and Germany, with an area of about 280,000 square miles, and a population roughly estimated at eleven and a half millions. It stood third in the list of European countries as regards its extent, and fifth as regards its population."[2] Poland's economic and military straits were dire, however. State revenue was equal to one-seventy-fifth that of France and smaller than England's revenue from stamp paper alone.[3] And in the first year of King Stanislas's reign, the Polish army numbered approximately twelve thousand ill-trained men—not even one-tenth the size of the Austrian army, and closer to one-twentieth that of the Russian forces.[4]

Conventional wisdom attributes the decline and eventual death of the Polish state to its paralyzing domestic structures.[5] In addition to an electoral monarchy, Poland was distinguished by a very powerful parliament, or *Sejm*. The first of the *Sejm*'s powers, after the election of the king, was the *liberum veto*. This institution allowed any single member of the *Sejm*

---

[2]Eversley 1915, 15.
[3]Zamoyski 1992, 5.
[4]Lukowski 1999, 10.
[5]See for example Eversley 1915, 18–19; Lukowski 1999, 8.

to veto any agreement on the floor of the diet. Given its frequent use in the eighteenth century, the *liberum veto* almost always served the cause of gridlock. The many direct consequences of the *liberum veto* included prolonged and unpredictable *Sejms*, kings reduced to figureheads, and a general inability to prevent or effectively deal with crises.

Another practice contributing to the difficulties of Polish politics was the common precedent of dissatisfied aristocrats, or *szlachta*, to form rival governments, or confederations. Frequently, these confederations were supported by the armies of the founding *szlachta* and any others they might recruit to their cause. More often than not, various confederations unintentionally functioned as crowbars used by neighboring powers to lever their way into Polish politics.

The duration of these paralyzing institutions cannot, however, be attributed solely to *szlachta*. The electoral monarchy, the *liberum veto,* and the right to confederate also served the interests of neighboring powers—in particular Russia and Prussia—who wanted to keep Poland weak enough to exercise indirect control with little or no contest. As shown below, repeated attempts to modify the Polish Constitution met with fierce resistance from external as well as internal powers.

In 1772, 1792, and 1795, Poland's neighbors slowly dismembered it until the Polish state vanished from the European map. The eighteenth-century partitions of Poland clearly illustrate Poland's status as a buffer; they also demonstrate how partition accelerated as rivals' fears of losing control over the Polish buffer became more acute. Poland's partitioners were not deterred by clear and consequential nationalist resistance, however. The Poles took advantage of numerous opportunities to express their resistance to partition and occupation, yet Russia, Prussia, and Austria forwent just as many opportunities to withdraw from Poland in the face of resistance. The Poles were virtually helpless in preventing the death of their state. In addition to the failure of revolt in deterring aggression against Poland, attempts at balancing also failed to save Poland. A victim of unfortunate geography, Poland disappeared from Europe for over a century and was not reborn until 1919, as the international normative landscape was dramatically changing.

Why Was Poland Partitioned?

THE FIRST PARTITION

The rivalries surrounding eighteenth-century Poland are easy to identify. As early as 1764, when the issue of succession to the Polish throne arose, nearby great powers were jockeying for influence over the Polish buffer. Despite various maneuverings among Poland's *szlachta,* what was clear from the outset was that Russia would, in effect, decide the question. It did not take long for Catherine, empress of all the Russias, to decide on her former lover, Stanislas Augustus Poniatowski. Catherine's message to Poniatowski illustrates the extent of her control: "I am sending at once Count Keyserling as ambassador to Poland to declare you king after the death of the present monarch and, in the event of his not proving successful so far as you are concerned, I want it to be Prince Adam [Czartoryski]."[6] The Russian choice was to be backed by approximately seventy thousand troops.

These tactics, as well as the choice, were initially objected to by neighboring powers. Both Austria and France preferred a king from Saxony, and particularly wanted a Poland independent of Russian influence, but both retreated in the face of Russian reassurance. The Turks also sought a Poland free of foreign influence but were in favor of a native king. And Frederick the Great of Prussia, despite an offer of the throne by a rival Polish party to his brother, supported the Russian decision in the interest of maintaining his good relations with Russia.[7] Indeed, Frederick's view of the succession was a prescient one, and illustrated the multiple rivalries that would shape Poland's fate. He had always planned to recapture the port town of Danzig (or Gdańsk, in Polish) but knew that he could not do so without the consent and collusion of his Russian rival.[8] Frederick outlined his strategy for acquiring Polish territory by quoting Victor Amadeus of Savoy: "My son, it is necessary to eat the Milanese like an artichoke, leaf by leaf. . . . That is how it is necessary to profit and gain . . . sometimes a city, sometimes a district, until all is eaten."[9]

Surprisingly, King Stanislas quickly demonstrated his desire to act as more than a figurehead by proposing a number of reforms, including amending the *liberum veto,* that could strengthen the Polish state. Ratification of such reforms would threaten surrounding rivals' control over an increasingly independent Poland. Not surprisingly, both Prussia and Russia objected to these changes in the Polish Constitution.[10] In response to these attempted reforms, Russia used the threat of invasion to encourage Poland to sign the Perpetual Treaty between the Polish Commonwealth and the Empire of All Russia. The most important elements of the treaty were a Russian guarantee of Poland's territorial integrity and preservation of the Polish Constitution.[11] Poland had tried to wriggle out of its shackles but had been caught and re-bound even more tightly.

---

[6]Quoted in Kaplan 1962, 13. Prince Adam was Poniatowski's cousin.

[7]Kaplan 1962, chs. 2 and 3.

[8]Virtually the same problem faced Adolf Hitler in 1939.

[9]Quoted in Kaplan 1962, 20–21.

[10]Indeed, in a 1764 treaty these two powers had codified their intention to maintain the Polish Constitution.

[11]Eversley 1915, 41; Kaplan 1962, 89–90.

The treaty was perceived as an outrage by key members of the *Sejm*, who confederated at the small fortress town of Bar. The Barists declared their intention to take up arms to defend the Polish state against internal treason and external oppression, objecting particularly to the imprisonment of several prominent political figures by Russia. The Barist revolt soon provided important opportunities for Russia's rivals to challenge, or at least chip away at, Russia's domination of Poland.

The first such opportunity fell into Turkish hands. The Turkish Porte had objected strongly to the 1768 treaty with Russia, concerned about growing Russian control in Poland. When the Barists appealed to the Porte for assistance against Russia, the Turks initiated war with Russia.

The Russo-Turkish War provided excuses for other states to intervene in Poland. The first to do so was Austria; with what appeared to be genuine concern to prevent war from spilling over its border, Austria cordoned off its border with Poland in such a way as to include the town of Zips (also known as Spisz), which was part of Polish lands, in 1768. This action was not objected or responded to until 1770, after Austria had begun levying taxes and reversed its original position (stated in 1769) that the rights of the Polish Crown would be preserved. Austria now claimed that Zips belonged to Hungary and, therefore, to Austria. Further, in August 1770, Austria extended its cordon deeper into Polish territory, occupying parts of the Polish Ukraine.

Although the Prussians had actively been considering a Polish partition for some time, Frederick stepped very carefully. He would not be the first to make a move into Polish territory, but the Austrian occupation afforded him a golden opportunity. In a letter to the Prussian ambassador to Russia, Baron Solms, on February 2, 1769, he wrote:

> Count Lynar has a rather curious idea concerning Russia that might appeal to the interests of the princes and that might improve the present conditions in Europe. He suggests that Russia offer to the court of Vienna for its assistance against the Turks the town of Lwów, with its environs, and Spisz; that Polish Prussia with Warmia and the right of protection over Gdánsk be given to us; and that Russia, to indemnify herself for the expenses of the war, take whatever part of Poland would be convenient; and then Austria and Prussia, neither being envious of the other would in emulation of each other, aid Russia against the Turks.
>
> This plan has some luster; it appears seductive; I believed it my duty to send it to you. Although it seems to me that it is more brilliant than sound, you know the way of Count Panin's thinking; either you will suppress all this, or you will judge what is opportune to employ.[12]

---

[12]Quoted in Kaplan 1962, 112. Count Panin was Catherine the Great's chief adviser on Poland.

Solms's response to Frederick's letter indicated a Russian commitment to preserve Poland intact. But as the war threatened Prussia's borders as well, Frederick needed little prompting to enclave the towns of Elblag and Warmia. By January of 1771, Frederick had received indications from Solms that the mood in St. Petersburg was now in favor of partition. Soon after, a conversation between Catherine and Frederick's brother, Prince Henry, confirmed Solms's perception: "Why shouldn't we all take something?' [Catherine] said to Henry—although he could not be sure that she was serious. Frederick, he pointed out, had set up a cordon sanitaire, but, unlike the Austrians, he had not annexed any land. 'But,' laughed the empress, 'why not take the land anyway?' A moment later Count Chernyshev came up to me and talked on the same subject. . . . 'Why not take the bishopric of Warmia? After all, everyone ought to have something."[13] Several months later, on June 14, Frederick sent a "Draft of a Secret Convention between His Majesty the King of Prussia and the Empress of all the Russias" to Solms in St. Petersburg. The convention stated Prussian and Russian "ancient rights" to specific Polish territories, provided mutual guarantees of Prussian and Russian possession of these territories, committed to offering similar territories to Austria, and declared that both states would work to win Polish consent for the plan.

Given that Austrian actions had precipitated Russian and Prussian plans for partition, it was surprising that the Austrian empress, Maria Theresa, now balked at the notion of dismembering Poland. She objected to the plan on moral grounds, and reassured King Stanislas's brother that she meant to guarantee Polish territory as well as see Poland extricated from Russian domination. Soon after making these promises, however, on the advice of their adviser Prince Kaunitz, both Maria Theresa and Emperor Joseph accepted that if Russia and Prussia were to carve up slices of Poland, Austria must have its share as well. Having agreed to the idea of partition, Austria now insisted on an exactly equal slice of the pie. Indeed, the Austrian claims were so extensive as to alarm first Prussia and then Russia. In response to Prussian and Russian objections, Prince Kaunitz argued that the particular territory at issue was the only truly valuable portion of Austrian spoils from the partition. Even with this territory, Polish Austria would be a "narrow . . . and exposed strip of land"; if this territory were not granted to Austria, Kaunitz contended, the balance of power in the region would be upset.[14] Frederick wryly expressed his concern to the Austrian ambassador: "Permit me to say that your mistress has a very good appetite." Similarly, in Russia, Catherine's adviser

---

[13]Quoted in Lukowski 1999, 64.
[14]Prince Kaunitz was referring to the economically valuable salt mines at Lwów. Kaplan 1962, 170–71.

Count Panin feared that the Austrian demands were so excessive that they would completely eliminate Poland as a buffer state. "Poland must remain for ever as an intermediary State destined to prevent collision between her three neighbors. We should therefore leave to it a force and existence suitable for such a destination."[15]

Faced with such strong opposition to its claims, Austria amended its demands; on August 5, 1772, all three powers signed the partition convention in St. Petersburg. According to the terms of the treaty, Prussia received 5 percent of Poland's territory—including Polish Prussia, which had previously divided the Prussian state from itself—and 580,000 inhabitants; Russia took 12.7 percent of the territory and 1.3 million people; Austria received 11.8 percent of Polish territory—including the valuable salt mine town of Lwów—and 2.13 million inhabitants. Approximately one-fourth of Poland was now transferred to Prussia, Austria, and Russia, and, under the terms of the treaty, the state that remained was required to retain its old Constitution.

The first Polish partition was characterized by great-power concerns about rivals' gains. Russia had exerted indirect control over Poland for many years prior to partition. When that indirect control was threatened, the response was advance, not retreat. Seeing the opportunity for territorial gain, first Austria, then Prussia, and finally Russia moved to permanently occupy various parts of Poland. They were attentive to distributing the spoils equally, so as to preserve the balance of power. But they also left a wounded Poland in their midst, to serve as a buffer between the three rivals—a buffer that would separate their territories but be unable to resist their wills in the future.

THE SECOND PARTITION

In 1782, ten years after the first partition, war pitted Russia against Sweden, Prussia, England, and the Netherlands. Frederick of Prussia, never missing an opportunity to undermine Russia's influence in Poland, proposed a new Prusso-Polish alliance. The *Sejm*'s reaction to this proposal was extreme in its expression of opposition to Russian domination. The *Sejm*, which had confederated itself so as to remove the possibility of use of the *liberum veto,* insisted on the withdrawal of all Russian troops from Poland and set about amending the Constitution.

The proposed constitutional reforms were drastic. The monarchy was to be made hereditary. Both the *liberum veto* and the right to confederation were abolished. A system of checks and balances between the monarch and various parts of the *Sejm* was established. Merchants were

[15]Quoted in Eversley 1915, 54–55.

to sit in the *Sejm*. And perhaps most important, the army was to be increased to one hundred thousand men.

The Russian reaction to these amendments was equally extreme. Once again, the Polish buffer had taken action that threatened Russia's indirect control. On November 6, Russia's ambassador Stackelberg warned the *Sejm* that "Her Majesty the Empress, giving up with regret the friendship which she had vowed to His Majesty the King and the Most Serene Commonwealth, cannot regard otherwise than as a violation of the treaty the least amendment of the constitution of 1775."[16] At the same time, Austria looked on the developments in Poland favorably, seeing a stronger Poland as a buffer state more likely to survive.[17]

The initial lack of reaction from Russia was due primarily to its involvement in war with Turkey. Catherine's attitude toward the new Constitution, however, was clear. "How dare they alter the form of a government that I guaranteed!" she cried upon hearing the news.[18] She instructed plans for an invasion of Poland to be drawn up against the end of the Turkish war. But even when peace with the Porte was achieved, Catherine still faced potential opposition from Austria and Prussia, both of which on February 7, 1792, signed an agreement to protect the territorial integrity and independence of Poland. Austria and Prussia also committed to protect a free Polish constitution, but not necessarily the one under which the king then governed. Austria in particular expressed a strong desire for Russia to accede to the treaty.[19]

Catherine's plan was to divert Austrian and Prussian attention by embroiling them in war with revolutionary France. Leopold II, Austria's emperor, obeyed; Frederick William II, Frederick the Great's successor, was more recalcitrant and soon took steps to betray two allies at once. Rather than encouraging Russia to accede to the treaty with Austria guaranteeing Poland's territorial integrity, Frederick William consented to Catherine's suggestion that Prussia and Russia engage in a new partition of Poland. Both parties understood that Prussia's share of the spoils was contingent on its involvement with the war against France.[20]

Instead of invading Poland outright, Catherine chose to exploit opposition to the new Constitution. High-ranking *szlachta* who had opposed the reforms were invited to St. Petersburg in March 1792. On May 14, they formed a confederation at Targowica and requested Russian aid. Catherine, of course, readily consented; she demanded that the Constitu-

[16]Quoted in Zamoyski 1992, 309.
[17]Lukowski 1999, 142–43, 146; also see Schroeder 1994, 26.
[18]Quoted in Zamoyski 1992, 347.
[19]Zamoyski 1992, 354.
[20]Lukowski 1999, 147.

tion of 1791 be rescinded and that the king and the *Sejm* accede to the Confederacy of Targowica.

Poland had little choice. Badly outnumbered and outarmed vis-à-vis the Russians, the king agreed to accede to Targowica. Historians agree that, initially, Catherine sought only to reestablish control over Poland. But she would be unable to manage her alliance with Prussia if she did not agree to a new partition.[21] At the same time, Austria, on the losing side of its war with France, began demanding indemnities in the form of Polish land. Austrian demands were rejected, however, and Prussia and Russia secretly signed a new treaty of partition on January 23, 1793. When revealed, this treaty was presented to an empty-handed Austria as a fait accompli.

As in the case of the first partition, Austria objected to the inequality of the settlement. Prince Kaunitz's replacement, Baron Thugut, instructed Austria's ambassador to Russia to broach the topic with Catherine. The ambassador stated, "with regret, that the Emperor will decide to seek in Poland, after the example of these two Courts, an acquisition which, by right and justice, is due to him, but this must be inevitable in default of some other scheme of indemnity." In the same vein, a letter from Emperor Francis (Leopold II's successor) to Catherine read, "I insist persistently in demanding for Austria an absolute equality of acquisition and other advantages with Russia and Prussia."[22] Indeed, Austria's concerns for equality outstripped its desire to maintain a Polish buffer state. In response to the Russian reply that, were Austrian demands to be honored, nothing of Poland would be left, the Austrian ambassador answered, "What does that matter in comparison with the danger that will arise to Austria, if she has not an equivalent to that obtained by Prussia?"[23]

THE THIRD PARTITION

Following the second partition, Poland's neighbors—and in particular Austria—were concerned for the survival of the Polish state only insofar as it affected their own. In a letter to the Austrian ambassador to Russia, Baron Cobenzl, Francis's adviser Thugut wrote:

> Still worse than the fear of the Polish insurgent is my dread of new measures of Prussian dishonesty and turbulence. The Prussian troops have begun their march towards Poland, and General Igelström makes no protest, but enters into an understanding with them. But we can by no means allow the Prussians to remain for any length of time in Poland, still less to take up a position in Cracow. The Emperor desires no change, and no acquisition in Poland, but only

[21]Zamoyski 1992, 389–90; Eversley 1915, 119.
[22]Quoted in Eversley 1915, 133.
[23]Quoted in Eversley 1915, 134–35.

the right of garrison in certain border fortresses. But all this would be changed by a fresh aggrandizement by Prussia. Russia will know how to prevent this, and we beg to be informed of what she intends to do in opposition to Prussian rapacity. . . . Above all, we must be fully assured that Russia will not share her favour between us and Prussia. If Russia were to allow Prussian troops in Poland, we too should have to march in to secure our portion in the last partition.[24]

Austria had less to fear on this score than in the second partition. Having favored Prussia in that instance, Catherine decided to approach Francis of Austria to conclude a secret treaty of partition in 1793 that would exclude Prussia, thereby reducing its share in the next partition. The only outstanding questions were, Which power would receive which territory? and, Would a Polish buffer be preserved?

Austria sought compensation for the second partition as well as a share of the third.[25] The main bone of contention appeared to be the disposition of Cracow, desired by both Austria and Prussia. At the same time, the notion of retaining a tiny Polish buffer state surfaced in Prussia and was considered in Russia and, later, in Austria.[26] For the Austrians, however, the value of Poland as a buffer state had been severely undercut by the second partition, which brought Russia and Prussia almost to Austria's borders.[27] Ultimately, after presenting Prussia with a fait accompli in the form of the secret Austro-Russian treaty, the Russian ambassador to Prussia rejected the plans to retain a buffer and referred "to the late outbreak in Poland, which had indisputably proved the necessity of partitioning so volcanic a territory."[28]

Poland was to be partitioned in its entirety. Russia received the most, with more than 46,000 square miles and 1.2 million people; Prussia and Austria both took approximately 18,000 square miles of Polish territory, but Austria gained 1.5 million new inhabitants as well as the prize of Cracow, while Prussia received about 1 million people. King Stanislas was forced to abdicate as well as, in one of his last acts as monarch, to inform all foreign diplomats that their commissions were ended, in view of the end of Poland. A train of diplomats from France, Russia, Prussia, Austria, Sweden, Spain, the Netherlands, and the Vatican left Warsaw one by one.

In the eighteenth-century Polish partitions, the net benefit of conquest had more to do with strategic concerns over rivals' gains than with the value of Polish territory per se. Although some territories were intrinsi-

---

[24]Quoted in Eversley 1915, 191.
[25]Eversley 1915, 205.
[26]Lord 1925, 487, 496.
[27]Schroeder 1994, 122.
[28]Quoted in Eversley 1915, 240.

cally valuable (the salt mines at Lwów were an important source of income, and Danzig was a critical port for Prussia), most of the wrangling over territory reflected Russia's, Prussia's, and Austria's desire to avoid a situation in which one of their rivals' power was augmented at their own expense. These three states—and Prussia and Austria in particular—were engaged in a true security dilemma. Had Poland abutted only one of these states, it is not clear that its demise would have been as certain or as complete. The competitive spiraling of rivalry sealed Poland's fate.

How can we explain the timing of the partitions? Poland was a buffer state for many years prior to the first partition—why did Russia, Austria, and Prussia wait so long to take it over? Part of the answer to this question must lie in the fact that Poland was very effectively controlled indirectly by Russia before 1772. It appears that, once this control was threatened, partition was imminent; and because Poland was surrounded by rivals on all sides, Austria and Prussia would not have countenanced a unilateral Russian partition. A related question regarding the Polish partitions is, why would Russia trade sole indirect control over all of Poland for direct control over part of Poland, loss of any control over other parts, and the resumption of indirect control over the rump state? Once again, the history of the partitions suggests that partition schemes were consistently initiated by Austria or Prussia. Wary of Russia's influence in Poland, the two German states preferred a clear division of the Polish pie to Russia's hazy domination.

At what point did concerns over rivals' gains outweigh the desire for a buffer state? To the end of Poland's life as a state, schemes for maintaining a shrinking Polish buffer were presented in the highest circles of Russian, Austrian, and Prussian government. The Poles themselves were convinced that their value as a buffer state provided an assurance of survival.[29] The fact that the negotiations over the third partition—the one that was to bring the three powers' boundaries into direct contact—were lengthier and more difficult than those over the first and second partitions further implies the rivals' nervousness about directly abutting each other.[30] It appears that, in each case, the independent action of one rival—Austria's occupation of Zips before the first partition, Russia's plan to divert Prussia and Austria while invading Poland before the second partition, and Austria's determination not to be left out of the final division of Polish spoils—induced sufficient fears of relative loss to overcome the desire to maintain a buffer state.[31]

---

[29]Lukowski 1999, 49.

[30]Lord 1925, 481.

[31]Paul Schroeder makes a similar argument. "Poland's weakness, combined with Russia's growing power and invulnerability and the rivalry between Prussia and Austria, which made

What did—and did not—drive the underlying dynamic of partition is clear. Poland's conquerors were determined to win—or at least stand their ground—in the game of great-power politics. One of the cardinal rules of this game was that a rival's gains must be matched.[32] Once one rival claimed a slice of Poland, the others must do the same. Thus Poland was a victim of geography. Caught between three powers jealous of their standing, there was literally nothing Poland could do to prevent itself from, in Frederick the Great's choice phrase, being eaten like an artichoke—leaf by leaf.

Did Poland's Conquerors Anticipate Nationalist Resistance?

Conventional predictors of nationalism, such as levels of ethnic homogeneity and the constitution of a mass army, would not have indicated high levels of Polish nationalism. The Poland of the mid–eighteenth century included not only Poles but also Lithuanians, Byelorussians, Ukrainians, and Germans, with an attendant diversity of religion and language.[33] The Polish army could hardly be described as "mass" in either size or composition. An unusually high proportion of the Polish population was ennobled, however, and elevation to the aristocracy was not particularly challenging. Both the large size of and the powers accorded to the Polish aristocracy inspired fierce loyalty to country in the noble class.[34] Thus, even with relatively low levels of ethnic homogeneity or popular participation in the military, Polish nationalism was clearly expressed—and therefore predictable to Poland's conquerors—in the nationalist revolts that accompanied plans for partition. Polish nationalism, while not predicted by conventional indicators, was strong and persistent.

Although Polish nationalism was evident during the course of the partitions, it was ineffective. Nationalist revolt and parliamentary resistance hindered, but did not halt, the conquest of Poland at each step. Jean-Jacques Rousseau suggested precisely this strategy. "You cannot possibly keep them from swallowing you," he wrote. "See to it, at least, that they shall not be able to digest you."[35] It was clear to Russia, Austria, and Prussia that the Poles would resist their occupation. Nationalist revolts

---

both of them seek an alliance with Russia, laid the groundwork for the first partition of Poland. They did not, however, make it inevitable or even probable. Catherine and her advisers would have preferred to maintain Poland outwardly intact under Russian domination. . . . Partition instead came about mainly as a by-product of events, a means to other ends." Schroeder 1994, 12.

[32]Schroeder 1994, 6–7.
[33]Lukowski 1999, 2.
[34]Lukowski 1999, ch. 1.
[35]Rousseau 1985, 11.

occurred between the first and second and second and third partitions, giving Poland's conquerors a taste of what was to come. The rivals' responses to this resistance were, however, not retreat but advance. Nationalism led only to greater repression in Poland.

The first example of nationalist revolt occurred in protest of Russia's strong-arm tactics in keeping Poland within the Russian sphere of influence. But this rebellion, instead of saving Poland from Russian domination, led to Poland's downfall. As mentioned earlier, in response to the unequal treaty recently imposed by Russia, Polish nobles confederated at Bar. The Confederation of Bar was clearly a nationalist revolt against Russian domination. The Russian response to the confederation was not restraint but repression; the potential costs of repressing a rebellious Poland were undaunting.

Further, Polish resistance to foreign domination and invasion continued to be fairly constant. The Russian, Prussian, and Austrian response to this resistance, was not, however, withdrawal. They were not deterred by the prospect of rebellious citizens. On the contrary, resistance was used as a justification for partition. Indeed, the preamble to the Treaty of Partition signed in St. Petersburg in August 1772 stated: "The spirit of faction, the troubles and intestine war which had shaken the Kingdom of Poland for so many years, and the Anarchy which acquires new strength every day . . . give just apprehension for expecting the total decomposition of the state . . . at the same time, the Powers neighbouring on the Republic are burdened with the rights and claims which are as ancient as they are legitimate."[36]

From 1772 to 1788, Poland appeared to have accepted its fate, returning in its truncated form to its position as a Russian vassal. Stackelberg, the Russian ambassador, was seemingly successful in maintaining his charge, but in truth he was helped considerably by the conservative *szlachta,* who opposed any change in the Polish Constitution. Poland was considered so stable that Catherine withdrew most of her troops in 1780.[37]

When a reforming Poland threatened to drift away from the Russian sphere in 1788, Catherine was delayed in taking action by her involvement in war with Turkey. Once the war concluded, she turned her attention to her wayward buffer. Surrounded by a threatening Russia and an indifferent Prussia, Poland had little choice. But once again, resistance emerged from many quarters. Allegedly spurred on by Jacobin sentiments, rebellious Poles were ruthlessly suppressed by Russian troops, and the now uncontrollable Targowicans ignited further strife. The embers of insurrection were again met with repression instead of retreat.

[36]Davies 1982, 1:521–23.
[37]Lukowski 1999, 117.

The events surrounding the conclusion of the second partition contain eerie echoes of the first. Like its forerunner, the second treaty of partition blamed Polish resistance for the fate of Poland. Catherine wrote to her new ambassador to Poland, Count Sievers: "From the beginning, we have endeavoured to found our relations to Poland on an enduring basis, but the Poles, instead of meeting our advances with corresponding friendship, have only manifested the bitterest hatred; and then it came to our first partition in 1772, our consent to which, as all the initiated know, was only wrested from us by the force of circumstances."[38]

Severe territorial losses and a return to the Russian yoke did not sit well with many of Poland's nobles and soldiers. Poland had lost almost half its territory and more than half its population. Warsaw was now barely more than thirty miles from Prussia.[39] Plans for insurrection began even before the treaties of the second partition were signed. In an attack led by Tadeusz Kościuszko, these plans came to fruition on March 24, 1794.

Weakened by war, occupied by foreign powers, and lacking a clear domestic authority structure, Poland was not expected to be able to raise a consequential revolt against its conquerors. But the rebels defied expectations, making their opposition to conquest both clear and costly. With mostly peasant irregulars, Kościuszko forced the Russians to withdraw from Warsaw in less than a month. Where Russia's General Igelström had failed, Frederick William arrived from the west to lay siege to the city. A combined force of forty thousand Prussians and Russians attacked twenty-six thousand Polish defenders, many of whom were citizen volunteers.[40] From late July to September 2, Prussia attacked and Warsaw held. Finally, Frederick William was forced to raise the siege.[41]

Kościuszko's uprising was clearly born of nationalist sentiment in opposition to the partitions of Poland. Just as clearly, the surprising success of the insurrection imposed serious and unexpected costs on both Russia and Prussia. But as in the days leading to the first and second partitions, the Russian and Prussian response to nationalist rebellion was not to give in but to make an even stronger effort to crush revolt. Even while the insurrection was ongoing, Catherine wrote to Austria's emperor Francis that "The time is come when the three neighbouring Courts must use their efforts, not only to extinguish the smallest spark of the fire which has been kindled in their neighborhood, but also to prevent its ever being rekindled out of the cinders."[42]

---

[38]Quoted in Eversley 1915, 125.
[39]Lukowski 1999, 159.
[40]Lukowski 1999, 169.
[41]Zamoyski 1992, 427–28.
[42]Quoted in Eversley 1915, 204–5; see also Lukowski 1999, 172–73.

With Warsaw safe for the moment, Kościuszko turned east to meet the advancing Russians. Barely a month after the Prussian siege of Warsaw had been lifted, Kościuszko was captured.[43] The Russians also captured Warsaw after routing the Polish army and, infamously, massacring the citizens of the nearby suburb of Praga. Poland could do little more than surrender.

On October 24, 1795, Austria, Prussia, and Russia signed the final treaties of partition. Poland was dead, and its conquerors meant it to stay that way. Included as a secret article in the treaties was the following: "In view of the necessity to abolish everything which could revive the memory of the existence of the Kingdom of Poland, now that the annulment of this body politic has been effected . . . the high contracting parties are agreed and undertake never to include in their titles . . . the name or designation of the Kingdom of Poland, which shall remain suppressed as from the present and forever."[44]

Poland's partitioners may have feared Polish nationalism, but they dealt with that fear by committing themselves to crush the Polish nation, rather than by allowing themselves to be deterred by the high costs that nationalists, left unchecked, were expected to impose.

Did Poland Balance?

Given Poland's situation in the late eighteenth century, what policies should Poland have followed to increase its odds of survival? The balancing argument suggests that states in threatening situations should build up their military power and form alliances to help counter potential enemies. Even before the first partition, King Stanislas recognized that Poland would have to change its ways in order to survive. The king proceeded to attempt a number of reforms, including amending the *liberum veto,* that could strengthen the Polish state. Once the general state structure was sufficiently strong, the king planned to move on to additional efforts at internal balancing. The plan to amend the Polish Constitution, however, backfired. Poland's neighbors supported the Constitution precisely because it made it easier for them to exert influence in Poland. Once this influence was threatened by the proposed constitutional reforms, surrounding rivals quickly moved in to slice away at various parts of the Polish state.

Although Poland was more successful in forming alliances than in increasing its own military strength, eighteenth-century Polish history underlines the point that allies cannot always be trusted. Following the first

[43]Lord 1925, 483.
[44]Davies 1982, 1:542.

partition, King Stanislas first sought an alliance with Russia that would also permit an increase in the Polish armed forces. Once his appeal was denied, the *Sejm* responded favorably to an alliance offer from Frederick William, while proposing extreme constitutional reforms that included the strengthening of the army. Once again, Russia opposed the reforms; and while Prussia claimed to support the new Constitution, Frederick William fully intended to betray his Polish ally as soon as it was in his interest to do so. As Frederick William's ambassador Lucchesini wrote to his master after the alliance treaty was signed, "Now that we hold these people in our hand, and the future of Poland depends only on our combinations, this country may serve your Majesty either as a theater of war and as an eastern screen for Silesia, or it can become in Your Majesty's hand an object of barter at the peace negotiations."[45] Lucchesini's word's were prophetic. By January 1792, after Russia had intimated its intentions to reward Prussia with additional Polish territory if Frederick William did not interfere with Russian plans, Lucchesini was again sent to Poland, where he indicated that Prussia would not honor its alliance; his protestations met with willful denial on the part of the Polish king and his ministers.[46] In response to a Polish appeal for help, Lucchesini replied, "My master does not consider himself bound by the treaty of 1790 to defend by his army the hereditary monarchy, as established by the Constitution of May 3, 1791."[47] Even when it seemed that allies—like Prussia and Austria—had strong incentives to balance against Russia by preserving the Polish state, these powers quickly betrayed their Polish ally when their rivals began Polish landgrabs. And other powers—like France or Britain —that might have had an interest in preventing Prussia, Russia, and Austria from gaining strength through partition were either incapable of assisting Poland at the time (as in the French case) or unwilling to jeopardize other alliances to fight for Poland's survival (as in the British case).[48] Although Poland attempted to balance, these attempts made Poland more vulnerable to partition, instead of more likely to survive. We begin to see that Poland's attempt to balance against power could not be realized precisely because the powers it could turn to for help were interested in taking over Poland themselves.

At the time of the second partition, the Polish army numbered at most sixty-five thousand men—well short of the intended one hundred thousand. Arms were scarce and difficult to come by. Reliable allies were even harder to find, with Austria tied up in France and Prussia disavowing its

[45]Quoted in Zamoyski 1992, 322.
[46]Zamoyski 1992, 355.
[47]Quoted in Eversley 1915, 100.
[48]See for example Lukowski 1999, 83, 94.

commitments. Poland was once again in dire straits. King Stanislas attempted to extricate his country by appealing to Prussia to honor its alliance commitment, by requesting aid from Britain, and by offering the Polish throne to Catherine's grandson, Grand Duke Constantine. Catherine rejected this suggestion, demanding once again that the king accede to the Confederacy of Targowica.[49]

Between the first and second partitions, then, Poland sought to behave as the balancing argument suggests, strengthening its military and reaching out for alliances. Although the Poles achieved limited success on both scores, this success was not sufficient. In Paul Schroeder's words, "There was no way Poland could have played the current game of international politics successfully, even had it been endowed with greater strength, skill, and realism; the game itself was stacked against Poland and other intermediary bodies."[50] At the mercy of its neighbors, efforts at balancing were futile for Poland.

Poland's failure to balance, coupled with the fact that Poland was in many ways a failed state during the partition period, appears to confirm two conventional wisdoms: first, that Poland died because it was unable to govern itself; and second, that states that fail to balance will, indeed, be selected out of the system. The facts as they stand suggest that Poland is a prime example of the balancing argument at work.

A further analysis of the facts, however, suggests that it is important to take a step back from the conventional wisdom and ask why Poland demonstrated such weakness, both internally and externally. After all, only a century earlier Poland had been counted among the great powers of Europe. How and why did Poland fall such a long way in such a short time?

Poland's strategic position—the fact that it was a buffer state between Russia, Austria, and Prussia—perpetuated if not caused its weakness to a large extent. It is true that Poland made multiple, unsuccessful attempts to balance—a finding that seems to corroborate the balancing argument. But the failure was, to a large extent, not Poland's, in that surrounding rivals worked to ensure Polish weakness. Attempts at the time to conclude a formal Anglo-Russian alliance were thwarted in part by Britain's refusal to "spend the king's money to finance Polish anarchy."[51] An interesting hypothesis generated from this case is therefore that being a buffer state is causally related to the weakness that is conventionally taken to be the cause of Poland's demise. But the key prior condition here is geography, rather than balancing or even the paralyzing effects of the *liberum veto*.

---

[49]There is no need to discuss further the Prussian response, and although British public opinion favored Poland, there was little Britain was willing to do on Stanislas's behalf.

[50]Schroeder 1994, 77–78.

[51]Roberts 1964, 3.

If buffer states are pushed to weakness, how are nonbuffer states in otherwise similar situations treated? Here, the case of mid-eighteenth-century Sweden—which is contemporaneous with the Polish case—is suggestive. Sweden, unlike Poland, was not a buffer state. Indeed, the two most likely rivals over Sweden—Britain and Russia—had concluded an informal alliance to preserve Swedish sovereignty. Like Poland, however, Sweden was weak internally, but was neither a collapsed nor a partitioned state. The Polish example was in the minds of Swedish politicians at the time, who sought "to avoid slipping into a Polish anarchy."[52] To this end, they were aided by both Britain and Russia. Both powers sought to shore up the Swedish state against possible failure, rather than undermine it to ease the process of control and partition. Neither state sought to take over Sweden, and thus they saw only costs, and no benefits, in the weakness of the Swedish state. In Michael Roberts's words, "Sweden became the example *par excellence* of the possibilities of joint Anglo-Russian action, the demonstration of an essential community of interest."[53] While this comparison is by no means conclusive, it does lend support to an important notion: generally speaking, buffer states may be manipulated in ways that undermine their ability to balance *and* to govern.

Surviving against the Odds: Persia's Near-Death Experiences

Both Poland and Persia are often considered classic buffer states. Their fates, however, have differed dramatically. Why was Poland officially partitioned and absorbed, while Persia retained its international legal sovereignty in the face of rivalry between Imperial Russia and Britain? This variation in outcome is due to the confluence of rare circumstances that altered the nature of the rivalry between Russia and Britain at key moments.

Persia's role as a buffer state dates back to at least the early nineteenth century. Although it was not a "continental" buffer in the sense of lying between the homelands of two enduring rivals, Persia was a critical imperial buffer. The extensive literature on the central Asian "Great Game" between Russia and Britain consistently refers to Persia—as well as Afghanistan and Tibet—as a buffer between the two empires.[54] Examining the dynamics of rivalry as they pertain to imperial buffers allows us

---

[52]Roberts 1964, 6.

[53]Roberts 1964, 5.

[54]Curzon 1892; Greaves 1959, 1965a, 1965b, 1968a, 1968b, 1986c; Ingram 1973; Kashani-Sabet 1999; Kazemzadeh 1968; Klein 1971, 1972; McLean 1979; Sahabi 1990; Sicker 1988; Siegel 2002; Thornton 1954, 1955; Williams 1966; Yapp 1987. In fact, the term "buffer state" was coined in reference to nineteenth-century Afghanistan.

to gain insight into a class of cases where one might imagine the rivalry to be weaker precisely because of distance from the homeland.[55]

Like Afghanistan, Persia provided a route between British India and Imperial Russia.[56] While Persia perceived itself as caught between the Russian and British empires, the British in particular were much more concerned about French advances—both on the continent and, to some degree, in Asia—than about Russian incursions into Persian territory.[57] In the early 1800s, the Anglo-French rivalry was much more acute than the Anglo-Russian rivalry. Thus, the British were eager to forestall the French and to placate their Russian ally. The combination of the British desire to keep the Russians friendly with Russia's tendency to expand southward meant that Persia's frontiers contracted just as the Persians themselves were seeking to delineate their own boundaries.[58]

With the fall of Napoleon, British attention was redirected toward Asia, and concern over Russian advances in the area began to mount, particularly toward the middle of the nineteenth century. Similarly, Russia viewed the region as a key area where Britain might be trumped; Russia's military attaché to London, General Nikolai Ignat'ev, wrote in 1858, "In the case of a conflict with England, it is only in Asia that we shall be able to struggle with her with any chance for success and to weaken her."[59] In Martin Sicker's words, "[Iran's] geostrategic position made it the natural frontier of the expanding empires of Britain and Russia, each of which sought to use it as a security buffer blocking the further advance of the other."[60]

But other than blocking each other's advances, what was it that Britain and Russia sought in central Asia? Historians appear to agree that Britain's position was defensive; Russia's goals are less clear,[61] although Russian behavior is certainly consistent with goals of expansion in the region. As for the British, the amount of time and money spent on defend-

[55]The small number of imperial buffer states in the data set, and the high correlation between the legitimacy variable and imperial buffer status, make it difficult to test hypotheses on imperial buffer states quantitatively.

[56]See figure 5.1 (adapted from McLean 1979, 38). Note that this map represents Persia just after the 1907 Anglo-Russian Convention. Persia's borders a century prior were more extensive, including much of what is southern Russia on the map.

[57]Yapp 1987, 651.

[58]Ingram 1973; for a discussion of Iranian historical cartography, see Kashani-Sabet 1999.

[59]Quoted in Carrere d'Encausse 1994, 150.

[60]Sicker 1988, 3.

[61]This ambiguity may be due to the fact that Russia's goals in Persia/Iran may have changed over time, particularly following the 1917 revolution. Also, given the language limitations informing this project, many more British than Russian sources are cited, which may create some bias in terms of goal assessment.

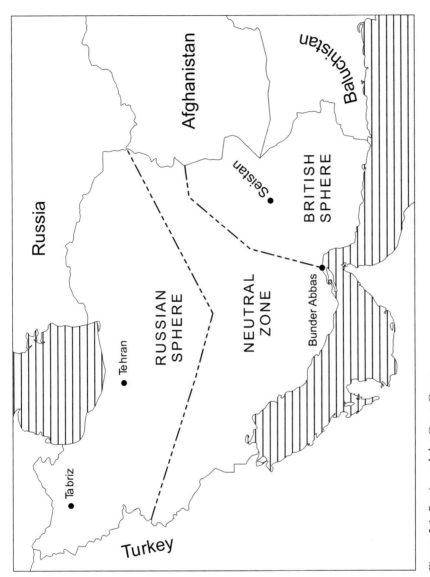

Figure 5.1. Persia and the Great Game

ing India may seem odd—after all, India was hardly the core of Britain. Nonetheless, India was the core of what made Britain an imperial power. A 1901 War Office memorandum argued that India, the empire's crown jewel, was also its most vulnerable colony:

> Speaking broadly, so long as the Navy fulfills its mission, the British empire is impervious to the great land forces of continental nations except in one point—India.
>
> Here alone can a fatal blow be dealt us. The loss of India by conquest would be a death-blow to our prosperity, prestige, and power. The damaging effects of even a near approach by hostile forces would be incalculable.
>
> We cannot doubt, therefore, that whatever may be done or left undone, the greatest and most determined effort will be made by Russia against India.

Next in importance then, and second only to the security of the United Kingdom itself, came the question of the defense of India.[62]

While maintaining the importance of defending India, Britain appears to have preferred avoiding any additional territorial acquisitions in central Asia. Prior to assuming official positions in India and in London, Lord Curzon wrote, "England neither wants to possess, nor ought to possess, nor ever will possess, those territories [Persia] herself."[63] David McLean echoes this sentiment, arguing that Britain was very concerned about the empire's trade relationship with Persia, which accounted for £5 million in some years.[64] Even more telling are the official instructions issued to Sir Henry Drummond Wolff, the new British minister to Iran in 1887: "It is to the interest of this country that the integrity of Persia should be maintained, that its resources should be developed, and that its Government should be strong, independent, and friendly. It is to the promotion of these objects that your attention should be directed, and so long, at least, as there is any reasonable hope of their being realized, the efforts of Her Majesty's Government would be to frustrate any policy incompatible with them."[65] These instructions summarized British goals and policy in Persia—to maintain the buffer against Russia for as long as possible.[66]

Russian intentions toward Persia were probably less honorable. Indeed, Russia's borders had expanded southward via the Caspian Sea and the Caucasus region. As a consequence, the shah's reach had decreased considerably.[67] The extent of Russia's ambitions in central Asia were un-

---

[62]Quoted in Greaves 1959, 192.

[63]Curzon 1892, 2:602.

[64]McLean 1979, 19–20.

[65]Quoted in Kazemzadeh 1968, 186.

[66]NB: Yapp argues that the British did not fear a Russian advance to India but, rather, Russian incitement of rebellion against Britain in India. Yapp 1987.

[67]Greaves 1959, 4–5.

STATE DEATH PRIOR TO 1945

known but regarded with considerable suspicion in both Tehran and London. Curzon was particularly wary of Russian motives: "It would be safe to assert that no Russian statesman or officer of the General staff would pen a report upon Russian policy towards Persia and the future of that country that did not involve as a major premise the Russian annexation of the provinces of Azerbaijan, Gilan, Mazanderan, and Khorasan—in other words, of the whole of North Persia, from west to east."[68] Persia was also attractive to Russia in that access to the Persian Gulf could provide the long-desired warm-water port.

Barring territorial annexation, Russia's intention appeared to be to make a virtual protectorate of Persia. In 1904, Russian foreign minister Count V. N. Lamsdorff instructed the Russian ambassador to Persia as to Russia's goals in Persia: "Our task is to make Persia politically obedient and useful, i.e., a sufficiently powerful instrument in our hands."[69] But it is not clear why Russia chose a policy of protection. Was it that Russia did not want to occupy any additional territory, or because of the strategic reality of seeing Britain on the other side of the buffer?

Britain and Russia therefore pursued a policy of maintaining the Persian buffer with varying optimism and zeal. Any skepticism about the viability of the buffer policy was due in large part to the two rivals' inability to trust each other. A loose agreement in 1834 to preserve the Persian buffer had been made and later reaffirmed, "but no one in Britain, or indeed in India, placed any faith in Russia's general expressions of goodwill."[70] In early 1885, before the House of Commons, Lord Salisbury was quite candid about his distrust of Russia:

Experience surely should have taught us that trustworthy engagements with Russia are not things which we can count upon obtaining. . . . I do not attribute to the Russian Government an intention to deceive. It is not necessary for my purpose that I should make any such disagreeable suggestion. When they said that they would not go to Khiva, and immediately did go to Khiva; when they said they would not extend their boundaries to the east of the Caspian, and immediately did so; when they said they would not take Merv, and allowed Merv to be surrendered to them, it is very possible that they were not acting with any intention to mislead the English Government, but that circumstances were stronger than men. But it really does not matter. If a man does not keep his promise in commercial matters, if he does it intentionally you say that he is a swindler; if he fails to keep his promise because he cannot keep it you say he is a bankrupt. But whether swindler or bankrupt you are very careful about trusting him the next time, and therefore, making the fullest allowance of the diffi-

[68]Curzon 1892, 2:594.
[69]Quoted in Sicker 1988, 16–17.
[70]McLean 1979, 15.

culties of the vast Russian Empire, and the impossibility of controlling the military element, which is the only sure foundation for the Throne—making all these allowances I still say that where we are now, with the lessons of history behind us, it was not wise to seek as the main object of our policy to rest the defence of India upon the guarantee of Russia. If we wish to defend the frontier of India we must do it as Lord Beaconsfield proposed—we must do it ourselves.[71]

Because the British appear to have feared a Russian incursion more than the Russians feared British advances in the area, British distrust of Russia is particularly well documented. Plans to respond to a potential Russian occupation of northern Persia, for example, included a reciprocal incursion on Persian sovereignty, with Britain occupying Seistan (strategically located near the Afghan border) and the port of Bundar Abbas.[72] Although the anticipated Russian occupation did not occur, mutual distrust persisted between the two rivals such that the negotiations over the 1907 Anglo-Russian Convention (see below) were drawn out because each state "was afraid to be the first to tip its hand to the Iranians, who might then be tempted to make a better deal with the other power."[73]

The development of Persia's infrastructure served as a focal point for Anglo-Russian rivalry, illustrating both the degree of competition as well as the lack of trust between the two powers. Railroad concessions and loans in particular created a number of minicrises in the Anglo-Russian-Persian relationship.[74] While each power saw at least some advantages to building railroads in Persia, Britain vociferously opposed any plans for railroad development by Russia that would link India and Russia via Persia, thereby obviating the Persian buffer. The Russians agreed with this assessment; when the Dutch minister in Tehran pointed out that Britain would almost definitely oppose Russian plans to build a railroad from the Caspian to Mohammerah, the Russian chargé d'affaires replied: "Then it will end by a partition of Persia between England and Russia."[75] But the issue of railroads continued to surface, as they could be commercially (and otherwise) valuable for all involved. For example, when a British railroad from Mekran to Seistan was considered, Lord Salisbury remarked: "It would not pay: but its military & political effect would be prodigious. . . . It would prolong the life of Persia a great number of years."[76]

Similarly, Britain and Russia often competed over loans to Persia, but

[71]Quoted in Greaves 1959, 104–5.
[72]McLean 1979, 46–47.
[73]Sicker 1988, 24.
[74]Kazemzadeh 1968, 148; also see Greaves 1965a.
[75]Quoted in Kazemzadeh 1968, 237–38.
[76]Quoted in Greaves 1986c, 93.

Britain was more constrained in its lending ability, a source of great concern to Lord Salisbury.[77] In 1894, Russia's establishment of the Discount Loan Bank constituted a real coup, as the new bank rivaled the British-backed shah's bank.[78] By 1905, Persia was indebted to Russia for over £3 million.[79] Persia's "bufferness" was not limited to territoriality; both Britain and Russia consistently leveraged tools that would allow them to exercise indirect control over Persia, either to preserve the Persian buffer or against the day when they could take over some or all of Persia.

Why Did Persia Survive?

Given the constant and intense competition between Britain and Russia for influence and power in Persia, how is it that Persia survived? As of the early twentieth century, it was not at all clear that Persia *would* survive. In fact, most states, including Britain and Russia, were convinced that Persia's death as a state was impending. This conviction was deepened and hastened by Russia's de facto occupation of and growing influence in northern Persia. It was not clear that Russian incursions would stop with the north. According to McLean, "Left alone, Persia would have quietly disintegrated. . . . By the end of the [nineteenth] century the disappearance of Persia as an independent state seemed to be imminent. The country was totally defenceless against Russian pressure from the north."[80]

A series of unpredictable (or, at least, unpredicted) and exogenous events constituted a string of luck for a Persia that seemed to be on its last legs. On several occasions when it appeared that Britain, Russia, or more likely both were about to take over Persia, the resources of the two powers were unexpectedly constrained, or circumstances forced them into temporary alliances. Both of these conditions gave what appeared to be temporary life support to a barely breathing Persia. The following sections focus on two such events: the Boer and Russo-Japanese wars leading to the 1907 Anglo-Russian Convention, and the perception of the German threat prior to World War I.

THE 1907 CONVENTION: TIRING HANDS AND DIVERTED RIVALRY

By the turn of the twentieth century, the general consensus was that Persia would not survive as an independent state. Yet, by 1907, Britain and Russia signed an agreement guaranteeing the survival of the apparently doomed. What caused this turn in events?

[77]McLean 1979, 12–13; Greaves 1965a, 288.
[78]Siegel 2002, 9–10.
[79]Williams 1966, 361; Greaves 1965b, 37.
[80]McLean 1979, 14, 8; also see Greaves 1965a, 305.

Two series of events appear to have led to an Anglo-Russian rapprochement with respect to Persia. First, both British and Russian resources had been sapped by wars in other theaters—the Second Boer War (1902) and the Russo-Japanese War (1904–1905). And second, both Britain and Russia feared Germany's entrance into the central Asian "Great Game"; they banded together to pledge (ostensible) support for Persian sovereignty and prevent a growth of German influence in the region. While one could argue that the Boer and Russo-Japanese wars had a greater impact on the decision to come to an agreement, both factors explain Persian survival as a function of "tiring hands" or "diverted rivalry." These circumstances greatly constrained Russia and Britain from taking over Persia when prior attempts at designing agreements were unsuccessful.

Britain had considered an accord with Russia for some time prior to the 1907 agreement. One stumbling block was the admission that Persia could not serve as a strong buffer state; another was that the Russians, already dominant in the north, had no incentive to come to the bargaining table. Both British and Russian incentives and credibility had changed by the beginning of the twentieth century. The Second Boer War in South Africa required four hundred thousand British troops by 1901, many of which were reassigned from the Indian Army. Britain's chances against Russia in central Asia were always uncertain, but at that time it was apparent that Britain would lose such a war.[81] At the same time that Britain was fighting a war in South Africa, London was confronting declining industrial growth and a rising national debt.[82] An agreement with Russia over central Asia seemed an increasingly attractive—and cheap—method of allowing a reallocation of British resources and easing British minds about Indian security.

Until 1904, the Russians were uninterested in such an agreement. But a humiliating defeat in the Russo-Japanese War, coupled with revolutionaries at home, prompted Moscow's receptiveness to British overtures.[83] Like the British, the Russians felt the pinch of strained resources and overextension both domestically and internationally.[84] Further, the recent Anglo-Japanese alliance gave Britain some leverage over future Russian behavior, or so the British believed.[85] While neither rival was able to tie its own hands prior to engaging in the 1907 convention, events in other theaters tired (and thus tied) their hands for them. Both knew each other's weaknesses, and could therefore be more confident in an agreement to se-

[81]McLean 1979, 46.

[82]Siegel 2002, 14–15; also see Williams 1966, 369.

[83]Kashani-Sabet 1999, 120; Sicker 1988, 23; McLean 1979, 73; Kazemzadeh 1968, 457; Siegel 2002, 15–16; Klein 1971, 127; Greaves 1965a, 306–7.

[84]Siegel 2002, 16.

[85]Klein 1971; Williams 1966.

cure Persia than in the past. Note that this result required that Russia and Britain be similarly constrained at around the same time; if only one of the rivals had been tied down in a war elsewhere, the other would have been likely to advance in Persia to its rival's detriment, and any agreement not to take over Persia would not have been credible.[86]

A second factor that helped the 1907 convention along was the rising German threat. A number of historians have argued that Britain and Russia came to an agreement in central Asia so that they could face Germany in Europe more effectively.[87] They may have also feared German involvement in central Asia itself, as German trade in the region was increasing and plans for a railroad concession appeared to be afoot.[88] Thus, it can be argued that Anglo-Russian rivalry in central Asia was, for the moment, subsumed, or diverted, against a third power.[89]

The 1907 convention itself dealt with Afghanistan, Tibet, and Persia. While Persian "integrity and independence" were to be maintained, at least ostensibly, the country was divided into three "zones": a Russian sphere of influence in the north, a corresponding (although smaller) British sphere in the south, and a relatively large neutral zone between the two. Each power agreed not to seek concessions in the other's sphere.

Thus, Persia's sovereignty appeared assured. In Jennifer Siegel's words, "for many, the Great Game appeared to have come to an end."[90] But the conditions that had led to the Anglo-Russian rapprochement were not permanent, and the credibility of the agreement could not withstand changes in those conditions. As Ira Klein writes: "the convention was a possibly naive and certainly incomplete British effort to end Anglo-Russian rivalry and to secure the status quo in Asia. Its terms for Persia did not prevent the continuance of serious friction there which served as a prelude to renewed Anglo-Russian rivalry in Central Asia."[91] In particular, as Russia regrouped its strength,[92] the north of Persia was again

---

[86]For example, Russia expanded at Iran's expanse while Britain was engaged in war in Sudan, and again between the start of the Second Boer and Russo-Japanese wars. Kazemzadeh 1968, 85; Williams 1966, 361.

[87]Kazemzadeh 1968, 592; McLean 1979, 80; Williams 1966.

[88]McLean 1979, 85; Siegel 2002, 18.

[89]NB: While the causal role of the "German threat" appears to have reached the status of conventional wisdom among historians of central Asia, I am more convinced by the argument that the Boer and Russo-Japanese wars weakened Britain and Russia sufficiently that they needed to retrench in central Asia, thus forcing them to come to an agreement. I find the argument about Germany less convincing for at least two reasons: first, the timing of the "German threat" seems somewhat ambiguous to me; and second, the prediction of this argument is that both parties should have worked to keep the 1907 agreement strong in order to contain Germany more effectively—this prediction is not borne out by the empirical evidence (see below).

[90]Siegel 2002, 19.

[91]Klein 1971, 128.

[92]McLean 1979, 75.

under threat, and by the time World War I began, it was obvious to all concerned that Persia could not survive.

THE GERMAN THREAT AND PRELUDE TO THE FIRST WORLD WAR

The honeymoon following the 1907 convention did not last long. By 1911, a Russian occupation of Tehran was in the offing. Northern Persia had been practically overrun, and the British were forced to consider the same strategy in the south. Persia again appeared to be on its deathbed, yet managed to survive. How can we explain Persia's continued resilience? Simply put, World War I saved Persia. Britain and Russia were forced to work together against Germany in Europe, and neither power wanted to sap its ally's strength by risking conflict in central Asia. The Anglo-Russian rivalry abated temporarily, giving the Persian buffer a second reprieve.

As Siegel argues, the Anglo-Russian Convention of 1907 was at best a stopgap measure. Within two years of the conclusion of the agreement, pressure in Russia began to build in favor of annexing Azerbaijan (then part of Persia).[93] Unstable conditions in northern Persia did not bode well for the future of Iran's sovereignty, as Russia used the pretext of anarchy interrupting trade routes to essentially occupy much of the northern part of the country. Such behavior clearly violated the spirit, if not the letter, of the 1907 agreement. While initially the British wondered if the aggressive behavior of Russian forces could be attributed to a few idiosyncratically belligerent officers, they were soon convinced that these actions were part of a systematic plan to take over the north—and perhaps more—of Persia.[94] The Russian absorption of northern Persia seemed imminent.

At first, the British reaction to Russian advances was one of disbelief. Then the British attempted to placate the Russians. In part, this policy was due to British unwillingness to occupy or annex southern Persia. But once it became clear that Russia intended to expand the depth and reach of its "sphere of influence," the British began to consider occupation as well. The problem with this strategy was twofold: it was both costly and, also, very likely to be extremely unpopular at home.[95] Another option was to amend the 1907 agreement by partitioning the neutral zone in such a way that the Russian and British spheres of influence would be more balanced.[96]

The situation in Persia caused Britain and Russia to reconsider the 1907

[93]Siegel 2002, 51.
[94]Siegel 2002, 166–67.
[95]McLean 1979, 108; Siegel 2002, 157.
[96]Siegel 2002, 177.

agreement. By 1913, Russian foreign minister Sazonov was expressing a desire for "more elbow-room and freedom of action in northern Persia" to the British ambassador; Sazonov suggested that Britain might exercise the same amount of "freedom" in its own sphere of influence.[97] At the same time, Sazonov claimed that Russia had no desire to annex Persian territory. Sazonov's assertion was not believed, and the British Foreign Office's Eyre Crowe argued: "There is only one possible way now of keeping Russia out of southern Persia: we must establish our own exclusive authority there ourselves. If we take the line that we cannot afford to incur expenditure for such Imperial interests, it will be like a declaration of imperial bankruptcy in respect of those regions."[98] Crowe later lamented, "To this necessity we must sacrifice the fiction of an independent and united Persia."[99] While British policy makers were reluctant to give up the goal of making a strong buffer state of Persia, the discovery of oil in the neutral zone and the British fleet's growing need for this resource helped them along in their acceptance of the need to renegotiate the 1907 agreement in ways that would most likely strip Persia of most, if not all, of its sovereignty.

Before the agreement could be reworked, however, World War I broke out in Europe. Partition had seemed inevitable, but fortune once again intervened to save Persia.[100] While the counterfactual of a world without World War I is difficult to conceive, historians appear to agree that, were it not for the First World War, the Persian state would have ceased to exist.[101] Anglo-Russian rivalry abated such that the two rivals could meet the German challenge in Europe together.

Persia's survival seems to have been almost a matter of happenstance. In both the very beginning of the twentieth century and again fourteen years later, wars in other theaters checked British and Russian advances in Persia by either rendering them incapable of making these advances or altering their incentives such that they preferred to pool and conserve their resources against a European threat. Following World War I, this pattern of behavior continued. With Russia mired in civil, as well as international, war, England extended its influence over all of Persia but refrained from annexation.[102] As Russian—now Soviet—strength renewed, Britain was again pushed south.[103] During the interwar period, Persia resumed its sta-

---

[97]Siegel 2002, 167–68.
[98]Quoted in Siegel 2002, 187.
[99]Quoted in Siegel 2002, 188.
[100]Siegel 2002, 194; Greaves 1968a, 307–8.
[101]McLean 1979, 145; Siegel 2002, 201.
[102]Sahabi 1990, 1–2, 6–7; Kashani-Sabet 1999, 152.
[103]Sahabi 1990.

tus as a buffer state. With the rise of Reza Khan, there was even some hope that Persia could be a strong, self-governing buffer state.[104] Nonetheless, rivalry over the buffer continued and, once again, was forestalled only by the coming of the second world war in Europe. Later on, of course, the decolonization of India after World War II meant that Persia was no longer a buffer state caught between British and Russian interests. Persia's survival can therefore be explained by employing the logic that predicts buffer state death, but only by admitting the role of exogenous shocks that incapacitated rivals and/or subsumed their rivalry, at least temporarily.

Did Persian Nationalist Resistance Deter Conquest?

To what degree were Britain and Russia deterred from—or at least hesitant about—taking over Persia in response to demonstrations of Iranian nationalism? Did a fear of occupying an unmanageable Persia prevent the death of the Persian state? The evidence suggests that this was not the case. Most key indicators of Persian nationalism were weak at best. The ethnic diversity in Persia was characteristic of central Asia, even given that Russia had absorbed parts of the north. The Persian military was not only poorly disciplined but also quite small. Indeed, the most reliable portion of the military was constituted by Russian Cossacks.[105] Persia scored similarly low on industrialization. Although Britain and Russia hatched a number of schemes to improve the country's transportation infrastructure through a series of possible railroad concessions, Persia was not valuable for its industry. Given that Persia was predicted *not* to be nationalist, the probability of conquest should have increased.

Persian nationalism did become evident in the form of revolt. But repeatedly, Persian nationalist movements led to great-power intervention rather than great-power retreat. The Russian response to a growing nationalist movement in Persia in 1907 contributed to some degree to Russia's seeking sanction of its role in northern Persia via the Anglo-Russian Convention.[106] The Russian fear was not that occupying Persia would be too costly because of nationalist elements but, rather, that Russia could not necessarily withstand a British response at the time. As the Persian nationalist/constitutionalist movement gained further momentum following the signing of the convention, the Russian foreign minister described the situation as "intolerable," and Russia intervened on the side of the royalists rather than withdrawing its forces.[107] Once the royalists were defeated, Russian troops remained in the north.

---

[104]Sahabi 1990, 196–97; Rose L. Greaves 1986, 101.
[105]McLean 1979, 8.
[106]Sicker 1988, 24; Kazemzadeh 1968, 511–12.
[107]Sicker 1988, 26.

While the British did not react to nationalist movements in Persia as belligerently as the Russians (indeed, the British supported the constitutionalists against the royalists), fear of nationalism did not lead to British retreat. Indeed, Klein argues that British support of the constitutionalists against the shah contributed significantly to the increase of anarchy in Persia.[108] Although perhaps unexpected, nationalist resistance did not save Persia from conquest.

Did Persia Balance?

Persia did not build up its military or form alliances to increase its survival prospects. The Iranian army remained weak and understaffed, and the few attempts at alliances were rebuffed. To the degree that Persia did make efforts to strengthen the state, these attempts were undermined by external powers. That Persia survived cannot be taken as confirmation of the balancing argument.

By the time that Anglo-Russian rivalry had clearly heated up in central Asia, the Persian military—indeed, the Persian government—was in a sorry state. The military, which Curzon numbers at around 30,000 men,[109] was unorganized, ill equipped, and an "undisciplined mob."[110] According to McLean, of the presumed 30,000 men counted by Curzon, only about 1,500 were truly reliable, and these were Persian Cossacks under Russian command.[111] In addition to low numbers in the military, Curzon was unimpressed by the mettle of the soldiers, pointing out numerous examples of cowardice on the field.[112]

Persia was weak militarily, but alliances can sometimes compensate for a lack of power. While Persia did attempt—numerous times—to form an alliance with Britain, the British were unwilling to commit themselves to the defense of Iran.[113] Persia's failed attempts here illustrate the difficulty of applying neorealist advice with respect to alliances. The benefits of balancing should be at their greatest when a state is threatened. Under these conditions, however, states may be unable to find friends and allies—this logic suggests that the effect of alliances on state survival is more ambiguous than a basic neorealist analysis would suggest.

[108]Klein 1972, 733.

[109]Curzon 1892, 1:590.

[110]McLean 1979, 8.

[111]McLean also illustrates the unfortunate condition of the Persian military with an anecdote: "When a British mission arrived at Tehran to confer the Order of the Garter on the Shah in 1903 a sentry at the imperial palace presented arms with a broken table leg." McLean 1979, 8.

[112]He also writes: "Finally, it may be said of the Persian officer, that on the battlefield he suffers from an ineradicable disposition to run." Curzon 1892, 1:605, 607.

[113]Thornton 1954, 569; Thornton 1955, 56; Ingram 1973.

In addition to attempting an alliance with Britain, Persia did make some efforts to strengthen its state. A few years before the Anglo-Russian Convention was signed, the shah was described as "'weak, capricious, and almost totally uneducated,' and surrounded by a group of courtiers whose sole interest was plundering the public revenues."[114] The shah's taste for luxury, coupled with his penchant for European tours, also took a toll on Persian finances, making the country extremely vulnerable to creditors.[115] The 1907 agreement, however, served as a real jolt to Persia. Persia had not been consulted when the convention dividing the country into spheres of influence was negotiated; instead, it was presented with a fait accompli. Soon after it was informed of the signing of the convention, the Persian government decided to take action to strengthen the state, thereby preventing any further incursions of sovereignty in what Siegel terms "a last ditch attempt to determine its own fate."[116] In so doing, Persia hired the American Morgan Shuster, as well as other foreign agents, to advise the state. Under Shuster's direction, Persia planned for both financial solvency and military improvements.[117] Both Russia and Britain, however, were uneasy about the involvement in Persia of advisers from another powerful state. And Russia in particular was vehemently opposed to any policy that would strengthen the Persian state. While Persia initially resisted Russian demands, Russian troop movements in the north eventually changed Persia's position. Thus, Persia was forced to fire Shuster, leaving itself in Russia's preferred condition of "a feeble and bankrupt Oriental neighbour."[118]

As in the case of eighteenth-century Poland, one can argue that Persia's internal and external weakness were causally related to the politics of geography. The British ideal was a strong Persian buffer, one that would be effective in separating the two imperial rivals. Lord Salisbury, serving concomitantly as prime minister and foreign secretary for much of the last fifteen years of the nineteenth century, placed great weight on the notion of a strong Persian buffer.[119] "What we have to do in Persia," he stated, "may be summed up in two sentences: we have to make Persia as strong as we can by internal development to resist the supposed aggression; & we have to obtain for ourselves the amount and the kind of influence which will enable us when the crisis comes to turn the efforts of Persia into the right direction."[120] While the British recognized that their policy

---

[114]McLean 1979, 8.
[115]McLean 1979, 8–9.
[116]Siegel 2002, 116.
[117]Siegel 2002, 104; Kashani-Sabet 1999, 140–41; McLean 1979, 83.
[118]Kazemzadeh 1968, 469.
[119]Greaves 1959, 51.
[120]Quoted in Greaves 1959, 224–25.

of strengthening the Persian buffer might well ultimately be ineffective,[121] they continued to pursue this policy until its inefficacy became obvious.

The Russians, on the other hand, did not hold a strong preference for the maintenance of a stable and healthy Persian buffer. Rather, they appear to have acceded to the buffer policy in deference to British power. Curzon argued that "Russia regards Persia as a power that may temporarily be tolerated, that may even require sometimes to be humoured or caressed, but that in the long run is irretrievably doomed. She regards the future partition of Persia as a project scarcely less certain of fulfillment than the achieved partition of Poland."[122] Indeed, Tsar Nicholas confirmed this view when speaking to a British diplomat in 1897, stating that "he did not believe in buffer States, unless they were strong and independent; and Persia, with its effete and corrupt Government, was too weak to play the role of such a State with advantage. Russia had already quite as much territory as she could manage, and he did not desire to acquire more; but he personally thought that our relations would be more friendly and satisfactory were there no Persia between us."[123] Perhaps to this end, Russia frequently interfered in Persian domestic politics, pressuring the government and pushing strongly for the maintenance of a weak monarchy.[124] Russia's attempts to maintain a manipulable Persia were evident from Moscow's insistence that Persia desist from any activities that might strengthen the state. Four years following the 1907 agreement, the Persian government barely functioned, a condition that was entirely acceptable to Russia.[125]

Russia's commitment to a weak Persia[126] did not go unnoticed by Britain. Britain's ambassador to Tehran, Alfred Townley, remarked to Foreign Secretary Edward Grey in 1914: "One is reluctantly forced to the conclusion that the Russian Government does not desire to see order re-established, either because it is in the interest of Russian trade that a valuable road into Persia should be blocked for British commerce, or because . . . Russia has some ulterior political object in wishing to see a state of anarchy maintained in a district into which she may wish to penetrate later on."[127] Persia, like Poland, seemed ripe for selection out of the system. Prior to 1907, there were few attempts to balance internally, and only failed attempts at external balancing. Thus, balancing did not save Persia from an apparently imminent doom around the turn of the twentieth cen-

[121]McLean 1979, 8.
[122]Curzon 1892, 2:593.
[123]Quoted in Kazemzadeh 1968, 311–12; also see Sicker 1988, 18–19.
[124]McLean 1979, 80–82.
[125]McLean 1979, 106.
[126]McLean 1979, 81.
[127]Siegel 2002, 186.

tury. Following 1907, Persia did make some effort to balance internally, but this effort was almost immediately denied in part because Persia was a buffer state. And yet, despite its failure to balance, Persia survived.

Was Neutrality an Effective Survival Strategy?

A common policy prescription for buffer states in particularly tense situations is to adopt a policy of neutrality. Should surrounding rivals fight, the buffer would then be "off limits." The problem with this policy, of course, is that it relies on the goodwill—or, at least, the propensity to obey international law—of states that have incentives to violate the buffer's neutrality. Persia did in fact declare its neutrality during World War I, but to little avail. While Britain and Russia were in favor of Persian neutrality, the Germans and Ottomans were not, and the Anglo-Russian buffer soon became a battleground.[128] Neutrality certainly did not save Persia prior to 1914, as the policy had not yet been adopted. During World War I, Persian neutrality was stated but not observed, and certainly did not assist in Persia's survival.

In times when Persia made efforts to promote its own survival, these attempts were consistently beaten back by Russia and/or Britain. In times when Persia failed to act to preserve its existence as a state, it continued to survive. Persian behavior did not therefore cause its survival. Caught between Russia and Britain, there was little or nothing Persia was able to do in its own defense. Persia survived because the rivalry between Russia and Britain either abated or was mitigated at key times. It is interesting to consider whether this type of abatement was more likely in imperial—as opposed to continental—rivalries. It may well have been easier to set aside rivalries farther from the homeland, making the preservation of imperial buffers more likely than the survival of continental buffers. Insofar as Persia's survival was a matter of luck, geography may have helped *and* hurt the survival prospects of the Persian state.

The Dominican Republic

Like Poland, the Dominican Republic has endured a series of occupations, annexations, and interventions throughout its history. It has been called by one scholar an "unsovereign state."[129] After gaining independence from Spain in 1822, the Dominican Republic was immediately annexed

---

[128]Kashani-Sabet 1999, 145; Sicker 1988, 29.
[129]Black 1986.

and occupied by Haiti for more than two decades. Following the resurrection of the Republic in 1844, Dominican leaders entered a phase of annexationism, seeking protection against the Haitians from virtually all the great powers operating in the Caribbean at the time. Annexationist schemes found a likely partner in Spain, which agreed to reannex its former colony in 1861. The renewal of this prior relationship, however, proved difficult, and the Dominican Republic regained its independence in 1865. Despite the failure of the Spanish venture, Santo Domingo continued to seek protectorate status through an available great power, this time the United States. US-Dominican negotiations for annexation went so far that in 1870 a treaty was presented for the Senate's ratification; congressional resistance, however, meant that the proposed annexation would not occur. Forty-five years later, in 1916, the United States began a military occupation of the Republic that would last eight years.

Unlike Poland (and Persia), the Dominican Republic is not obviously positioned between two or more great powers. Indeed, the only great power in the vicinity is the United States. The reach of great powers, however, can be quite long; in both the nineteenth and twentieth centuries, other great powers found bases in nearby colonial possessions or proxy states that challenged US hegemony in the Caribbean and Latin America. As in the colonization of Africa and Asia, we see here that great-power rivalry is not confined to the immediate backyard of great powers.

The Near Annexation of 1870

In the late 1860s, following the US Civil War, both the United States and the Dominican Republic faced serious international problems. The United States needed to reassert its leadership in the Western Hemisphere and to provide some teeth to the Monroe Doctrine. The Dominican Republic, riddled with debt and concerned once again about the possibility of Haitian incursion, needed a protector.

Dominican president Buenaventura Báez, aided by American filibusters[130] General William Cazneau and Colonel Joseph Fabens, concluded that a mutually beneficial solution to this problem would be for the United States to annex the Dominican Republic. Báez would receive a handsome payoff, Cazneau and Fabens could further exploit their Dominican investments, and the United States could assert its primacy in the Caribbean. President Ulysses S. Grant was favorable to the idea, seeing a legacy of expanding American territory in the offing. Negotiations

---

[130]The term "filibuster" referred to US adventurers for profit, as well as to the strategy of stalling votes in the Senate by giving long speeches.

went so far that a treaty of annexation was sent to the Senate floor. The treaty, however, was soundly defeated. Strong opposition dictated that the United States would not annex the Dominican Republic.

Why Did the United States Consider Annexation?

In July 1868, Dominican president Báez played on Secretary of State William Seward's fears by suggesting that Spanish influence was building in the Dominican Republic.[131] Seward, already concerned about the US retreat from the region during the Civil War, was committed to preserving and strengthening the Monroe Doctrine.[132] Upon hearing Báez's suggestion for a US annexation of the Dominican Republic, Seward—a great expansionist—lent his full support to the plan, and was able to convince President Andrew Johnson of its merits as well. On December 9, 1868, Johnson stated in a message to Congress:

> It can not be long before it will become necessary for this Government to lend some effective aid to the solution of the political and social problems which are continually kept before the world by the two republics of the island of St. Domingo, and which are now disclosing themselves more distinctly than heretofore in the island of Cuba. The subject is recommended to your consideration with all the more earnestness because I am satisfied that the time has arrived when even so direct a proceeding as a proposition for an annexation of the two Republics of the island of St. Domingo would not only receive the consent of the people interested, but would also give satisfaction to all other foreign nations.[133]

Despite his position, Johnson's influence was limited because of his recent impeachment and low popularity. The annexation question was therefore deferred to the next administration.

Fortunately for Báez, Cazneau, and Fabens, President Ulysses S. Grant was a strong proponent of expansionism and, therefore, eager to implement the annexation plan. In a memorandum titled "Reasons why San Domingo should be annexed to the United States," Grant listed the Dominican Republic's promise of agricultural productivity; its strategic position as "the gate to the Caribbean Sea"; the desire of its population to join the United States; the possibility of former US slaves emigrating to the Dominican Republic; and the possibility of England taking it over if the United States did not.

---

[131]Nelson 1990, 54.
[132]Welles 1928, 1:315–16; Theodore Smith 1901.
[133]Richardson, 1911, 6:689.

A glance at the map will show that England has now a cordon of islands extending from southern Florida to the East of the Island of Cuba, with Jamaica,
and Grand Cayman south of that island, and a foothold upon the main land in
Central America, thus commanding (on both sides of Cuba) the entrance to the
Gulf of Mexico, both sides of Cuba, a gulf which borders upon so large a part
of the territory of the United States. Again she has a succession of islands run-
ing [sic] from the East of St. Thomas to South America, with another foothold
upon the main land, British Guiana, thus nearly surrounding the Caribbean Sea.
The coasting trade of the United States, between the Atlantic seaboard and all
ports West, and South west of the Cape of Florida, has now to pass through
forin [sic] waters. In case of war between England and the United States, New
York and New Orleans would be as much severed as would be New York and
Calais, France.[134]

Although Grant referred to the Monroe Doctrine in his justification for
annexing the Dominican Republic, this argument was one among many
marshaled to support the scheme. As discussed below, evidence of rivalries—and, in particular, a threat from the British—was as unconvincing
to Grant's contemporaries as it is to historians of the case.

General Orville Babcock was commissioned by Secretary of State
Hamilton Fish to evaluate the prospects for annexation.[135] Babcock's
mission quickly turned into a treaty negotiation that included relief of Dominican debt, Grant's promise to use his influence to convince Congress
to accede to the treaty, a payoff to the Dominican government, and a
backup clause that provided for the US purchase of Samaná Bay in the
event that the annexation treaty was not approved.[136]

It appeared that the major players were all agreed. The Dominican and
US presidents, pushed along by the mercenary Cazneau and Fabens, had
put their full weight behind the treaty. Notably, their motives were similar. Báez wanted to be bought off, to rule a US colony in comfort without
having to worry about Dominican security. Grant saw the Dominican
venture as key to his legacy as an American expansionist. Cazneau's and
Fabens's motives were perhaps the simplest; if the United States annexed
the Dominican Republic, the value of their investments on the island
would increase by orders of magnitude. Money and pride were the driving goals of the US and Dominican annexationists.

---

[134]Quoted in Simon 1995, 20:75–76.
[135]Welles 1928, 1:371–72.
[136]Nelson 1990, 74.

Why Did the United States Decide against Annexation?

The Dominican scheme failed because of opposition from the Senate. In particular, Charles Sumner, chair of the Senate Foreign Relations Committee, took a very hard—and public—stand against annexation.

Sumner articulated a number of arguments against annexation. A survey of the historiography on this case suggests that his principal objection was related to preserving the power of the legislature against that of the executive. Annexationist schemes prior to the Dominican plan—such as the acquisition of Alaska—had been surrounded by secrecy.[137] Sumner and his fellow senators feared that the Senate's foreign policy powers were slipping away from them, and when Grant took actions like dispatching US ships to guard the Dominican coastline, these fears were only deepened. General antiannexationist sentiment in the Senate was due in part to the large US debt at the time, the perceived expense of annexation, and the broad sentiment that the United States needed to focus on reconstruction rather than expansion.

While protecting the power of the legislature may have been the main reason for the Senate rejection of the annexation treaty, it was only one among a host of reasons. The entire scheme left a sour taste in the mouths of many due to the perceived motives of the proannexationists. The involvement of mercenaries like Cazneau and Fabens, who fabricated information to support their own financial interests, reflected poorly on the scheme. Grant's expansionist tendencies also were frowned upon. Accusations of corruption fueled a political war between Grant and Sumner that tarnished the former's reputation and led to the latter's removal as chair of the Foreign Relations Committee.

Issues relating to race and slavery also generated opposition—from many different fronts—to annexation. Prior to the US Civil War, Latin American and Caribbean states were seen as potential new slave states by a number of expansionists.[138] Now, after the war, the fact that the Dominican Republic had abolished slavery made it unattractive to southerners in particular who opposed increasing the population of free blacks in the United States, or even in a US empire.[139] Northerners like Sumner approached this issue from a very different perspective, arguing that annexing states such as the Dominican Republic would be akin to reviving slavery, while Senator Schurz contended that the "republican institutions" of the United States could not survive in tropical climates.[140]

[137]Theodore Smith 1901.
[138]Nelson 1990, 38–39.
[139]Martínez-Fernandez 1993, 575, 579.
[140]For a survey of the role of race in this case, see Love 2004, esp. ch. 2.

A final, but quite important, reason behind the Senate's rejection of the treaty was the perception that there was no strategic imperative to annex the Dominican Republic. This claim may be somewhat controversial, as the Caribbean basin was a hotbed of great-power rivalry for much of the period from 1844 to 1865.[141] These rivalries gave Dominican leaders many options for protectors, and allowed them to play various great powers with interests in the region against each other. It was the presence of a variety of European rivals in the Caribbean, rather than the self-interest of Dominican leaders, Martínez-Fernández argues, that explains Dominican fickleness in courting various potential protectors.

With respect to the Dominican Republic, Seward and particularly Grant frequently invoked the Monroe Doctrine, warning of a mysterious European threat to Dominican sovereignty.[142] But the history of this case reveals little in the way of a rival for US control over the Dominican Republic. The greatest potential rival to the United States in the Caribbean was Britain. But at the time of the treaty negotiations, Secretary of State Hamilton Fish was negotiating the Treaty of Washington with Britain. This treaty was meant to settle US claims against England. The United States had (rightly) accused England of having violated the laws of neutrality by aiding the Confederate navy during the US Civil War. Any US-British rivalry was, for the time being, suspended in the interest of concluding what was perceived to be a much more important international agreement than the US absorption of the Dominican Republic.[143]

At least in part, then, the failure of the United States to annex the Dominican Republic in 1868–1870 can be explained by the absence of rivals in the area at the time.[144] In arguing against annexation, Senator Sumner also noted this point. Sumner's two main arguments against annexation were, first, that annexing the Dominican Republic would *create* unwanted rivalries with European powers and, second, that (absent annexation) European powers were very unlikely to interfere in Dominican affairs.[145] Sumner's colleague, Missouri senator Carl Schurz, in arguing against annexation, dismissed the notion that European rivals threatened US hegemony in the region: "And finally, the great bugbear of foreign interference is again raised before our eyes. We are told that if we do not take San Domingo, some foreign power will do so and in annoying proximity enjoy all the sweets we reject. Why, sir, is there a sensible man willing to believe it? I am ready to assert here, on my responsibility as a Sen-

[141]Martínez-Fernandez 1993.
[142]Ulysses S. Grant, letter to the Senate, May 31, 1870, in Simon 1995, 20:153–59.
[143]Nelson 1990, 67–68. Also see J. Smith 1979, 58–59.
[144]Martínez-Fernandez 1993, 596–97.
[145]Pierce 1893, 4:441.

ator, my confident belief that there is no European Power that will ever dare again to set its foot upon a square inch of American soil in the northern hemisphere against our pleasure."[146] Rivalry in the region was not only absent but was also recognized as such by the major opponents to annexation.

Given the lack of a strong strategic impetus for the annexation of the Dominican Republic—even a voluntary annexation, as was planned—Congress did not approve the plan. In the Senate's eyes, the reasons to vote for annexation were hard to find, but the reasons to vote against annexation were hard to miss. Even if additional evidence of rivalry around the Dominican Republic at the time could be shown, the main reasons for senatorial opposition were related more to domestic than to international politics. Grant's hands would have been effectively tied by Sumner's objections, providing another route for the Dominican Republic to survive.

Did Dominican Nationalism Affect US Decision Making?

To what degree is the ultimate decision not to annex the Dominican Republic attributable to anticipation of Dominican nationalist resistance? Proannexationists knew that the Dominicans might resist, but were not deterred by this possibility. Antiannexationists like Senator Sumner, on the other hand, used the fear of nationalist resistance to help convince the Senate to vote against annexation.

The Dominican Republic in 1870 scores fairly low on basic indicators of nationalism. The population was primarily mulatto, mixed but without a particular national origin. The military was more feudal than mass, with armed forces bearing allegiance to specific caudillos. And the economy was agricultural rather than industrial. According to these measures, we should expect that Dominican nationalism—and, therefore, the likelihood of resistance to annexation—would be fairly low.

Nonetheless, Senator Sumner argued against annexation partly on the grounds that US forces would face Dominican resistance and even the possibility of civil war.[147] His argument was supported by the conventional wisdom that the efforts of Dominican freedom fighters had imposed sufficiently high costs on their Haitian and Spanish occupiers and had led to Dominican resurrections in 1844 and 1865. Available sources do not indicate, however, that President Grant took these previous cases as indications of what might happen in a Dominican Republic under US protection.

Grant did, however, make feeble efforts to reassure himself that the Do-

---

[146]*Congressional Globe*, 41st Congress, 3rd Session, January 11, 1870, Annex, 32.
[147]Nelson 1990, 97–98.

minican people were in favor of the annexation plan. When Báez realized
that the Dominican Congress would not support the annexation treaty,
he decided to put the treaty to a popular vote. Although Grant may not
have been aware of the reason for Báez's decision, he supported the notion of Dominican consent to annexation. The fraudulent nature of the
vote, however, was clear to high-level US policy makers.[148] Even if Grant
was not apprised of the conditions surrounding the plebiscite, suspicions
must have been raised by the outcome of the vote, which was 15,169 in
favor of annexation and 11 opposed.[149] The administration's ostensible
concern for Dominican consent to annexation reflected a regard for ap-
pearances rather than actual worry about the response of the Dominican
people to annexation.

The actual resistance the United States would have encountered had it
annexed the Dominican Republic remains unclear. The Dominicans had
certainly resisted previous occupiers. Nonetheless, most Dominicans were
completely ignorant of these decisions and simply followed the instructions of their caudillos.[150] The role of nationalism in influencing the decision against annexation is therefore nebulous but, apparently, at least
slightly positive.

Did the Dominican Republic Balance?

A post hoc analysis might suggest that the Dominican Republic survived
as a state in 1870 because it was a successful balancer—because it built
up its power, forged alliances, and generally did what needed to be done
in order to survive. History belies this claim. In many ways, Dominican
leaders' behavior was in direct opposition to the basic principles of the
balancing argument.

The Dominican Republic in the nineteenth century challenges the assumption that states seek survival. Schemes for annexation originating in
the highest circles of Santo Domingo began with independence from Haiti
in 1844 and continued throughout the nineteenth century.[151] A primary
motive for giving up sovereignty was gaining protection against Haiti.[152]
Another important motive for annexationism was that annexation would
offer Dominican presidents more resources and security than if they had
to steer a struggling state on their own.[153]

Dominican leaders were not particularly picky about which state they

---

[148]Nelson 1990, 79.
[149]Martínez-Fernandez 1993, 596.
[150]Nelson 1990, 60–61.
[151]Atkins and Wilson 1998, 15; Nelson 1990, 17; Martínez-Fernandez 1993, 574.
[152]Nelson 1990, 47; Martínez-Fernandez 1993, 577.
[153]Martínez-Fernandez 1993, 588.

would have yielded sovereignty to, so long as it was not Haiti. They approached many of the major European powers, as well as the United States, several times. Dominican annexationist efforts became much more intense around 1849, when Haiti's new dictator proclaimed a policy of retaking the Dominican Republic. Finally, when the United States was distracted by the Civil War, Spain acceded to Dominican requests for recolonization. Although the reabsorption of the Dominican Republic into the Spanish Empire was ultimately short-lived, this experience did not prevent the leaders of the Republic from seeking another protector. Again, multiple powers were approached, and in 1870 it appeared as if the United States would take the bait.

The endemic annexationism of the Dominican Republic in the mid- to late nineteenth century runs contrary to the balancing argument. It is clear that the survival of the Dominican Republic was entirely unrelated to attempts at balancing. In fact, the Dominican Republic was willing to die, but could not find a state with sufficient strategic motives to help it meet its end.

Military Occupation, 1916–1924

By the time Teddy Roosevelt gained the US presidency in 1901, the fragility of the Dominican Republic had become acute. The Monroe Doctrine alone was no longer sufficient to preserve the US sphere of influence; European creditors were insistently knocking at the doors of Caribbean debtors. To forestall European intervention in the region in general and the Dominican Republic in particular, Roosevelt enunciated the Roosevelt Corollary to the Monroe Doctrine in his annual message to Congress in 1904:

> It cannot be too often and too emphatically asserted that the United States has not the slightest desire for territorial aggrandizement at the expense of any of its southern neighbours and will not treat the Monroe Doctrine as an excuse for such aggrandizement on its part. We do not propose to take any part of Santo Domingo or exercise any other control over the Island save what is necessary to its financial rehabilitation in connection with the collection of revenue, part of which will be turned over to the Government to meet the necessary expenses of running it and part of which will be distributed pro rata among the creditors of the Republic upon a basis of absolute equity. The justification for the United States taking this burden and incurring this responsibility is to be found in the fact that it is incompatible with international equity for the United States to refuse to allow other Powers to take the only means at their disposal of satisfying the claims of their creditors and yet to refuse, itself, to take any other steps.

> . . . Under the Monroe Doctrine [the United States] cannot see any European
> Power seize and permanently occupy the territory of one of these Republics;
> and yet such seizure of territory, disguised or undisguised, may eventually af-
> ford the only way in which the Power in question can collect any debts, unless
> there is interference on the part of the United States. . . . The conditions in the
> Dominican Republic not only constitute a menace to our relations with other
> foreign nations, but they also concern the prosperity of the people of the Island,
> as well as the security of American interests.[154]

In stating this new policy, Roosevelt authorized the creation of a US customs receivership in the Dominican Republic to manage that country's finances. One could certainly argue that this level of interference constitutes
a formal loss of control over foreign policy making to another state. Despite the fact that this case would fit my argument,[155] I do not include the
establishment of the US customs receivership in the Dominican Republic
as an instance of state death, because the Republic continued to exercise
an independent foreign policy in many other respects, including negotiating deals and security loans and contracts with a number of European
powers, often without US consent.

In 1916, however, the United States—now led by President Woodrow
Wilson—did formally strip the Dominican Republic of its foreign-policy-
making powers by implementing a large-scale—and long-term—military
occupation. According to the terms of the occupation, Dominicans were
ineligible to hold key foreign-policy-making positions, such as the minister of war and marine, and Dominican diplomatic representation was also
controlled by the military government.[156] Unlike the prior receivership,
the occupation commencing in 1916 entailed US control over Dominican
foreign policy. Thus, the Dominican Republic truly lost its foreign-policy-
making powers to another state.

Why Did the United States Intervene in 1916?

The reason the United States gave for intervening in the Dominican Republic was the Dominican violation of the US-Dominican treaty of 1907,
which governed repayment of Dominican foreign debt.[157] The principal
cause for US intervention, however, was the German threat in the Caribbean. Recent German actions from Venezuela to Mexico challenged US

[154]Quoted in Welles 1928, 2:621–23.
[155]In that the Roosevelt Corollary and its attendant policies were clearly a reaction to the
threat of European intervention in the region.
[156]Welles 1928, 2:797–98.
[157]Frequent leadership and regime changes meant that the Dominican government was
not able to uphold its end of the agreement. Black 1986, 21.

hegemony in the region. Bruce Calder writes, "The most important immediate cause of the US occupation of the Dominican Republic, aside from the logic of its ever increasing involvement in Dominican affairs, was strategic: the desire of the United States to protect the approaches to its southern coast and the Panama Canal against unfriendly powers, especially Germany."[158] In a contemporary account, Carl Kelsey wrote, "Prominent Americans and Dominicans have told me that they believe that Washington knew of certain plans of Germany to use the island if opportunity offered and, inasmuch as we were not then at war, thought it better to forestall such a possibility."[159] Germany was also alone among the European powers in refusing to accept the basic principles behind the Monroe Doctrine. This created a rivalry between the United States and Germany that would be played out in both Latin America and Europe.

What precisely were the grounds behind the American fear of the German threat? First, Germany—like the United States—was a rising power. The kaiser's policy of *Weltpolitik* was threatening to all states, as was his commitment to his navy. In the early 1900s, it was also clear that naval superiority favored the Germans over the Americans. Germany had missed out on the first wave of colonization, but Latin America seemed to provide an opportunity for a second wave. Second, as Nancy Mitchell shows, increased trade between Germany and the United States by the end of the nineteenth century had led to as much conflict as cooperation. The US-German relationship, which had previously been friendly, was now characterized by tariff wars and mutual suspicion.[160] Third, Germany did not accept the Monroe Doctrine. One of the kaiser's marginalia on a memo after the German gunboat *Panther* downed a Haitian ship in 1903 reads: "South America is our aim, old boy!" Fourth, and more specifically, in 1902 Germany participated in a blockade of Venezuela in response to Venezuelan default on a number of European debts. In retrospect, Teddy Roosevelt described the incident as follows: "Germany intended to seize some Venezuelan harbor and turn it into a strongly fortified place of arms . . . with a view to some measure of control over the future Isthmaian Canal, and over South American affairs generally."[161] Fifth, as Friedrich Katz has argued, Germany was actively increasing its influence in Mexico. Katz suggests that this activity culminated with the Zimmermann telegram, sent in January 1917, which proposed that Mexico help Germany by miring the United States in a regional war to prevent US involvement in World War I.[162]

[158]Calder 1984, xii.
[159]Kelsey 1922, 178.
[160]N. Mitchell 1999, 18.
[161]Quoted in N. Mitchell 1999, 98.
[162]Katz 1981.

Thus, the United States had ample reason to fear German invasion in the region. The Caribbean, in particular, was pregnable because of its poorly managed states, such as the Dominican Republic and Haiti, which were vulnerable to the demands of outside creditors. Indeed, the German navy had war plans to invade both the Caribbean and the United States. Suspecting this possibility, the General Board of the US Navy drew up responses, the most detailed of which was the Hi-Sd (Haiti–Santo Domingo) Plan.[163] The expectation was that if Germany was going to attack, it was most likely that Hispaniola would be the target.

Although there is no direct evidence linking an imminent German attack to the US intervention in the Dominican Republic in 1916, the incident was practically a textbook case for German action. In a number of cases, German gunboats had steamed into the ports of countries that were about to default on loans to Germany. Similarly, the Dominican economy was in dire straits. To preserve its influence in the country and prevent the interference of European powers, the United States insisted on increased decision-making power in the Republic. The newly elected president Jimenez refused, knowing that accession to such demands would amount to political suicide. Such combinations of domestic and financial instability had created clear targets for German intervention in the past. To forestall such intervention, the United States acted preventively, landing 150 marines in the Dominican Republic on May 5, 1916.[164]

Did Dominican Nationalism Affect US Decision Making?

The nationalist resistance argument makes two key predictions with respect to the Dominican Republic in 1916. The first prediction is that the United States would be more likely to take over the Republic in 1870 than in 1916, as Dominican nationalism would have been more developed in the later period. The second prediction is that if the United States anticipated nationalist resistance from the Dominicans prior to its intervention in 1916, it would not have occupied the Republic.

The first prediction is clearly not supported by the evidence. The United States failed to annex the Dominican Republic in 1870 but occupied it for eight years beginning in 1916. The second prediction, however, is supported by available evidence. Thus, of all the cases presented in this chapter, the 1916 US occupation of the Dominican Republic best supports the nationalist resistance argument.

Both just prior to and just after the US intervention, Dominican resis-

---

[163]N. Mitchell 1999, 46, 54–56.

[164]Fuller and Cosmas 1974, 7. Note that, under similar circumstances, and for similar reasons, the United States had invaded Haiti the previous year.

tance was practically nonexistent.[165] Basic indicators of nationalism suggest this outcome: the population of the Dominican Republic was primarily a mixed (mulatto) one (at a minimum, it was not a traditionally homogeneous population); there was no mass army; and levels of industrialization were extremely low. Although the US Marines experienced light casualties in the first days of the occupation, the resistance they met was very dispersed and weak.[166] One US concern at the time was to quell the domestic unrest that had broken out in the country, but this unrest was not sufficient to prevent US occupation. At least initially, the nationalist resistance argument seems effective in this case—the lack of anticipated resistance makes the US decision to intervene a sensible one.

Although the signs pointed to low levels of nationalism and resistance, a longer-term effect of occupation was the generation of fairly high levels of resistance, as discussed in the following chapter. This outcome suggests at least two potential problems with the nationalist resistance argument. First, the indicators that policy makers (and social scientists) use to predict resistance prior to invasion may not be particularly apt. The inefficacy of these measures may be due to the fact that it is easier to gauge the prospects of resistance once boots are on the ground. In other words, even if policy makers are concerned about meeting nationalist resistance, their tools for evaluating the probability of resistance may be inadequate.

Second, even if perfect measures of nationalism were available to policy makers, resistance may be more a result of the nature and fact of occupation than any *ex ante* features of the occupied society. Thus, potential occupiers might find themselves in a quandary in that they must balance the goals of occupation/conquest against the possibility of resistance.

Did the Dominican Republic Balance?

Faced with mounting debts to European creditors, a United States very protective of the Monroe Doctrine, and a US occupation in Haiti the previous year, it is not at all clear that the Dominican Republic *could* balance in 1916. The government of the Dominican Republic acceded to the relatively minor (when compared to the 1916 occupation) incursions of sovereignty that required US supervision of the Dominican economy around the turn of the century. Although the president ultimately refused to turn over control of the military, thus evincing some form of a survival instinct, the financial state of the country, coupled with the growing US role in the economy, prohibited increased military spending. Further, the Roosevelt

[165]Calder 1984, 10.
[166]Fuller and Cosmas 1974, 9–10.

Corollary to the Monroe Doctrine only reinforced the US commitment to preserve its influence in the hemisphere, virtually closing down the option of a European alliance.

The case of the US occupation of the Dominican Republic in 1916 is consistent with the Polish and Persian cases in that it is not clear that the Dominican Republic *could* balance to enhance its prospects for survival. But while the Dominican occupation is characterized by a failure to balance followed by state death, the failure to balance was a direct consequence of being in the very situation that should most encourage balancing.

Did the Norm against Conquest Affect US Decision Making?

The norm against conquest influenced US decision making with respect to the 1916 intervention in one critical way: the intervention was always intended to be temporary, and the United States was explicit in denying territorial ambitions in Hispaniola. Nonetheless, the nature and duration of the occupation seem to belie Woodrow Wilson's principles of territorial integrity and self-determination. How—if at all—can we reconcile Wilson's principles with his actions?

Wilson's pre–World War I policy had been characterized by a commitment to improving US–Latin American relations. In an address on October 27, 1913, he argued:

> The dignity, the courage, the self-possession, the self-respect of the Latin American States, their achievements in the face of all these adverse circumstances, deserve nothing but the admiration and applause of the world. They have had harder bargains driven with them in the matter of loans than any other peoples in the world. Interest has been exacted of them that was not exacted of anybody else, because the risk was said to be greater; and then securities were taken that destroyed the risk—an admirable arrangement for those who were forcing the terms! I rejoice in nothing so much as the prospect that they will now be emancipated from these conditions, and we ought to be the first to take part in assisting in that emancipation. . . . We must prove ourselves their friends and champions, upon terms of equality and honor.[167]

Later in the same speech, he stated: "the United States will never again seek one additional foot of territory by conquest."[168]

The commitment to a policy against conquest was, in fact, a theme of the Dominican occupation. When constitutional government faced a

---

[167]"An Address on Latin American Policy in Mobile, Alabama," in Link 1966, 28:448–52.
[168]Quoted in Welles 1928, 2:716. Also see Gilderhus 1986, 8.

breakdown in the Republic, the US government stated: "The Government of the United States desires nothing for itself from the Dominican Republic and no concessions or advantages for its citizens which are not accorded citizens of other countries. It desires only to prove its sincere and disinterested friendship for the republic and its people and to fulfill its responsibilities as the friend to whom in such crises as the present all the world looks to guide Santo Domingo out of its difficulties."[169] Similarly, upon actually occupying the Republic, Rear Admiral W. B. Caperton declared to the Dominican people: "It is not the intention of the United States Government to acquire by conquest any territory in the Dominican Republic nor to attack its sovereignty, but our troops will remain here until all revolutionary movements have been stamped out and until such reforms as are deemed necessary to insure the future welfare of the country have been initiated and are in effective operation."[170] Indeed, Wilson himself acceded to the occupation only because he saw it as his only option. Responding to the suggestion that the United States occupy the Dominican Republic, he wrote to his secretary of state, Robert Lansing, "It is with the deepest reluctance that I approve and authorize the course here proposed, but I am convinced that it is the least of the evils in sight in this very perplexing situation."[171]

The US occupation of the Dominican Republic did not constitute a territorial conquest, but neither did it reflect a respect for the Dominican right to territorial sovereignty. If the argument in this book is correct—that a norm against conquest has prevented violent state death after 1945—how can it be that the primary entrepreneur for this norm, Woodrow Wilson, himself failed to follow the norm strictly?

Wilson's commitment to the right of self-determination played a particularly odd role in his decision making with respect to Latin America. As argued in chapter 3, the self-determination principle caused Wilson problems because it could conflict with the norm against conquest. But because he saw war as the greatest evil, and because he saw territorial aggression as the principal cause of war, Wilson established a bright-line rule against conquest. Nonetheless, Wilson also attempted to promote the right to self-determination when possible. In his relations with Latin American states, however, Wilson's perception of these rights took on a paternalistic bent. Latin Americans certainly possessed the right of self-determination, but Wilson himself stated that "I am going to teach the South American republics to elect good men."[172] To teach them such

---

[169]Quoted in Welles 1928, 2:736.
[170]Quoted in Welles 1928, 2:777.
[171]Quoted in Welles 1928, 2:792.
[172]Ninkovich 1999, 52.

lessons, intervention was justified. Sumner Welles conjectures that Wilson assumed that observers understood his motives. Because Wilson had disavowed territorial conquest, he expected that the Dominicans and Latin Americans both accepted that disavowal and believed that his intentions in occupying the Dominican Republic were good.[173] Wilson's brand of Latin American self-determination was promoted through the military occupation of certain states, but the norm against conquest was preserved because the United States renounced the right of conquest.

Wilson's restraint in 1916 is further exemplified by the lack of a policy of occupation for the Dominican Republic.[174] Had the United States planned to acquire the territory, it is likely that policies of political assimilation and resource extraction would have been implemented in the years from 1916 to 1924. None were. Thus, the norm against conquest did play a role in the US occupation of the Dominican Republic. Although, on the surface, this case appears to challenge my argument, Wilson made a reluctant decision to temporarily violate Dominican sovereignty in the face of a strategic imperative. His principles severely constrained the nature of the intervention, both by depriving the occupation forces of an occupation plan and by obliging them to teach the Dominicans how best to exercise their right to self-determination.

The Role of Legitimacy

Along with buffer state status and survival to 1945, the level of international recognition a state received emerges in the previous chapter as one of the strongest predictors of state survival and death. While this chapter focuses primarily on more detailed exploration of the buffer state, balancing, and nationalist resistance arguments, the cases presented above also afford an opportunity to discuss the role international legitimacy may have played in the partitions of Poland, in the "Great Game" played around Persia, and in the near annexation and actual occupation of the Dominican Republic.

At first glance, these cases might appear inconsistent with the logic of the legitimacy argument. The two states that died—eighteenth-century Poland and the Dominican Republic in 1916—were clearly members of the interstate system. Of the two states that survived, both (Persia in the late nineteenth/early twentieth centuries and the Dominican Republic in 1870) were fully recognized by Britain and France.[175]

[173]Welles 1928, 2:738–39.
[174]Calder 1984, 23.
[175]Note that the Dominican Republic is not included in the list of revisions to the Corre-

In these cases, the role of legitimacy seems to be overwhelmed by the strategic imperative governing rivals surrounding buffer states. Nonetheless, we still might expect to see a limited role for legitimacy even when it does not prevent state death. Specifically, states contemplating partition or annexation might feel the need to justify such acts differently depending on whether the object of their intentions is considered a fully legitimate member of the interstate system. The case of the Polish partitions is consistent with this logic in that Russia, Austria, and Prussia often offered historical justifications for their claims to Polish territory. Likewise, the Wilson administration expended a great deal of rhetorical energy justifying its occupation of the Dominican Republic. Conquerors of "legitimate" states may therefore feel bound to explain why their actions are appropriate in ways that conquerors of "illegitimate" states do not.

The role of legitimacy is murkier for the two cases of state survival considered here. Although Persia was a fully recognized member of the interstate system, Russia did not appear to harbor any reservations about partitioning Persia, and Britain's reservations appear to have been driven more by strategic than legitimacy concerns. Quite possibly, Russian and British attitudes were driven as much by the distinction between Europeans and non-Europeans as by the status achieved by fully recognized states. Like the reasoning of Britain and Russia, the US reasons for not taking over the Dominican Republic in 1870 do not appear to have included concern for the legitimacy of their actions (or the legitimacy of the Dominican state).

The relationship between international status and state survival/death in the cases considered in this chapter suggest that, while the level of international recognition a state received played *a* role in conditioning the process of that state's survival or death, any concerns about legitimacy were in fact trumped by strategic imperatives facing would-be or actual conquerors. That said, the varying justifications of conquest in each case do imply that conquering powers were at least aware of a norm against taking over fully recognized states. Moreover, these reservations seemed heightened for European and twentieth-century cases; the prospect of taking over Persia in the late nineteenth century or the Dominican Republic in 1870 (or indeed precolonial Asian and African states) tended not to excite these types of concerns. This result is consistent with the findings from chapter 4 in suggesting that the effect of legitimacy is weaker than the effect of buffer state status and, further, that legitimacy might be measured in terms of distance and difference from Europe as well as through international legal instruments that accord recognition.

---

lates of War in appendix A, because it did not meet the population threshold of 500,000 at the time. It did, however, meet the recognition threshold of having concluded a treaty of commerce, alliance, or navigation with Britain or France.

Conclusion

In Poland, Persia, and the Dominican Republic, the dynamics of rivalry governed state survival and death. This chapter illustrates the vulnerability of buffer states in cases of clear rivalry and geography (such as Poland in the late eighteenth century) as well as in murkier instances of rivalry (as in the Dominican Republic in 1916). The decision to focus on the pre-1945 period in this chapter is due in large part to the fact that violent state death virtually ceased after World War II. But even before 1945, not all states at risk of dying went the way of the grave. The Dominican Republic in 1870, for example, survived the annexationist schemes of a few US filibusters because the United States faced no strategic imperative to take over the Dominican Republic (which is to say, it was not a buffer state). And yet even buffer states like Persia could get lucky, if the dynamics of the rivalries surrounding them were mitigated by extenuating circumstances that made threatening states incapable or wary of taking over the buffers that lay between them.

Alternative explanations for state death and survival do not fare as well. The performance of the nationalist resistance argument in explaining the outcomes in Poland, Persia, and the Dominican Republic is relatively poor, particularly when compared to the geographical argument involving the security dilemma surrounding buffer states. The words of the rulers and advisers of the day demonstrate an utter indifference to—even an abhorrence of—nationalism. Nationalist uprisings were not to be feared; they were to be crushed.

The assessment of the balancing argument is more complex. Both Poland in the late 1700s and the Dominican Republic in 1916 failed to balance against power, and these failures were followed by state death. Persia in the late nineteenth and early twentieth centuries and the Dominican Republic in 1870, however, also failed to balance, but survived. None of these states balanced, and only some died. What is most interesting about this finding is that none of these states balanced. Especially in the Polish, Persian, and twentieth-century Dominican cases, the balancing option was foreclosed by surrounding rivals. If states—especially threatened states—are supposed to balance against power in order to survive, how useful is this prescription if threatened states are unable to act on this advice *because* they are threatened? The evidence suggests that buffer states can do very little to promote their own survival. The pessimistic result is that the politics of location and timing hamstring states' strategies to cheat death.

PART III

THE NORM AGAINST CONQUEST
AND STATE DEATH AFTER 1945

Chapter 6 _____

Resurrection

BETWEEN state death and state birth is an important, and fascinating, category—state resurrection. More than half of all states that die violently later reenter the international system in something very close to their original form. Poland is a classic example of this phenomenon; in addition to being a quintessential buffer state, Poland is also a model of the phoenix state. Partitioned in 1795, Poland was reborn in 1919. Partitioned again in 1939, a resurrected Poland reappeared on the world map (albeit with a westward shift) after the Second World War.

Resurrection is also an important phenomenon in the history of colonialism. Algeria, conquered in 1830, reentered the international system as an independent state in 1962. Similarly, Burma regained its independence from Britain in 1948, but Sind did not reemerge as an independent state. How can this variation in state resurrection be explained?

Some explanations for state death can also be applied to state resurrection. The normative argument that explains the decline of violent state death after 1945 may also predict resurrection. Norms are typically slowly developing phenomena; they do not emerge overnight. The close of the Second World War was a key turning point in the history of the norm against conquest. For the first time, the chief proponent of this norm—the United States—had both the will and the means to enforce it. But the tenure of this norm precedes the end of World War II. We can date its presence in the international system to at least the end of World War I, when Woodrow Wilson championed the principle of territorial integrity for all nations. With the US retreat into isolationism during the interwar period, however, the full power of the norm was not realized. Even a tempered norm can exert some effect on international politics, though. If we do not expect the norm against conquest to prevent violent state death until after 1945, we might still expect that such actions might be frowned upon. To the degree that disapprobation was forthcoming, it might have led to reversals of state death. Thus, one corollary hypothesis of the normative argument is that violent state deaths that occurred after 1920 were more likely to be reversed than those that occurred prior to 1920.

A second corollary hypothesis of the normative argument is that *all* state deaths are more likely to be reversed after 1920, and particularly after 1945. With the United States as a new superpower disapproving conquest generally, past conquests might be more likely to be reversed. The US commitment to this norm, along with other factors, certainly helped in promoting the decolonization movement after World War II. Related, the nationalist resistance hypothesis might be better suited to predict resurrection as opposed to state death. The nationalist resistance argument places a heavy burden on would-be conquerors in its explanation for state death. It requires that conquering states predict accurately the degree of resistance they will face after conquest. The ability of conquerors to predict nationalist resistance beforehand may in fact be quite poor. Once conquest has occurred, however, conquerors can experience resistance to their rule. The nationalist resistance hypothesis predicts that states that are more nationalistic will be more likely to be resurrected than their less nationalistic brethren because the more nationalistic states will exhibit greater resistance to conquest.

Finally, the absence of the primary cause of state death might lead to state resurrection. States that died as buffers might be resurrected when the rivalries surrounding them have faded away.

The remainder of this chapter focuses on assessing the impact of nationalist resistance and the norm against conquest on state resurrection. The first section of the chapter presents several quantitative tests of the propositions outlined above. The results support both the nationalist resistance and the normative arguments. A brief discussion of the buffer status of resurrected states is also included. Recognizing the inadequacy of purely quantitative measures of both nationalism and norms, I turn to two case studies of resurrection in the second half of this chapter: the 1919 resurrection of the Polish state and the US withdrawal from the Dominican Republic in 1924. While nationalism does not appear to have had an effect on conquest in either case, it does appear to have promoted the Dominican resurrection. The claim that nonbuffer states are more likely to be resurrected than buffers also receives some support. The Dominican Republic was resurrected only after the perceived rivalry between the United States and Germany concluded with World War I. Poland, on the other hand, continued its existence as a buffer state upon its reentry into the international system in 1919; the timing of Poland's resurrection coincides with the early emergence of the norm against conquest, hinting that the strategic imperatives of rivalry may interact with the norm in interesting and important ways.[1] The conclusion of this chapter is therefore threefold: that nationalist resistance can increase the probability of resurrection; that buffer states may have a particularly difficult time regaining their sovereignty; and that the early effects of the norm against con-

---

[1] Although Poland was resurrected as a buffer state in 1919, it was repartitioned twenty years later.

quest are visible in the increased reversals of state deaths in the early twentieth century.

Quantitative Analysis of State Resurrection

In this section, I conduct tests of hypotheses drawn from the normative and nationalist resistance arguments as they apply to state resurrection. The variables associated with each argument vary slightly from the variables used to predict state death in chapter 4. Because the universe of cases is restricted to violent state deaths, variables that gauge the relationship between conquered and conquering states can be included. Also, in order to test the effect of the norm against conquest on state resurrection, an indicator variable for death after 1920 (as opposed to 1945) is included, as the hypothesis here is meant to test for early effects of the norm.

Variable Measurement

STATE AGE AT TIME OF DEATH

Nationalism may be affected by the age of a state. Older states may enjoy greater cohesion and therefore a stronger sense of national unity. The nationalist resistance hypothesis suggests that older states will be more likely to generate resistance and, therefore, impose costs on their conquerors that will lead to resurrection.[2] State age at time of death was obtained by subtracting the state's date of independence or founding from the year of death. Data on state independence and founding were taken from the *CIA World Factbook* and the *Encyclopedia Britannica* in most cases.[3]

LINGUISTIC PROXIMITY

An additional variable that captures elements of the nationalist resistance argument is the cultural distance between conquered and conquering states. According to the nationalist resistance argument, we should expect that, as the cultural distance between conquered and conqueror increases, the probability of state resurrection also increases.

One measure of cultural distinctiveness is linguistic proximity between

---

[2]Note that this variable could not be included in the duration analyses presented in chapter 4, because age is collinear with survival time.

[3]Consulting secondary sources was particularly important for states whose dates of founding or independence precede the start of the data set used here (1816). Where these data were not available from standard sources, histories of the states in question were used to determine dates of founding/independence.

conquered and conqueror. Using standard linguistic charts, I first identified the primary languages of each dead state and the state to which it lost
its control over foreign policy. I then counted the number of language fam-
ilies shared by the two states. A state whose population spoke a language
that was in an entirely different family from that of a conquering state received a 0 on the linguistic proximity scale. When the conquering and conquered state had the same primary language, the linguistic similarity score
ranges from 5 to 9, depending on how developed that particular branch
of a language tree was.[4] The greater the linguistic proximity between conquered and conquering states, the lower the probability of resurrection.[5]

ADDITIONAL VARIABLES

As in chapter 4, data on economic development and democracy—which
are meant to predict nationalism—are taken from the Correlates of War
and Polity projects. The main variable that is meant to test for the early
effects of the norm against conquest is a dummy variable for whether the
state died in the post-1920 period.

Analysis

Two striking features of the twentieth century emerge with respect to state
death: the virtual absence of violent state death after 1945 and the visible
increase in state resurrections that begins around the turn of the twentieth century and continues to the present. Figure 6.1 illustrates these
trends, showing violent state deaths and resurrections of violent state
deaths by decade, for 1816 to 2000. The increase in the number of resurrections in the early twentieth century adds further support to the
norms hypothesis: post-1945 deaths are few, and pre-1945 state deaths
are more often reversed as a norm against conquest becomes more widely
supported.

One corollary hypothesis of the norms argument is that all violent state
deaths are more likely to be reversed as the norm gains in strength. A
Mann-Whitney test confirms that the number of state resurrections is different before and after 1920 at $p = .0004$. If we extend the cutoff to a
date when the norm against conquest was even stronger—if we consider
resurrections before and after 1945—the result is even more dramatic. We

[4]Grimes 1996–1999.

[5]Note that this variable could not be used as a measure of the nationalist resistance argument in chapter 4, because the analysis in chapter 4 is a monadic one, where features of
states themselves—rather than features of states related to *specific* conquerors—are examined as predictors of state death.

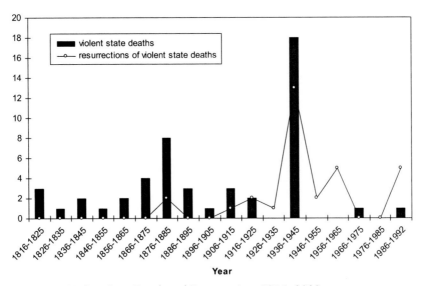

Figure 6.1. Violent State Death and Resurrection, 1816–2000

can reject the null hypothesis that the number of resurrections is the same before and after 1945 at $p = .0000$.[6]

More sophisticated tests allow further analysis of both the normative and nationalist resistance arguments.[7] Unlike the duration analyses presented in chapter 4, each state (death) is represented by only one observation in this data analysis, and the dependent variable is dichotomous, making logistic regression an appropriate statistical model.[8] Table 6.1 lists the variables used in the analysis and the expected sign of their coefficient in logistic regressions on state resurrection.

[6]It is difficult to compare rates of state resurrections, because it is unclear what the denominator would be for the ratio. One reasonable denominator might be the number of states in the system; in this case the results of the Mann-Whitney test indicate that we can reject the null that the pre- and post-1945 rates are the same at $p = .0272$.

[7]It should be noted that testing the nationalist resistance hypothesis on state resurrection presents a potential selection bias. The expectation of the argument with regard to state resurrection is that, among states that die violently, those states best able to generate resistance will be most likely to be resurrected. In general, though, the argument suggests that states able to generate resistance would not have been killed (or would have faced a lower probability of dying); thus, the argument should apply to the question of state death and not state resurrection. This potential bias, however, has been redressed by the general tests of the nationalist resistance hypothesis presented in chapter 4.

[8]The values of time-varying covariates are taken for the year of state death. Duration analysis is not possible, because data for years after death are unavailable.

TABLE 6.1
Expected Effects of Variables on the Probability of State Resurrection

Variable	Associated hypothesis	Expected effect
Death after 1920	Norm against conquest	Positive
Linguistic proximity	Nationalist resistance	Negative
Economic development	Nationalist resistance	Positive
Level of democracy	Nationalist resistance	Positive
Age	Nationalist resistance	Positive

TABLE 6.2
Logistic Regression on State Resurrection

	1	2	3
Nationalism			
Linguistic proximity	−0.58**	−0.50**	−0.48**
Energy consumption[a]	0.00	0.00	
Iron and steel production[b]	−0.00	−0.00	
Democracy (at death)	1.20*	1.06*	0.89
Age at death	0.00	0.00	
Norm against conquest			
Death after 1920	3.15**		3.69***
Constant	−0.30	0.18	0.13
N	50	50	50
Prob $> \chi^2$	0.00	0.00	0.00
Pseudo-R^2	0.42	0.30	0.37
Percent correctly predicted	88.00	80.00	88.00

[a]Measured in thousands of coal-ton equivalents.
[b]Measured in thousands of tons.
*Significant at the .1 level.
**Significant at the .05 level
***Significant at the .005 level.

TABLE 6.3
Marginal Effects for Resurrection

Variable	Prob. of resurrection changes by
Death after versus before 1920	+59%
Linguistic proximity from 25th to 75th percentile	−61%
Nondemocracies to mixed regimes	+28%
Mixed regimes to democracies	+17%
Nondemocracies to democracies	+46%

Interestingly, the nationalist resistance argument performs relatively well in predicting state resurrection, especially when compared to its apparent lack of relationship with the probability of state death. While the economic development variables do not appear to be related to the probability of resurrection, the linguistic distance and democracy measures are significant in the models above (see tables 6.2 and 6.3). The democracy variable is somewhat more tenuously related to the probability of resurrection, but moving from the 25th to 75th percentile in the distribution of linguistic proximity decreases the probability of resurrection by about 60 percent (table 6.3). Even with these imperfect predictors of nationalism, we observe an important effect—nationalist resistance, while an ineffective deterrent, may nonetheless be a useful strategy in reversing conquest.

The results are also consistent with the hypothesis that the early effects of the norm against conquest might be visible in the history of state resurrection. The indicator variable for death after 1920 is always significant; further, state deaths after 1920 are almost 60 percent more likely to be reversed than are deaths prior to 1920 (table 6.3). The results suggest that early in the norm's "life" it does not prevent state death, but it might prevent state death from becoming permanent.

Assessing the role of buffer state status in predicting state resurrection is more challenging. What we would like to know is, for any given buffer state death, does the continuation or conclusion of the rivalry surrounding the buffer state increase the probability of that state's resurrection? Regression analysis would be inappropriate given the number (twenty-one) of violent buffer state deaths. Nonetheless, a summary look at the data is telling. Of the twenty-one buffer state deaths, five states were never resurrected, eight were resurrected despite the fact that the rivalry surrounding them continued, and another eight were resurrected only following the conclusion of the rivalry around them. Further, of the eight states resurrected as buffer states, all were resurrected after 1920. Selecting on the dependent variable of resurrection, of the thirty-five resurrections of violent state deaths, ten states were buffers when resurrected, and all ten were resurrected after 1920. Thus, buffer status could have some effect on state resurrection. But even if states are more likely to be resurrected when they are no longer (or never were) buffer states, the norm against conquest might temper the desire of conquering states to continue the subjugation of absorbed buffers; the norm might, in effect, insist that these buffers be allowed to reenter the international system. The consequences of continued tension between the strategic imperative to take over buffer states and the norm against conquest that promotes all states' survival is discussed at greater length in chapter 7.

Case Studies of State Resurrection

A question that emerges from the previous chapter's case studies of Poland in the late eighteenth century and the Dominican Republic in 1916 is, why were these states resurrected? Nationalist resistance theorists would expect that nationalist revolts in occupied societies should lead conquerors to withdraw owing to the high costs of resistance. The norms argument predicts that resurrection should be more likely to occur after World War I, when the norm against conquest starts to gain support from major powers. These two arguments could be viewed as complementary, rather than competing, in instances of resurrection, especially given Woodrow Wilson's commitment to both the norm against conquest and the principle of self-determination. It would be easiest to distinguish the predictions of the arguments in situations of revolt and resurrection before 1919, or in situations of no revolt but resurrection after 1919. The former case would support the nationalist resistance argument but not the norms argument, and the latter case would support the norms argument but not the nationalist resistance argument. But what if resurrection was both preceded by nationalist revolt and decided during or after 1919? In this type of case, it is more difficult to assess the relative explanatory power of these two arguments without examining cases in greater detail.

Why Was Poland Resurrected in 1919?

The 1795 partition of Poland endured for over a century. During this interregnum in Polish statehood, the Polish nation was expressed in several incarnations, from the autonomous Duchy of Warsaw and Congress Kingdom, dominated by France and Russia respectively, to the rebirth of an internationally recognized Polish state in 1919. Given the length of the partition period, the survival of a Polish nation—although not a Polish state—that continued to seek resurrection is truly surprising, and represents strong evidence of Polish nationalism. During 124 years of occupation, the Poles rose up against the partitioning powers on multiple occasions. In many cases, these uprisings were well organized and costly to the occupiers. In none of these cases, however, did rebellion lead to resurrection. Resurrection of the Polish state was instead dependent on a change in the international normative and strategic landscape that made the plight of the Poles both more convincing and less acceptable to the great powers of the day.

THE ROLE OF NATIONALISM

The history of the interregnum period was characterized by a series of nationalist revolts against Poland's conquerors. These revolts were most intense under the government of the Congress Kingdom, a Polish region with limited autonomy under Russian rule. On the night of November 29, 1830, Polish revolutionaries stormed the Warsaw Palace where the Grand Duke Constantine resided. The grand duke was Tsar Nicholas's proxy in the Congress Kingdom. Despite initial confusion as to which side they should support, the citizens of Warsaw ultimately rallied behind the revolutionaries, denying the city to its Russian occupiers. An insurrectionary government was established, and the *Sejm* officially took the Polish throne away from the tsar, thereby violating the 1815 Constitution of the kingdom.[9] Once again, Poland sought independence.

For the next nine months, Polish and Russian forces fought throughout the kingdom. The Poles' efforts to gain external support were in vain; for obvious reasons, neither Prussia nor Austria could support the uprising, and other powers were leery of getting involved in a conflict with Russia. Under the circumstances, fighting alone, the Poles were surprisingly successful, routing their Russian foes in several key battles. By September 1831, however, Warsaw capitulated.

That the Poles, few and friendless, were able to fight the Russians for so long is a testament to their commitment to the cause of national independence. That the Russians were relatively unsuccessful against the Poles until about August 1831 speaks to the costs inflicted on the Russian army. But the response to the 1830 insurrection was not a granting of, or even an increase in, Polish independence or autonomy. Instead, the rights and privileges accorded the Congress Kingdom in the 1815 Constitution were

---

[9]The 1815 Constitution essentially made the Congress Kingdom an autonomous region of Russia, and a kingdom of the tsar.

severely curtailed. The Polish language was eliminated from official use, local self-government in Lithuania was abolished, and wide-reaching policies were established to eradicate all remnants of a Polish state. Resistance led to results opposite from the one the Poles had hoped for. Lest the lesson was not clear, Tsar Nicholas spoke to Polish nationalists in 1835: "If you persist in nursing your dreams of a distinct nationality, of an independent Poland . . . you can only draw the greatest of misfortunes upon yourselves."[10]

For the moment, at least, it seemed that Nicholas's lesson was not lost on Russian Poland. But in 1846 another uprising appeared in Cracow, which had been absorbed by Austria. The insurrectionaries succeeded in freeing Cracow, raising an army of six thousand, and engineering outbreaks in additional parts of partitioned Poland, once again inflicting significant and clear costs on the occupying powers. But after seven months of fighting, Austrian and Russian forces suppressed the revolt.

The January Insurrection of 1863 was the most widespread and the most intense revolt. At the start of the insurrection, organization was poor, and leaderless Polish forces faced twenty-to-one odds against the Russians in the Congress Kingdom. But by spring the Poles had regrouped, and the insurrection started to spread to parts of Poland that had been absorbed by Austria and Prussia. And by the summer of 1863 the underground "National Government" essentially controlled the kingdom, despite the continued presence of Russian forces. The Russian response to this improbable success was to continue fighting the Poles for more than a year. The insurrection was finally put down in October 1864.

Once again, Polish nationalism had reared its head and demonstrated its ability to inflict severe costs on Poland's conquerors. And, once again, Poland's conquerors responded to nationalist uprising by attempting to eradicate, rather than accommodate, Polish nationalism. Thousands of people were executed, imprisoned, or deported to Siberia. The title of "Kingdom of Poland" was eliminated; the Congress Kingdom was to be known henceforth as "Vistula Land." Intensive Germanization and Russification campaigns were launched in the various sectors of partitioned Poland. Any vestiges of local self-government were eradicated. Official, or even public, use of the Polish language was severely restricted. Polish property was confiscated. At the same time, particularly in Russia, ethnic minorities that had resided in prepartition Poland were siphoned away from the Polish nationalist cause; Lithuanians, Ukrainians, and Ruthenians began to find their own nationalities.

Nineteenth-century Poland was characterized by insurrection and revolt against the partitioning powers. Although these rebellions varied in

[10]Quoted in Wandycz 1974, 122–23.

success and strength, it must have been clear to the occupying states that Poland would not, as Rousseau had suggested at the time of the first partition, be easy to digest. Continued nationalist revolts made Poland a costly conquest. But the reaction to the repeated violent expression of Polish nationalist sentiment led, without fail, to a backlash against the Poles. Indeed, if the partitioning powers were going to be deterred by the threat of nationalist insurrection, it is unlikely that they would have executed the second and third partitions in the eighteenth century. The Poles, however, never seemed to learn the lesson that revolt alone would not gain them freedom; instead, revolt would lead to a curtailment of whatever liberties they retained. The actions that the Poles (and nationalist resistance theorists) expected would lead to a resurrection of the Polish state were met with brutal repression in every instance of insurrection.

THE ROLE OF THE NORM AGAINST CONQUEST

During the First World War, debate and conflict eddied about Poland from the inside and out. Polish nationalists disagreed on the best strategy to reunite and free Poland; some favored an alliance with the Central Powers, while others looked to Russia (help from the West was not considered until later in the war). At the same time, each of the three partitioning powers sought to tempt the Poles to its cause by offering various packages of autonomy and even independence. Poland was a literal and figurative battleground.

Schemes for a new Poland ran a narrow gamut; it was proposed that Poland would be an independent state closely "allied" with Russia, Austria, or Germany, depending on the nationality of the author of the plan. Bethmann-Hollweg considered both a Poland united with Austria and an independent Polish buffer state, while Tsar Nicholas claimed support for a unified Poland under Russian suzerainty. When in the spring of 1915 the Central Powers succeeded in pushing eastward, all of Poland came under their rule. As the Polish economy was subjected to the needs of the German war, Bethmann-Hollweg began considering a new set of proposals that would link a semi-independent Polish buffer state to Germany instead of Austria. In November 1916, Germany and Austria issued the Two Emperors' Manifesto declaring the establishment of an autonomous Polish kingdom carved out of Russian Poland.

Backed into a corner, Russia responded to the manifesto with appeals to the West. Stating its support for a unified, independent Poland, Russia was able to recruit allies for this cause from London, Paris, Rome, and Washington. The "Polish Question" was no longer restricted to Central Europe. In Western democracies with large Polish populations, policy makers were particularly sympathetic to arguments for resurrection of the

Polish state in some form. Polish nationalists leveraged this dynamic as well as commitment to the norm against conquest.[11] Well-connected Polish-Americans appealed directly to President Wilson's idealism.[12] As World War I drew to a close, international support for the self-determination of Poland had gained strength, as evidenced by Wilson's January 22, 1917, speech to the US Senate:

> No peace can last, or ought to last, which does not recognize and accept the principle that governments derive all their just powers from the consent of the governed, and that no right anywhere exists to hand peoples about from sovereignty to sovereignty as if they were property. I take it for granted, for instance, if I may venture upon a single example, that statesmen everywhere are agreed that there should be a united, independent, and autonomous Poland, and that henceforth inviolable security of life, of worship, and of industrial and social development should be guaranteed to all peoples who have lived hitherto under the power of governments devoted to a faith and purpose hostile to their own.[13]

While Wilson's commitment to the restoration of a Polish state was probably sincere, Russian rhetoric was shallow at best. Russia's strategy was to gain Western support for its cause against the Central Powers, while at the same time to plan for a resumption of control over Poland after the war.

When the tsarist regime was overthrown on March 12, 1917, the Bolsheviks also stated their commitment to an independent Poland based on the principle of self-determination. The manifesto of the Provisional Government declared that "the creation of an independent Polish state, comprised of all the lands in which the Polish people constitute a majority of the population, would be a reliable guarantee for lasting peace in the new Europe of the future."[14] This new Polish state was, of course, to be allied with Russia.

The retreat of the Central Powers in the fall of 1918 was unexpectedly quick and peaceful. The occupiers left, literally handing Poland back to the Poles. Certainly, the facts that Austria-Hungary itself no longer existed, that Germany was badly wounded, and that Russia was undergoing a revolution created an auspicious situation for the Poles. While Poland was still a buffer state, the rivalries surrounding it at the time of its resurrection were not nearly as intense as those in the late eighteenth

---

[11]Karski 1985, 21.

[12]Karski 1985, 17.

[13]Woodrow Wilson, Address to the Senate, January 22, 1917, in Link 1966, 40:536–37.

[14]Quoted in Wandycz 1974, 355. Similarly, Gerhard Weinberg argues that the major powers operated under the assumption that the oppressed nationalities of central and eastern Europe would be granted their own statehood. Weinberg 1994, 9–10, 15.

century or, for that matter, as they would become in the coming years. In the midst of these fortuitous circumstances, the remaining great powers—and in particular the United States—took advantage of the opportunity to apply an emerging norm and resurrect the Polish state. The 1919 resurrection of Poland was not preceded by revolt but by idealism, coupled with a dramatic change in the strategic environment surrounding Poland.

The US Withdrawal from the Dominican Republic

The US occupation of the Dominican Republic lasted for only eight years. The years of occupation were formative, however—they witnessed the withdrawal of the German threat to the Dominican Republic, an increasing concern about the status of the United States as an occupying state, and Dominican revolts against occupying US forces. More than in any other case examined in this book, the nationalist resistance argument is supported in this case by the fact that resistance did have an important, positive effect on the US decision to withdraw from the Dominican Republic.

THE ROLE OF NATIONALISM

The United States anticipated very little resistance to its planned occupation of 1916. By 1917, however, these expectations had been revised dramatically. Particularly in the eastern part of the country, large bands of organized nationalists denied US Marines entry into various rural areas.[15] Poorly armed Dominican guerrillas met and consistently defeated the marines who by all accounts should have outmatched them.

The initial US reaction to Dominican resistance was to send more marines to the eastern part of the Republic.[16] Fighting continued throughout 1917 and 1918. By 1919 the conflict was so intense that three times the original number of marines were stationed in the east.[17] Thus, the first US response to nationalist revolt was to fight back, not to withdraw. In addition to sending more troops, the US military double-crossed nationalist leaders seeking to negotiate, herded many rural Dominicans into internment camps, air-bombed the east, and not infrequently abused civilians. This type of behavior only elevated the level of fighting.

By 1920, plans for withdrawal began to surface. Thus, it appeared that nationalist resistance had been successful. At that point, the marines had given up on controlling the east, seeking only to contain the fighting. And

[15]Calder 1984, 120–21.
[16]Fuller and Cosmas 1974.
[17]Calder 1984, 133.

indeed, violent opposition to the occupation halted by May 1922, when it was clear that the US intent was to withdraw soon.[18]

Renewed resistance affected the plans for withdrawal in a way that neither side wanted. The US preference was to withdraw as quickly and cleanly as possible. This was also the Dominican preference. But the original US terms (stated in 1921) included provisions for continued US control over various parts of the Dominican economy and government. The Dominicans rejected this plan, and four years of negotiation ensued. For every plan suggested by the United States, the Dominicans appeared willing to wait for something better. At times the US response was violent, and included threats to extend the occupation until the Dominicans acceded to US demands. Ultimately, though, the US decision was to withdraw from the Republic rather than to continue fighting. The resistance mounted by Dominican nationalists against their American occupiers appeared to have been successful.

THE ROLE OF THE NORM AGAINST CONQUEST

In addition to constraining the duration of the intervention, the norm against conquest influenced the US decision to withdraw from the Dominican Republic. As argued in chapter 3, one of the mechanisms by which great powers in particular are encouraged to adhere to norms is reputational. The Soviet Union, for example, refrained from outright conquest after World War II in part because such behavior would have damaged its relationships with other states it sought to recruit to its ideological cause. Similarly, the United States suffered, in its relationships with other Latin American states, for violating Dominican territorial sovereignty. By 1919, as Secretary Lansing was reconsidering the Dominican situation because of the end of World War I, Latin American voices of protest against the occupation were getting louder.[19] In 1920, a series of events underlined the general protest. The Colombian Congress passed a resolution in favor of ending the occupation, the Brazilian and Uruguayan ambassadors to the United States told Lansing they hoped the occupation would soon end, and most of the Latin American press launched a campaign against the occupation.[20] The US intervention made other Latin American states nervous for a good reason; if the United States could find a legitimate excuse to occupy the Dominican Republic for so long, might another Latin American state be next?[21] The negative repercussions of the

---

[18]Calder 1984, 179–80.

[19]Welles 1928, 2:823.

[20]Welles 1928, 2:829.

[21]Mark Gilderhus makes this broad argument with respect to US policy toward Latin America in the early twentieth century. Gilderhus 1986.

occupation were felt domestically as well. In the 1920 presidential election, Warren Harding frequently criticized Wilson on his Latin American policy in general and the Dominican occupation in particular.[22] The impact of violating the norm against conquest was keenly felt by the Wilson administration, particularly in the absence of a continued strategic threat to the Dominican Republic. As in the Polish case, both the change in buffer state status and the emergence of the norm against conquest worked to promote the Dominican Republic's return to the international system.

One puzzle concerning the US occupation remains, however: why did it last so long? The reasons for the extended duration of the Dominican occupation are related to the reasons for the occupation (and withdrawal) itself. Because the United States did not intend to annex the Dominican Republic in 1916, there were no plans beyond occupying the island to protect it from Germany. Soon after the occupation, the United States became involved in World War I. High-level attention was directed across the Atlantic, not the Caribbean.

In the absence of direction from Washington, the US Navy began to implement a number of programs to improve Dominican government and society. These included public works, education, sanitation, and military projects. Inertia seems to have carried the day until about 1920. Once opposition to the occupation was voiced—both internally and externally—the US government made the easy decision to withdraw. The conditions of withdrawal were, however, more difficult to determine. From 1920 to 1924, the United States negotiated with the Dominicans, going through at least three major plans for withdrawal until one was accepted. Interestingly, during the process of negotiation, it was the US—facing domestic and international pressure, as well as the threat of renewed violence—and not the Dominicans that made major concessions. Thus, both US inertia (at first) and intransigence (later) account for the duration of the Dominican occupation.

Conclusion

Resurrection is a puzzling, and sometimes unexpected, phenomenon, suggesting critical changes in the incentive structures facing conquering states. From the arguments presented in this book, we can derive a number of possible explanations for state resurrection. Among the most important are the early effects of the norm against conquest and the ability

[22]Welles 1928, 2:836.

of nationalist resistance to inflict costs on conquerors. Quantitative and qualitative evidence suggests roles for both in our understanding of state resurrection. For nationalist resistance theorists, this finding should be particularly interesting and, coupled with the evidence presented in previous chapters, implies a reconfiguration of the theory. Even if nationalism has been on the rise in the twentieth century, it may not be an effective deterrent to conquest. Resistance can, however, be an effective strategy for a conquered people. The analysis of state resurrection also supports the claim that early effects of the norm against conquest were consequential prior to 1945. At times the norm worked in tandem with buffer state status, as when states that had been buffers were resurrected when the rivalries surrounding them abated and the power of the norm was on the rise. But the power of the norm also sometimes appears to have trumped—or at least conditioned—the strategic imperatives of rivals, leading to state resurrection even when the resurrected states continued as buffers. This line of reasoning continues into the next chapter, which considers additional corollaries of the normative argument and the general question of state death in the post-1945 era.

Chapter 7

State Death and Intervention after 1945

ONE OF THE MOST striking trends of post–World War II international relations is the relative absence of conquest and annexation. State death has changed dramatically, with voluntary unifications (à la Germany and Yemen) and dissolutions (à la the Soviet Union and Czechoslovakia) far outpacing the rate of violent state death. The incidence of coercive territorial change also seems to have decreased markedly.[1] Concomitantly, we have seen a rise in external interventions to replace regimes and leaders. Both the degree to which states are willing to violate their fellows' sovereignty and the nature of that violation have seen significant changes. If we consider sovereignty violations on a continuum, with violent state death on one end and nonintervention on the other, the conduct of international politics seems to have shifted dramatically since World War II. The means that states employ to exert control over one another have changed. How can we understand and explain this dramatic shift in state behavior?

This chapter assesses the causes of the post-1945 shift away from violent state death both quantitatively and qualitatively. The difficulty of measuring key explanatory variables—particularly, nationalism and the norm against conquest—poses serious challenges to the goal of explaining this shift, however. This chapter attempts to meet these challenges in two ways.

First, several corollary hypotheses of the normative argument (as discussed in chapter 3) are considered. Precisely because the rise of the norm is concomitant with a number of other trends unique to the post–World War II era, it is important to consider what additional behaviors the norm should promote. Second, cases of actual or would-be conquest or intervention after 1945 are examined to see why and whether these states experienced death, intervention, or no violent incursions of sovereignty.

Recent events have highlighted the importance of a deeper understanding of state death after 1945. For the most part, the late twentieth century was fairly uneventful in terms of cases of violent state death. US actions in Iraq, however, suggest a precedent of conquest that may reverse the trend of the past sixty years. As compared to, for example, the US intervention in Panama in 1989, recent US actions in Iraq have been extra-

---

[1]Zacher 2001.

ordinary in the degree to which they captured Iraqi (as opposed to Panamanian) sovereignty.[2] The ongoing possibility that violent state death may
reemerge as a fact of life of international relations heightens the need to
understand violent state death more generally.

Corollary Hypotheses of the Normative Argument

The quantitative analyses in chapter 4 show a dramatic decline in violent
state death after 1945 but do not explore the causes or consequences of
this trend. The basic finding—that violent state death has declined since
1945—is consistent with the argument that a norm against conquest has
emerged since World War II but is ultimately inconclusive because the post-
1945 period has been characterized by a number of important trends, some
of which (like the norm against conquest) are unique to the era.

   Before we can test for effects of the norm against conquest, it is important to establish its presence in the international system. The norm is
most clearly codified in Article 2.4 of the UN Charter, which states, "All
Members shall refrain in their international relations from the threat or
use of force against the territorial integrity or political independence of
any state, or in any other manner inconsistent with the Purposes of the
United Nations." At the conclusion of World War I, the Covenant of
the League of Nations contained a similar provision in Article 10: "The
Members of the League undertake to respect and preserve as against
external aggression the territorial integrity and existing political independence of all Members of the League." Given the League's limited membership—especially as compared to the United Nations—the commitment to the norm against conquest as expressed in the League Covenant
should be taken as an indication that the norm was beginning to be institutionalized in the international system. But without more widespread
support, deeper internalization of the norm would have to wait for the
post-1945 era.

   The codification of the norm against conquest in the League Covenant
and UN Charter contrasts with key earlier treaties that were more likely
to institutionalize conquest than to prevent it. In 1748, Article XXII of
the Treaty of Aix-la-Chapelle stated, "The Duchy of Silesia, and the
county of Glatz, as his Prussian Majesty now possesses them, are guar-
antied to that Prince by all the powers, parties and contractors of the present treaty."[3] As discussed in chapter 5, the treaties following each parti-

---

[2]The ceremonial handover of sovereignty to the Iraqi governing council has no parallel in
the Panamanian case. Filkins 2004.
   [3]Israel 1967–1980, 1:283. Also see Korman 1996, 72.

tion of Poland carefully delineated which partitioning power was to receive which part of the shrinking Polish state. The Congress of Vienna similarly redrew the map of Europe (including parts of the then-defunct Polish state). Fifty years later, the 1864 Treaty of Vienna provided for Denmark's surrender of Schleswig-Holstein to Austria and Prussia. In 1866, Austria ratified Prussia's conquest of Northern Germany (Treaty of Prague) and Sardinia/Piedmont's conquest of the Italian States (Treaty of Vienna). Even the 1878 Treaty of San Stefano, which created Serbia, Bulgaria, and Romania as independent states, included a number of territorial indemnities to be transferred from the Ottomans to Russia. As Sharon Korman argues, the right to conquest was the norm in international society through at least World War I.[4]

The change in language employed in major treaties that discuss territorial conquest is clear. The norm against conquest had become somewhat accepted by the time the League of Nations was formed but needed to be reiterated at the founding of the United Nations. By the time the United States had ascended to superpower status, the ascendancy of the norm was also clear. The norm's clear presence in the international system, however, is no guarantee of its power to prevent conquest. How can we distinguish the effects of the norm against conquest from those of other trends unique to the post-1945 era?

Corollary Hypotheses

If the norm against conquest accounts for the drop in violent state death, we should see additional consequences of this norm. Tests of corollary hypotheses derived from the normative argument build on the analysis presented in the previous chapter (which focuses on the early effect of this norm on state resurrection) by illustrating the extent of the effect of the norm against conquest.

At least five corollary hypotheses can be derived from the proposition that a norm against conquest has prevented violent state death after 1945. While some of these observable implications of the norms argument are also consistent with alternative explanations for the post-1945 decline in state death, as a group these corollary hypotheses are uniquely predicted by the claim that this shift is caused by a norm against conquest. Because only the norms argument generates *all* these hypotheses, if they all are supported by available evidence, we should be more likely to accept the claim that a norm against conquest has prevented violent state death after 1945.

1. The decline in violent state death after 1945 will be accompanied by a rise in the number of external interventions to replace regimes and leaders in

4Korman 1996, ch. 3, 99–100.

buffer states. The logic behind this hypothesis is that would-be conquerors will turn to alternative means to achieve the ends formerly sought through conquest. The norm against conquest functions as an intervening variable that rechannels the drive to conquest. This logic also suggests that buffer states will be vulnerable to this type of intervention after 1945, just as they were vulnerable to conquest before 1945.

2. The decline in violent state death after 1945 will be accompanied by a decline in all forcible territorial change. This latter change, however, will not be as significant as the change in the number of violent state deaths. The logic behind this hypothesis is that forcible territorial change is similar to, but not as severe as, conquest of an entire state. Thus, forcible territorial change will be frowned on but not punished as severely as conquest of a state.

3. After 1945, the rate of state collapses should increase. The logic behind this hypothesis is that where past (impending) state failures may have been preempted by forcible territorial change or by state death, such behaviors are prohibited today. In addition, leaders of weak states may succumb to a moral hazard problem, plundering state resources in ways that are likely to lead to collapse in part because they know that their states are safe from conquest.

We also should expect to see early effects of the norm against conquest. Although the norm came into its own with the US rise to superpower status after 1945, the norm was weakly institutionalized following World War I, as evidenced by Wilson's commitment to preserving interstate borders from predation. Because the process of norm internalization is typically a slow one, we should observe changes in behaviors related to the norm before it is widely accepted in the system. Specifically:

4. As discussed and demonstrated in chapter 6, reversals of previous violent state deaths should increase as the norm emerges in the international system. All violent state deaths should be more likely to be reversed after 1920, and those deaths that occur after 1920 should be particularly likely to be reversed.

5. The manner of violent state death should change as the norm against conquest emerges in the international system. Insofar as the norm specifically prohibits territorial conquest, states should be more inclined to engage in (or label) state death via occupation as opposed to annexation. We should observe an increase in occupations as opposed to annexation or other types of conquest in the first half of the twentieth century, as the norm begins to gain international traction.

Analysis

Tests of corollary hypotheses generated by the argument that a norm against conquest has prevented violent state death since 1945 are presented below.

REGIME/LEADER CHANGE

The first hypothesis is that states should turn to alternative means of achieving the same goals after traditional methods are denied them. After 1945, states should cease to "kill off" other states and should instead replace regimes and leaders. Thus, there should be an increase in external replacement of regimes and leaders after the conclusion of World War II.

Available evidence seems to support this hypothesis. Other scholars have done an excellent job of defining and identifying regime and leader changes. There are no obvious biases in their coding criteria, and available data sets on regime and leadership changes already attribute them to internal or external causes. In this book, the Polity IIId data set on regime transitions and the Archigos data set on leadership change were combined to identify over five hundred cases of regime change and leader replacement.[5] Changes caused by actors external to the state, as well as changes independent of state deaths, were then identified.[6] Polity IIId codes an externally caused regime change when the polity is "terminated in circumstances of international war, threat, or intervention . . . [and] if the nation or its component parts maintain their autonomy."[7] Goemans identifies a state leader as "the person who held ultimate authority and was held accountable [for policy]."[8] Coding a leader change is definitionally straightforward; if the person holding ultimate authority in the state changes,

---

[5]Goemans et al. 2004. The Archigos data set begins at 1875. The list of world leaders from Bueno de Mesquita et al. and secondary sources such as the *Encyclopedia Britannica* were used to backdate the list of leader changes via external intervention to 1816. Bueno de Mesquita et al. 2003. Note that this data set does not include country-years added to COW. For this reason, it is not possible to test claims related to the role of international legitimacy and recognition on conquest and intervention here. One such claim could refer to the changing importance of legitimacy with respect to regimes and leaders as opposed to states. If recognition today is most disputed (and most used as a diplomatic tool) as it pertains to regimes and leaders, we might expect that this shift in the role of legitimacy would be paralleled by a shift in the object(s) of attack. In other words, rather than "illegitimate" states being targeted today, perhaps it is "illegitimate" (sometimes known as "rogue") regimes and leaders that are most likely to be targeted after 1945.

[6]In other words, I did not double- or triple-count regime or leader changes that occurred simultaneously with regime changes or state deaths.

[7]Gurr 1990, 19.

[8]H. E. Goemans 2000, 54.

then the leader has changed. Table B.4 in appendix B lists externally caused regime and leader changes from 1816 to 1998.[9] From 1816 to 1945, there were twenty-one such events, almost one every six years. From 1946 to 1998, there were fourteen cases of regime and leader replacement by external powers, or one every four years.

A Mann-Whitney test allows comparison of the means of the rates of regime and leader replacement before and after 1945. Essentially, the Mann-Whitney test assigns a rank to each year's rate and then compares the pre- and post-1945 cumulative ranks to see if they are different.[10] The results of a Mann-Whitney test confirm that, after 1945, states are indeed more likely to experience external replacement of regimes and leaders. The null hypothesis that the rates of regime and leader replacement before and after 1945 are the same can be rejected at a level of $p = .015$.

It is important to assess whether the putative effect of the post-1945 era remains when other variables are controlled for. As discussed in chapter 3, a number of additional variables could account for the shift from conquest to intervention. For instance, democracies might be less likely to conquer other democracies but more willing to intervene. This logic suggests that democracy should be positively and significantly related to the probability of being subject to intervention as opposed to conquest. Similarly, the nationalist resistance argument implies that states that are able to generate higher levels of nationalism should be more likely to experience intervention versus conquest. Variables linked to nationalism, such as democracy and economic development (measured here by energy consumption and iron and steel production) should therefore also be related positively and significantly to the probability of intervention versus conquest. Finally, we might expect the balancing argument to shed some light on this shift. Perhaps balancing cannot prevent attack but can mitigate its effects; in other words, more powerful, allied states might be more likely to suffer intervention as opposed to conquest. Note that testing for a role for alliances captures to some extent the possible effect of the Cold War, given the broad membership of both the Warsaw Pact and NATO.

---

[9]The data used in this study are based on very conservative estimates of the death of states, leaders, and regimes. I am confident that the cases identified as externally caused state, regime, and leader political death are accurate, though I recognize that I may not have included additional cases. For example, I did not include cases of suspected (or known) covert foreign intervention, such as the US involvement in the Iranian coup of 1953, unless foreign troops were on the verge of implementing these changes themselves. See "Secrets of History: The CIA in Iran," *New York Times*, April 16, 2000, 1.

[10]Another method to test this hypothesis would be to conduct a Poisson test. The difficulty with the Poisson test, however, is that while it can account for the number of states in the system in any given year, it cannot account for the uneven number of years under study before and after 1945.

Unlike standard duration models, which code failure dichotomously, competing risks models offer the possibility of multiple types of failure. A competing risks model is used here to test the claim that the norm against conquest has led to a shift from conquest to intervention.[11] This model helps assess whether buffer states are vulnerable to both types of events. If buffer states are not vulnerable to intervention (particularly after 1945), the claim that intervention substitutes for conquest would be disconfirmed.

Table 7.1 suggests several conclusions. First, buffer states are vulnerable both to conquest and to interventions that replace regimes and leaders. This result supports the claim that a substitution effect between conquest and intervention does, in fact, exist. Second, the post-1945 indicator variable suggests a significant decline in conquest after 1945 but does not suggest as strong an increase in interventions to replace regimes and leaders following World War II. This finding could be consistent with the normative argument in that challenges to sovereignty may be frowned on in general as the norm takes hold in the international system. When an interaction term is included that tests for the effects of buffer states before and after 1945 (see models 6 and 7), the models perform as predicted; the probability that buffer states will experience intervention after 1945 is significant and positive, while the probability that buffer states will experience violent state death after 1945 is highly significant and negative. Third, and consistent with earlier quantitative results from chapter 4, variables associated with alternative explanations for (the decline in) conquest do not appear to bear a significant relationship to conquest *or* intervention. The one exception is that, when energy consumption is included in the model, allied states seem to be more likely to suffer intervention than unallied states.[12]

[11]Multinomial logit is used to predict conquest or intervention. The base category is "no event" but does include cases of nonviolent state death. Note that I have corrected for serial correlation through the use of splines and panel-corrected standard errors, but I do not report the relevant counting variables or splines here. Beck, Katz, and Tucker 1998.

[12]A simpler analysis of the shift from conquest to intervention restricts the universe of cases to states that have experienced conquest and/or intervention, and tests to see which variables might affect the probability of intervention as opposed to conquest. Results from a logistic regression along these lines indicate that, far from being overwhelmed by other variables, only the post-1945 indicator exerts a significantly positive effect on the shift from conquest to intervention. In fact, states after 1945 are over 50 percent more likely to experience intervention as opposed to conquest. These results are consistent with a key corollary hypothesis derived from the normative argument and, further, suggest that important alternative explanations are not particularly useful in understanding the shift from conquest to intervention.

TABLE 7.1
Competing Risks Model of Conquest and Intervention

Variable	(1)	(2)	(3)	(4)	(5)	(6)	(7)
Intervention							
Log of power	−0.11	−0.08	−0.13	−0.15	−0.09	0.10	0.11
Alliance (dummy)	0.82	0.84	1.08*			0.89*	
Alliance (type)				0.42*	0.32		0.32*
Buffer State	1.25**	1.25**	1.40**	1.37**	1.22**		
Post-1945	−0.62	−0.56	−0.67	−0.80	−0.64		
Buffer × post = 1945						1.02*	0.97*
Democracy	−0.01	−0.01	−0.00	−0.01	−0.01	0.00	0.00
Iron & steel		0.00			−0.00		
Energy			−0.00	−0.00		−0.00	−0.00
Constant	−7.29***	−7.13***	−7.76***	−7.85***	−7.19***	−6.19***	−6.17***

Conquest

Log of power	-0.13	-0.13	-0.17	-0.17	-0.12	0.16	0.16
Alliance (dummy)	-0.12	-0.13	0.16			-0.14	
Alliance (type)				0.05	-0.06		-0.07
Buffer state	1.17**	1.17**	1.38**	1.37**	1.19**		
Post-1945	-3.23***	-3.23***	-3.38***	-3.38***	-3.21***		
Buffer × post = 1945						-35.84***	-33.82***
Democracy	-0.03	-0.03	-0.02	-0.02	-0.03	-0.01	-0.01
Iron & steel	0.00	0.00			0.00		
Energy			0.00	0.00		-0.00	-0.00
Constant	-11.95**	-11.95**	-12.78**	-12.78**	-11.94*	-11.65	-11.64
N	12,000	12,000	11,691	11,691	12,000	11,691	11,691
Wald χ^2	77.27	122.71	99.95	100.90	119.34	17893.33	16301.64
Pr $\chi^2 > 0$	0.00	0.00	0.00	0.00	0.00	0.00	0.00
Pseudo-R^2	0.11	0.11	0.12	0.13	0.11	0.06	0.06

Note: In additional specifications, the number of states in the international system in any given year were included, and the results were stable.
* Significant at the .1 level.
** Significant at the .05 level.
*** Significant at the .001 level.

FORCIBLE TERRITORIAL CHANGE

Mark Zacher's work provides evidence in favor of the hypothesis that forcible territorial change decreased after 1945, but that this decrease is smaller than the decrease in violent state death. Zacher compiled a list of conflicts from 1648 to 2000 during which territory was redistributed.[13] Zacher finds that the number of territorial redistributions has halved from the nineteenth to the late twentieth centuries. He also notes at least seventeen forcible territorial changes since 1946.[14]

Data on forcible territorial change are also included in the Territorial Exchange Data Set, which codes for the use of military conflict in territorial exchanges from 1816 to 2000.[15] The Territorial Exchange Data Set codes 180 territorial changes as a result of conflict from 1816 to 1945, but only 41 such changes after 1945. A Mann-Whitney test on the Territorial Exchange Data Set also indicates a statistically significant difference in forcible territorial exchanges before and after 1945, at a level of $p = .0097$.

It is clear that, as predicted, the frequency of forcible territorial changes has declined significantly since 1945. But how does this decline compare to the decline in violent state death? A simple calculation and comparison of the rates of forcible territorial change and violent state death is telling. According to both Zacher and the Territorial Exchange Data Set, the rate of forcible territorial change has approximately halved since 1945, with about 1.4 such changes occurring per year from 1816 to 1945, and about 0.75 such changes occurring per year after 1945. Violent state death, on the other hand, is about ten times less frequent after 1945 as compared to before, with about 0.37 violent state deaths per year from 1816 to 1945 and 0.03 per year after 1945. These findings conform with the hypothesis that coercive territorial change will decrease concomitantly with—but to a lesser degree than—violent state death after 1945.

STATE FAILURE

Another corollary hypothesis of the norms argument that can be tested here is that the rate of state collapse should increase after 1945. State collapse is "a situation where the structure, authority (legitimate power), law and political order have fallen apart."[16] It can also be described as the "complete or partial collapse of state authority, such as occurred in So-

---

[13]Zacher 2001.
[14]Zacher 2001.
[15]Tir et al. 1998.
[16]Zartman 1995, 1.

malia and Bosnia."[17] Before proceeding, it is important to raise a key labeling issue. "State collapse" and "state failure" are sometimes taken to mean different conditions, and other times taken to mean the same condition. Rotberg, for example, distinguishes the two, arguing that state collapse is an extreme version (or end state) of state failure.[18] Other scholars appear to use these terms interchangeably, defining state failure as state collapse. The phrases "state collapse" and "state failure" are used interchangeably here.

To date, the Polity IV project is the only data set that includes pre-1945 observations of state failure/collapse. Polity IV codes a state failure "for each year during which a standardized code denoting Interregnum, or 'complete collapse of central regime authority,' is recorded."[19] The advantage of using Polity IV is that it allows for comparison across a very long period of time (1800–2000). The inclusion of this variable in Polity IV does, however, raise some questions. It appears that the state failure coding is taken from the State Failure Task Force (SFTF) findings.[20] The SFTF categorizes and analyzes four types of state failure: ethnic war, revolutionary war, adverse regime changes, and genocide/politicide. Within the category of adverse regime changes is a subcategory of "collapse of central state authority," coded "1" "when a regime lacks the strength of authority to effectively govern at least half its sovereign territory (that is, provide essential services and security)."[21] The SFTF begins its analyses at 1955; thus, confidence in the pre-1955 codings of state failure should be lower than for the post-1955 period. Because the data on state failure appear less comprehensive for the pre-1945 period than for after 1945, it will be difficult to compare pre- and postwar trends in state failure, although we may be able to uncover trends in the post–World War II era.

According to Polity IV, there are forty-five cases of state failure over the past two centuries. Included in this list are six states conquered by Germany or Italy during World War II. These cases were dropped from the analysis because the "complete collapse of central regime authority" was a loss of authority to another state without any type of interregnum where the "failed" state itself could not control its territory. Dropping the World War II cases leaves thirty-nine cases of state failure (see table B.5 in appendix B). A Mann-Whitney test on pre- and post-1945 state collapses lends statistical support to the claim that state collapses have increased

[17]King and Zeng 2001a, 1.
[18]Rotberg 2003.
[19]Marshall, Jaggers, and Gurr 2002.
[20]The SFTF is also known as the Political Instability Task Force (PITF).
[21]Esty et al. 1995. Also see the Political Instability Task Force Problem Set Codebook, available at http://globalpolicy.gmu.edu/pitf/pitfcode.htm #30, accessed on November 17, 2006.

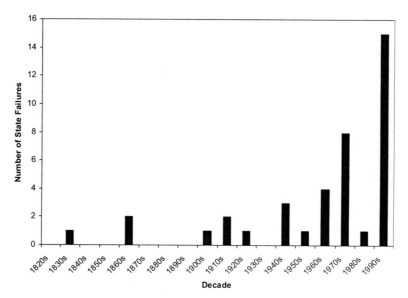

Figure 7.1. State Failure, 1800–2000

since 1945. We can reject the null hypothesis that the number of state collapses is the same in the pre- and post-1945 periods at $p = .0018$.

Figure 7.1 graphs the incidence of state collapse over the past two centuries. This graph might overstate the increase in state failures because the number of state failures has increased with the number of states in the international system. But the norms argument proposed here is also consistent with an increased number of state entries. As shown in chapter 6, state resurrections should increase as the norm against conquest gains in strength. As resurrections—particularly in the form of decolonization— become more frequent, the number of state entries into the international system will rise. Thus the norms argument suggests two complementary logics that could predict an increase in state failure. First, if the rate of state failures for any given number of states is constant, the absolute number of state failures will still increase with the number of states. Second, if conquest is prohibited, and predatory leaders of weak states are aware of this prohibition, such leaders might face incentives to plunder their states because there is little risk of reprisal in the way of territorial conquest. The increase in state failures could therefore be an indirect and direct consequence of the norm against conquest.

OCCUPATION

For the purpose of this book, occupation is considered as a subset of state death. While many cases of occupation have occurred without the formal loss of control over foreign policy making to another state, I mean to consider the extent to which occupation (as one form of violent state death) replaces other types of conquest and violent state death, such as annexation. To assess this claim, an adapted version of David Edelstein's definition of occupation as "the temporary control of a territory by another state that claims no right to permanent sovereign control over that territory" is employed here.[22] In order to qualify as a state death, the territory occupied must itself be an entire (or nearly so) state, and the occupation must be included in the list of state deaths employed in this book.

Cross-referencing Edelstein's list of occupations with the list of state deaths yields five cases of state deaths as occupations: Egypt in 1882, Cuba in 1906, Haiti in 1915, the Dominican Republic in 1916, and Japan in 1945. Several interesting features of this list emerge. First, and consistent with the corollary derived above, these occupations appear to be clustered in the first half of the twentieth century, as the norm against conquest was emerging in the international system. Second, in four of these five cases, the occupier was the United States—the primary sponsor of the norm, and therefore perhaps the most likely to change its behavior with respect to the norm early in the norm's life. Third, of Edelstein's full list of twenty-seven occupations (not only those that are coded as state deaths), sixteen occurred in the first half of the twentieth century, with only five occupations from 1815 to 1900 and six after 1945.[23] As predicted, occupation seems to have been a relatively frequently used tool in the beginning of the twentieth century—as the norm against conquest was emerging in the international system, and territorial conquest was slowly becoming taboo—as opposed to other historical eras.

All the corollary hypotheses of the argument that a norm against conquest works to prevent violent state death after 1945 are supported by the analyses presented above. As before, while some of the alternative explanations for the post-1945 shift away from violent state death predict some of these behaviors, only the claim that a norm against conquest caused this shift predicts all these outcomes. Ultimately, however, the normative argument is best explored using qualitative as well as quantitative data. In the next section of this chapter, I turn to case studies to probe both the

[22]Edelstein 2004, 52.
[23]Edelstein 2004, 84–89.

normative argument and the nationalist resistance argument as possible explanations for the post-1945 shift away from violent state death.

Case Studies

The remainder of this chapter examines four cases of post-1945 (would-be) intervention and state death. As in chapter 5, the cases are selected with two variables in mind. The first (independent) variable remains buffer state status. The second (dependent) variable is now divided into cases of conquest, intervention, and nonevents. The cases discussed in this chapter are summarized in table 7.2.

More specifically, I examine the first two cases—Hungary and Poland in 1956—together, given the many similarities between them. If we resolve the difficulty of coding Cold War buffer states by treating all European states as buffer states in the postwar period, both Hungary and Poland could be considered buffer states. Following revolt in Eastern Europe, the USSR considered intervening in both states but attacked only Hungary. Between two possible explanations for this variation in outcome, nationalism does not predict variation, while the argument that the strategic threat presented by Hungarian moves was much greater than that presented by Poland is more convincing. Because my argument predicts that buffer states will be especially likely to experience intervention after 1945, the Hungarian case represents an easy test, but the Polish case presents a real conundrum, especially when contrasted to its fellow satellite state. The third case discussed in this chapter, the 1965 US intervention of the Dominican Republic, is the case of an intervention in a non-buffer state; as such, it serves as another hard test of my theory. The United States intervened in the Dominican Republic because it was extremely concerned about losing another Caribbean state to its Communist rival. Extensive primary evidence reveals that, as compared to US relations with the Dominican Republic in 1870 and, to a lesser extent, 1916, the norm against conquest—and not concerns about nationalist resistance—constrained US action in 1965.[24]

---

[24]Focusing on Hungary and Poland (and, to some extent, the Dominican Republic) raises an important question: if, for example, all European states could be considered buffer states after 1945, why were interventions conducted only in some European states (indeed, one could narrow this question further, asking why it is that the Soviets intervened military in some satellite states but not others)? The answer to this question admittedly relies on contingency to the extent that the United States and the USSR tended to react to perceived threats to control. I do not attempt to explain here why Poland, Hungary, and Czechoslovakia—along with Cuba and the Dominican Republic—experienced coups and revolutions that nearby superpowers viewed as threatening, while Romania and Bulgaria did not expe-

TABLE 7.2
Case Selection for Post-1945 Cases

	Buffer	*Nonbuffer*
Violent death	No cases	Kuwait 1990
Intervention	Hungary 1956	Dominican Republic 1965
No intervention/death	Poland 1956	Most states

The final case discussed here constitutes an exception to the rule that violent state death tends not to occur after 1945. On its face, this case is inconsistent both with the claim that buffer states are particularly likely to die, or suffer intervention, and with the claim that a norm against conquest prevents violent state death in the post-1945 era. The Iraqi annexation of Kuwait is also, however, the exception that proves the rule. In the absence of information that violations of the norm against conquest would be enforced, Iraq attempted to annex Kuwait. The flaws in the Iraqi perception that the norm against conquest was no longer operational were underlined by the international response to the annexation of Kuwait.

1956: October Spring and the Fall of Budapest

The Polish so-called "Spring in October" of 1956 does not fit the pattern of the eighteenth-century partitions or the World War II annexation of Poland. In response to Polish moves toward greater independence, the Soviet Union did not take over Poland, nor did it intervene militarily. This outcome is particularly puzzling in light of events in Hungary occurring at about the same time. Like the Poles, the Hungarians sought greater independence from Soviet control. In many respects, the two rebellions look very much alike. The USSR intervened in one country, however, but not the other.

The Soviet decision to invade Hungary but not Poland speaks directly to the argument about the dynamics of rivalry advanced here. Fears of losing Hungary to the West were much stronger than fears of losing Poland. Both were buffer states, but the threat to Soviet control was more acute in Budapest than in Warsaw. While Poland sought greater freedom domestically, including the recall of Soviet "advisers" and officers, Hungary's Imre Nagy sought neutrality and withdrawal from the Warsaw Pact. Hungary was therefore at greater risk of being co-opted by a rival

---

rience such events. But what we can discern from these cases is that greater apparent threats to a rival's control over a state lead to greater levels of intervention.

of the Soviet Union. The dynamics of the security dilemma surrounding buffer states were much more acute in the Hungarian versus the Polish case. The USSR could concede Poland's demands without worrying about keeping it in the Soviet bloc; the same was not true for Hungary.

WHY DID THE SOVIETS CONSIDER INVADING POLAND IN 1956?

With Joseph Stalin's death on March 5, 1953, came confusion and, for many in the Soviet bloc, the hope of an era of increased freedom. Signs of such freedom quickly emerged in Poland. Lieutenant Colonel Józef Światło of the Polish Security Police defected to West Germany in December 1953 and, within a year, began broadcasting to Poland on Radio Free Europe.[25] Światło's broadcasts condemned the ruling leadership of Poland and painted the most accurate picture to date of the repressiveness of the regime, as well as its level of dependence on the Soviet Union. Konrad Syrop notes that the only Communist whom Światło praised was the then-imprisoned Władyslaw Gomułka; ironically, Światło himself had arrested Gomułka three years earlier.[26]

By December 1954, Gomułka had been quietly released from his imprisonment. Then, in 1955, the next bombshell struck. Poet Adam Ważyk published the "Poem for Adults" in the August 21 issue of *Nowa Kultura*, the official journal of Polish writers. Ważyk's work constituted an explicit criticism of the hypocrisy and injustice underlying the Communist regime.[27] Despite negative reaction from the authorities, that the censors had permitted Ważyk's poem to be published at all seemed to herald a time of greater artistic, intellectual, and perhaps political freedom.

Events in the Soviet Union reinforced this sentiment. In February of 1956, the Polish interwar Communist Party was rehabilitated. One week later, in his famous "secret speech," Nikita Khrushchev denounced Stalin, revealing many of his more ruthless policies and accusing him of creating a "cult of personality." According to Tony Kemp-Welch, Khrushchev's speech led to a storm of questions in Poland about how to view the Polish and Russian roles in World War II, the trustworthiness of the Politburo (whose members, by virtue of having supported Stalin in the past, had just committed an about-face by applauding Khrushchev's speech), Poland's territorial boundaries, and, most important, Poland's future.[28] The Polish government's ability to respond to these questions was hindered by the mysterious death of Poland's First Secretary, Bolesław Bierut, in Moscow approximately two weeks after Khrushchev's speech. Edward

[25]Syrop 1957, 20–21.
[26]Syrop 1957, 22.
[27]Adam Ważyk, "Poem for Adults," reprinted in Zinner 1956, 40–48. Original translation by Lucjan Blit.
[28]Kemp-Welch 1996.

Ochab was quickly selected to replace Bierut and, by June, had announced the release and rehabilitation of thousands of prisoners.

Less than a month later, in late June 1956, the workers of the ZISPO Locomotive Factory in Poznań began to express loudly their dissatisfaction with Poland's current economic situation. Faced with price inflation and wage depreciation, and rebuffed by the Warsaw authorities, the workers began a labor action on Thursday, June 28. Before long, the ZISPO workers were joined by others from all over Poznań. Quickly, what had started as a peaceful demonstration turned into a violent riot. The local Party offices, prison, and radio-jamming station were attacked. The workers carried signs reading "BREAD and FREEDOM" and "RUSSIANS GO HOME."[29] Fighting between the workers and militias continued for two days; "Black Thursday" finally ended on the night of Friday, June 29.

Both the Soviet and, for obvious reasons, the Polish leaderships were very much concerned by the Poznań riots. Although force was used to suppress the demonstration, the government's official response acknowledged the legitimacy of the workers' grievances and the need to pursue a new economic policy in Poland. As the Poles sought new leadership to meet these challenges, the Soviets looked over their shoulders, concerned that Poland remain within the Communist fold.

On October 19, the Eighth Plenary Meeting of the Polish Central Committee commenced. First Secretary Ochab made two announcements. The first was that Gomułka and two of his supporters, formerly imprisoned, were to be inducted into the Central Committee. The second announcement was that Khrushchev, accompanied by a high-ranking Soviet delegation, was scheduled to arrive in Warsaw that very day.

Khrushchev's visit and Gomułka's rehabilitation were not independent. The Soviet premier was very much concerned by events occurring in Poland, particularly by information that the Central Committee members closest to the Soviet Union—like Marshal Rokossovski[30]—were to be booted out and replaced by Polish nationalists like Gomułka. Indeed, Gomułka demanded Rokossovski's removal as a condition of his assuming the position of first secretary. Gomułka also demanded that Soviet advisers and officers be recalled from the Polish armed forces.[31] Partly in response to these demands and partly in response to an apparent rise in anti-Soviet sentiment in Poland,[32] Khrushchev decided to take action by scheduling an unprecedented trip to Warsaw.

Although the precise details of the meeting between Khrushchev and his delegation and the Polish Party members remain unclear, documents

[29]Davies 1982, 2:584.

[30]Rokossovski, a Soviet citizen of Polish descent, was the Soviet-appointed head of the Polish armed forces.

[31]Gluchowski 1995, 38.

[32]For a description of Polish anti-Soviet sentiment at this time, see Machcewicz 1997.

have recently come to light that reveal many of the key moments. Khrushchev's own memoirs reveal the nature of his concern regarding events in Poland:

> It looked to us as though developments in Poland were rushing forward on the crest of a giant anti-Soviet wave. Meetings were being held all over the country, and we were afraid Poland might break away from us at any moment.
>
> In Warsaw, an important meeting of the [Polish] Central Committee was under way. We had no time to lose. We expressed our urgent desire to meet with the Polish leadership, to hear their side of the story, and to let them know how we viewed the situation. . . .
>
> The situation was such that we had to be ready to resort to arms if the threat of an armed struggle in Poland became real and if we were in imminent danger of being cut off from our army.[33]

That the Soviets were very close to an armed invasion is also supported by the notes of the meeting taken by a member of the Polish Central Committee:

> Khrushchev's first words were as follows: "We have decided to intervene brutally in your affairs and we will not allow you to realize your plans." We immediately thought that if someone puts a revolver on the table we will not talk. . . . The subsequent talks were somewhat calmer. Comrade Mikoyan reported the perspective of the Soviet delegation. He said that the Soviet Union has certain military forces on GDR [German Democratic Republic] territory and is concerned that changes by us after the VIII Plenum might lead to a difficult situation, with a loss of communications to those military forces, especially if Poland wants to break away from the bloc uniting our states.[34]

Indeed, a Soviet invasion appeared imminent. Soviet battleships had taken up position in the Bay of Gdańsk and, as further noted by the Central Committee:

> At this time, we received reports that the Soviet army stationed in Poland began to march on Warsaw. As to our question about what this means, the Soviet comrades explained that it was part of some military exercise planned a long time ago. We explained to the Soviet comrades that, notwithstanding the facts, in the eyes of Polish society this military exercise will be understood as an attempt to put pressure on the Government and Party. We demanded the return of the Soviet armored units to their bases. The Soviet comrades told Marshal Rokos-

---

[33]Khrushchev 1974, 199, 200. The army Khrushchev refers to in the last sentence is the Soviet army in East Germany.

[34]Notes from the completed discussions of January 11 and 12, 1957, between the delegates of the Chinese People's Republic and Poland, included as "Document 4" in Gluchowski 1995, 44, trans. by L. W. Gluchowski.

sowski, who was taking part in the discussions, to transmit to Marshal Konev the wishes of the PUWP [Polish United Workers' Party] Politburo, to halt the military exercises, which of course did not happen. Smaller units of the Polish armed forces were also moved in the direction of Warsaw, on the orders of Marshal Rokossowski, who, when asked, admitted: "I wanted to secure selected positions in Warsaw." Of course, Rokossowski did not inform the PUWP Politburo about his orders, merely confirming, after we asked about it, that he had given the orders.

The talks with the Soviet delegation went on for the whole day. The atmosphere was very unpleasant, inhospitable. Our side was calm but determined. Near the end of the talks, now calmly, comrade Khrushchev explained: "It doesn't matter what you want, our view is such that we will have to restart the intervention." We again assured the Soviet comrades that their fears concerning Poland's departure from the bloc of socialist states was groundless.[35]

Despite the threatening actions of the Soviets, Gomułka appears to have been able to call their bluff, convince them of his intentions to keep Poland within the Soviet bloc, or both. Central Committee member Aleksander Zawadzki's notes of the meeting support the first interpretation:

> At this point, 9:00 [p.m.], Comrade Gomulka vehemently protests against the movement of Soviet and Polish tanks—[which brings about] sharp clashes with the Soviet comrades. Comrade Khrushchev—that in Germany [there is] a huge Soviet army . . . Comrade Mikoyan—go ahead, do it, but you will assume a great responsibility in front of the Party, the nation and the brother countries! (directed at Gomulka). Again, about the list of new Politburo [members] . . . [and its] distribution in Warsaw.
>
> Comrade Khrushchev. 1) regarding the [Soviet] advisers—that rather reluctantly they will give it to us [Soviets will concede]. That he [Khrushchev] feels pained by the position of Comrade Gomulka on the issue of the advisers. That the Soviet Union saw it as its duty [to send advisers to Poland]. He [Khrushchev] admits that they [Soviets] travelled here with the purpose of telling us their views, interpretations, and to influence us . . . But we [the Poles] will not entertain anything. Very determined concerning the issue of Comrade Rokossowski. [Soviets concerned] That this is how Gomulka has come [to join] the leadership of the [Polish] Party, with such a position.[36]

Why did Khrushchev ultimately give in? Mark Kramer has found evidence that, as Soviet troops moved toward Warsaw, Polish units loyal to

---

[35] Notes from the completed discussions of January 11 and 12, 1957, between the delegates of the Chinese People's Republic and Poland, included as "Document 4" in Gluchowski 1995, 44, trans. by L. W. Gluchowski.

[36] Aleksander Zawadzki's notes, included as "Document 3" in Gluchowski 1995, 43. NB: Ellipses and bracketed/parenthetical notes are from the original translation.

the new regime made threatening countermoves. Engaged in a prolonged game of chicken, Khrushchev and Gomułka returned to the negotiating table. Stalemate, however, continued, and Khrushchev and his cohort returned to Moscow on October 20 without having gotten what they had come to Warsaw for.

Voting for the new Polish Politburo took place on October 21. The hated Rokossovski and his fellow pro-Soviet comrades were not elected; Gomułka became first secretary, replacing Ochab. Syrop reports the comments of a radio broadcaster just prior to the voting: "This is spring in October—the spring of awakened hopes and of awakened national pride, the spring of true international proletarianism and of determined will to mark out our own Polish way to socialism."[37] By the next day, Khrushchev had conveyed assurances that the Soviet advisers would be recalled from Poland.[38]

WHY DID THE SOVIET UNION INTERVENE IN HUNGARY IN 1956?

Ten years after the close of the Second World War, a Communist regime seemed well entrenched in Budapest. The Warsaw Pact was signed, reformists like Imre Nagy were booted out of office, and the western borders of the USSR's quasi empire appeared secure. But in the fall of 1956, Soviet tanks rolled into Budapest twice to quell large uprisings. Hungary was on the verge of seceding from the Soviet bloc in terms of both domestic and foreign policies.

Hungarian discontent with the Soviet-imposed regime was not new in 1956.[39] Nagy had been a particularly popular leader, and his expulsion from the Party certainly bred resentment. But following the crackdown on Nagy, Khrushchev's "secret speech," which denounced many of the "mistakes" of the Stalin era, appeared to signal a political opening. The first sign of change in Budapest was the replacement of Prime Minister Mátyás Rákosi, who was widely disliked among the populace, with the less controversial Ernö Gerö in July of 1956.

Such changes, however, seemed marginal when compared to citizens' grievances. Led by students at the Budapest Technical University, a large crowd demanded sixteen "points," including Nagy's return to government, the abolition of the secret police, and the removal of Soviet troops from Hungarian soil. As the crowd toppled Stalin's statue in Budapest, Gerö and his inner cabinet requested Soviet military intervention. The first Soviet intervention, then, was an invasion by invitation.

[37]Quoted in Syrop 1957, 136.
[38]See letter from Khrushchev to Gomulka, included as "Document 5" in Gluchowski 1995, 45–46, trans. by L. W. Gluchowski.
[39]Granville 2004, 35.

By the morning of October 24, Imre Nagy was reinstituted as prime minister. Demonstrations and strikes continued, despite his pleas for calm. By October 25, Soviet troops had killed or wounded more than one hundred peaceful demonstrators at the parliament building. Three days later, following the reconstitution of the Hungarian government such that some of the least popular Communists were now out of office, a truce was called. Nonetheless, fighting in the streets continued, raising fears in Moscow that Nagy was unable to control the situation.

A Soviet declaration of intent to begin negotiations to withdraw troops from Hungary was meant to quell rebellion and prevent a reintervention that neither side wanted. Presidium members were apparently willing to make this concession.[40] One day later, however, the Soviet position was reversed. Fears about the Hungarian Revolution were exacerbated, not only by the situation on the ground, but also by the pace and content of reforms proposed by Nagy. Multiparty democracy was very high on Nagy's list of proposed changes, but more troubling to Moscow was the proposal that Hungary chart its own course in foreign policy. As Mark Kramer notes, archival sources released in the 1990s reveal that calls for neutrality and Hungarian withdrawal from the Warsaw Pact preceded Nagy's November 1 announcement of these policies. Béla Kovács, a close colleague of Nagy's, called for a neutral Hungary [and the end of Hungary's] ties to military blocs" on October 30.[41] According to Kramer, "that same day, Nagy himself endorsed the goal of leaving the Warsaw Pact, and he opened talks about the matter (and about the withdrawal of all Soviet troops from Hungary) with Mikoyan and Suslov, who promptly informed their colleagues in Moscow about the decisions. It seems likely that Nagy's expressed desire to renounce Hungarian membership in the Warsaw Pact was one of the factors that induced the CPSU Presidium on 31 October to reverse its decision of the previous day."[42]

As Soviet troops turned back toward Hungary, and Nagy appealed to the United Nations for a recognition of Hungarian neutrality,[43] a new Hungarian leadership was already being instructed by Moscow. At the

---

[40]Further, they determined on October 30 that they would not intervene in Hungary. Kramer remarks that the Soviet Union may "have been willing to accept the collapse of Communism in Hungary." Kramer 1996b, 38.

[41]Quoted in Kramer 1996b, 369.

[42]Kramer 1996b, 369. Note that Granville casts doubt on the impact of Nagy's intention to declare neutrality and withdraw from the Warsaw Pact by noting that the Soviet decision to reintervene in Hungary was taken prior to Nagy's official announcement of these policies. "Where Nagy's decision making is concerned, the Soviet invasion was clearly the cause, his declaration of neutrality the effect." Granville, however, does not mention the upper-level cabinet discussions of this policy shift, to which key Soviet decision makers were privy. Granville 2004, 71.

[43]Litván 1996, 79.

same time, the Soviet Union continued to negotiate with Nagy's government for the removal of Soviet troops. The intention was to deceive Nagy; while only five Soviet divisions had been deployed in October, the Soviets were sending seventeen divisions to Hungary in November.[44]

On November 4, the establishment of János Kádár's new "Revolutionary Workers' and Peasants' Government" was announced. Kádár, unlike Nagy, was a more reliable friend of the USSR and had, in fact, been spirited away to Moscow in late October to be primed for this new position. On the same day, Soviet troops attacked Budapest. While Nagy and many of his closest colleagues fled to refuge in the Yugoslav embassy, fighting in Budapest continued until the eleventh, leaving over twenty thousand dead and wounded Hungarians.[45] By November 7, Kádár was sworn in as prime minister and, by the end of the month, Nagy and his cohort had been kidnapped to Romania, where they remained until their return to Budapest for trial and execution.

WHY DID THE SOVIET UNION INVADE HUNGARY BUT NOT POLAND?

The events of Poland's October Spring were watched closely by neighbors in Hungary. Indeed, the Hungarian Revolution of 1956 began with demonstrations meant to convey solidarity with Polish reformers. As in Poznań in June, however, demonstrations quickly turned to riots. Like Gomułka in regard to Poland, Hungary's Imre Nagy demanded the removal of Soviet troops from Hungary. The two revolutions appeared to be following parallel courses. But when, approximately one week after the Hungarian Revolution had started, a full-scale Soviet invasion commenced, it was clear that the revolutions would in fact meet very different fates.

What accounts for Soviet invasion in Hungary and restraint in Poland? One argument that has been suggested to explain the variation in Soviet behavior toward Hungary and Poland in 1956 refers to the negative demonstration effects of revolution. Granville argues that Hungary was perceived by Moscow as "The First Domino," one that could topple the entire Soviet empire.[46] Relatedly, Kramer notes that the Soviets were receiving reports from Czechoslovakia and Romania that the revolution was spilling over Hungary's borders.[47] Such a spillover would certainly

---

[44]Granville 2004, 96–97.

[45]Granville 2004, 96.

[46]Granville 2004.

[47]Kramer 1998, 192–93. Also see "Minutes of the 55th Meeting of the Romanian Workers' Party Political Committee, October 26, 1956," document no. 36 in Békés, Byrne, and Rainer 2002, 246–49.

threaten the stability and cohesion of the Warsaw Pact. While spillover concerns may have been genuine, what is not clear is why the Soviets would have selected Hungary, rather than Poland, as their target. After all, the Polish revolution had itself spilled over into Hungary, thus serving as the original cause of the spillover. Ruthless suppression of the Poles would therefore have been expected to suppress all the revolutionaries taking action in their image, while an invasion of Hungary would leave the Polish reformists to continue to implement their new agenda.

Jakub Zielinski advances an interpretation of this puzzle that relies heavily on the role of signaling by the Soviet military to the Polish and Hungarian leaders, respectively. It was made clear to the Poles, argues Zielinski, that too much independence would not be tolerated; the Hungarians, on the other hand, received the opposite signal—that reform was acceptable. The relevant signal to the Poles, according to Zielinski, was Khrushchev's threatening visit to Warsaw on October 19. Nagy, by contrast, received assurances that he could reform in peace. "[Nagy] explicitly asked whether a concession with regard to multiparty democracy and Soviet military withdrawal would be acceptable to Moscow. The Soviets answered in the affirmative. Their only condition was that Hungary did not become an anti-Soviet state and that people associated with the prewar regime be barred from power."[48] The problem with this analysis is that Khrushchev conceded to Gomułka much more than Zielinski admits. As noted above, Khrushchev agreed to the withdrawal of Soviet advisers and troops from Poland; no such concession was forthcoming with respect to the Hungarian case. By contrast, the importance of Hungary's remaining in the Warsaw Pact was clearly stated to Nagy. Thus, if anything, the Poles received a "green light" for reform, while Nagy was given an explicitly limited set of conditions under which Hungarian reform could take place.

The puzzle of the Soviet invasion of Hungary but not Poland can be solved by analyzing the respective roles of Poland and Hungary as buffer states in the Cold War between the Soviet Union and United States. Hungary, not Poland, threatened to secede from the Soviet bloc. Although Gomułka fought for the removal of Soviet advisers and officers from the Polish military, he explicitly and frequently endorsed the alliance with the Soviet Union, in part because he associated the survival of Poland with the maintenance of the alliance. Gomułka was particularly concerned about the stability of Poland's western border against German revanchism, arguing that "Poland needs friendship with the Soviet Union more than the Soviet Union needs friendship with Poland. . . . Without the Soviet Union we cannot maintain our borders with the West."[49]

[48]Zielinski 1999, 222.
[49]Quoted in Granville 2004, 46.

Unlike Poland, Hungary's borders had not been redrawn following World War II in ways likely to inspire territorial revisionism. Thus, Nagy was in a better position to state explicitly a desire to withdraw Hungary from the Warsaw Pact and declare neutrality.[50] Further, this desire was increasingly supported by public sentiment in Hungary.[51] Once Nagy had communicated his intentions to Soviet Presidium members Mikoyan and Suslov, the Soviet decision against intervention was reversed immediately; this course of action could only have been reinforced by the public statement of Hungarian neutrality. It was neither the desire to prevent spill-over, nor poor signaling on the part of the Soviets, but the fear of losing Hungary to the other side—a fear not present with respect to Poland— that sent Soviet tanks to Budapest rather than Warsaw.

That Hungary was more likely to secede from the Soviet bloc than Poland in 1956 is clear. But to what extent does this potential secession generate—or perhaps represent—the type of security-dilemma dynamic between the United States and Soviet Union that would create Soviet incentives for intervention? To answer this question, we must examine both US behavior and Soviet perceptions of that behavior.

Among US propaganda efforts to wean away Soviet satellite states was Radio Free Europe (RFE). To the degree that RFE broadcasts could be taken as indicative of US policy, the broadcasts surrounding the Hungarian Revolution must have sent a dangerous signal to the Soviet Union. For example, an October 28 broadcast—occurring between the original invasion and the decision to undertake the second invasion—offered tactical advice to Hungarian insurgents.[52] Further, the stated position of the Eisenhower administration prior to the invasion was "based on the assumption that if they [Soviet satellites] gained independence they would in reality join the western world, which also meant joining NATO."[53] Public attempts to reverse this policy and send a more comforting signal to the Soviets were made repeatedly, but in extremely watered-down form.[54] The United States also protested the Soviet invasion of Hungary in the UN Security Council.[55] While the US response to the invasion certainly could have been more threatening than it was, it is not difficult to see how Soviet decision makers might have viewed US actions with alarm.

---

[50]See Békés, Byrne, and Rainer 2002, 332–34.

[51]Granville 2004, 71–72.

[52]"Transcripts of Radio Free Europe Programs, Advising on Military Tactics to Use Against a Superior Enemy, October 28, 1956," document no. 45 in Békés, Byrne, and Rainer 2002, 286–89.

[53]Békés, Byrne, and Rainer 2002, 209–10.

[54]Békés, Byrne, and Rainer 2002, 209.

[55]See for example document 158: "Telegram From the Mission at the United Nations to the Department of State, November 2, 1956," in Glennon 1990, 368–69.

Such alarm was clearly expressed by Krushchev during an October 31 Presidium meeting:

> We should take the initiative in restoring order in Hungary. If we depart from Hungary, it will give a great boost to the Americans, English, and the French—the imperialists.
>
> They will perceive it as weakness on our part and will go onto the offensive.
>
> We would then be exposing the weakness of our positions.
>
> Our party will not accept it if we do this.
>
> To Egypt they will then add Hungary.
>
> We have no other choice.[56]

The weak US attempt to signal its restraint to the Soviet Union failed.[57] US and Soviet policy makers saw the Hungarian Revolution as, respectively, an opportunity and a crisis. Importantly, the shared perception seemed to be that the Soviets were truly in danger of losing control over Eastern Europe.[58] In the words of Békés, Byrne, and Rainer, "in Soviet eyes, cracking the East European buffer zone would create an intolerable security threat."[59]

DID ANTICIPATED RESISTANCE LEAD THE SOVIETS TO INTERVENE
IN HUNGARY BUT NOT POLAND?

The conventional wisdom regarding the varying outcomes in Budapest and Warsaw in 1956 is that Khrushchev chose to intervene in Hungary rather than Poland because he anticipated greater nationalist-driven popular resistance in Poland. If supported, this explanation would offer considerable ammunition to the argument that a rise in nationalism accounts for the decrease in violent state death. This interpretation is incorrect, however. Although the Soviets did anticipate resistance in Poland, anticipated nationalist uprisings cannot account for a variation in outcome, because the nationalist resistance anticipated by the Soviets in Budapest and Warsaw were virtually the same.

Poland and Hungary look very similar on various measures of nationalism. Both states were fairly homogeneous, with the dominant ethnic group comprising over 90 percent of the population. Both states were industrial, although Poland's per capita energy consumption was higher

---

[56]"Working Notes and Attached Extract from the Minutes of the CPSU CC Presidium Meeting, October 31, 1956," document no. 53 in Békés, Byrne, and Rainer 2002, 307–10.

[57]Békés, Byrne, and Rainer 2002, 213.

[58]"Memorandum of Discussion at the 301st Meeting of the National Security Council, October 26, 1956, 9–10:42 a.m.," document no. 34 in Békés, Byrne, and Rainer 2002, 240–43.

[59]Békés, Byrne, and Rainer 2002, 210.

than Hungary's. The critical question, however, refers to the history of resistance and expectations regarding the loyalties of the Polish and Hungarian armies.

Khrushchev hesitated in ordering an invasion of Poland in part because it appeared that the Polish military was not entirely loyal to Rokossovski and the Soviet Union. Furthermore, it was expected that the Poles would violently resist any such interference. Kramer suggests that Khrushchev anticipated high levels of nationalist resistance in Poland and, for this reason, decided not to intervene:

> [Quoting Khrushchev on October 20/21:] "Finding a reason for an armed conflict [with Poland] now would be very easy, but finding a way to put an end to such a conflict later on would be very hard." The stand-off on 19 October had demonstrated to the Soviet leadership that most of the Polish troops who were not under Rokossowski's command, especially in the KBW [Polish Internal Security Forces] were ready to put up stiff resistance to outside intervention. Khrushchev and his colleagues also seem to have feared that Polish leaders would begin handing out firearms to "workers' militia" units who could help defend the capital. . . .
>
> . . . Khrushchev's reluctance to pursue a military solution in such unfavourable circumstances induced him to seek a modus vivendi with Gomulka whereby Poland would have greater leeway to follow its own "road to socialism." Gomulka reciprocated by again assuring Khrushchev that Poland would remain a loyal ally and member of the Warsaw Pact.[60]

Khrushchev had good reason to worry about both the loyalty of the Polish military and the reaction of the Polish people. Apparently, many Polish troops resisted the suppression of the Pozń riots in June, and continuing demonstrations clearly exhibited the mood of Polish civilians.[61] If the loyalty of the Hungarian military and populace was (relatively) assured, then this explanation would be a convincing one for the Soviet decision.

To assess the loyalty of the Hungarian military and population, it is helpful to start with the initial demonstrations in Budapest on October 23, during which Hungarian first secretary Ernö Gërö requested Soviet military aid to quell the insurgents. Although they initially were uncertain as to their response, the Soviets ultimately acceded to Gërö's request. According to Grzegorz Ekiert, the Soviets believed that the mere demonstration of force would quell insurrection.[62] Kramer describes an extensive deployment of the Soviet forces.[63] Despite its firepower, this first

---

[60]Kramer 1998, 172–73.
[61]Kramer 1998, 168.
[62]Ekiert 1996, 63.
[63]Kramer 1998, 184–85.

intervention was a clear failure. Resistance was not only evident but also very effective against the vulnerable Soviet tanks and artillery. Hungarian troops, rather than fighting in cooperation with the Soviets, fought alongside their countrymen. Instead of repressing the revolution, the intervention only aggravated it.

Thus, it was demonstrably clear to the Soviets that the Hungarians also would resist invasion. Further, the loyalties of the Hungarian army were in question.[64] Soviet envoys Anastas Mikoyan and Mikhail Suslov reported from Budapest on October 30 that

> The political situation in the country, rather than improving, is getting worse. . . . The peaceful liquidation of the remaining centres [of resistance] can effectively be excluded. We will try to liquidate them using the armed forces of the Hungarians. But there is a great danger in this: the Hungarian army has adopted a "wait-and-see" position. Our military advisers say that the attitude of Hungarian officers and generals toward Soviet officers has deteriorated in recent days, and that there is no longer the trust which existed earlier. It may well be that if Hungarian units are used against the uprising, they will go over to the side of the insurgents, and it will then be necessary for the Soviet armed forces to resume military operations.[65]

The evidence thus does not suggest that the anticipated resistance generated by Polish, as opposed to Hungarian, nationalists, was significantly higher. Both populations and, importantly, both militaries were considered unreliable in their support of a Soviet intervention. Further, while the Polish military was larger than its Hungarian counterpart (300,000 versus 215,000), the ratio of military personnel to population and area indicates that it might have been more favorable for the Soviets to invade Poland as opposed to Hungary. If both militaries were equally likely to resist a Soviet invasion, the Hungarians held the defensive edge in being able to field twice as many soldiers per square kilometer, and per civilian, as opposed to the Poles.[66] The likelihood of resistance that could have been foreseen by the Soviets therefore appears to be roughly equal.

(HOW) DID THE NORM AGAINST CONQUEST AFFECT SOVIET DECISION MAKING?

A major element of the argument advanced in this book is that a norm against conquest has prevented violent state death after 1945. It is important to note that, while the Soviets considered taking military action

[64]Ekiert 1996, 54.

[65]Quoted in Kramer 1998, 188.

[66]Data on Hungarian and Polish military personnel and population are from Bennett and Stam 2000. Data on area are from the 2004 *CIA World Factbook*.

in Poland in 1956, and did take such action in Hungary, in neither case did they attempt to annex their wayward satellites. Can Soviet restraint be explained by the power of the norm against conquest? To what degree did this norm affect the decision to execute a military intervention at all?

The role of the norm against conquest in restricting Soviet behavior appears to be positive, but small. A survey of the documentary evidence on the Polish and Hungarian events of 1956 does reveal conversations among the Soviet leadership that refer to the option of occupation, but as a tool to be avoided, if at all possible.[67] Soviet reluctance to exercise this option is particularly interesting in this case, as the Soviets displayed few scruples in annexing half of Poland and all of the Baltic states in 1939 and 1940.

The norm against conquest explicitly prohibits the violent conquest of states. While military interventions that replace regimes and leaders do not constitute blatant violations of the norm against conquest, they are hardly consistent with the principles underlying the norm. Ironically, however, it does seem that the norm played a role in *permitting* the Soviet invasion of Hungary. At the same time that the Soviets were managing the Polish and Hungarian revolutions, the French, British, and Americans were facing an emerging crisis in the Middle East. Following Gamal Abdel Nasser's announcement of the nationalization of the Suez Canal, the French and British blockaded and launched air raids on Egyptian cities. The Western military intervention in Egypt could have been taken as justification for the Soviet invasion of Hungary—a sort of tit for tat in the game of norm infringement.[68] It is clear that Soviet Presidium members considered the Suez crisis as they determined how to handle the Hungarian rebellion in particular. Khrushchev, for example, remarked: "The English and French are in a real mess in Egypt. We shouldn't get caught in the same company."[69] This statement suggests real concern for how Soviet aggression might have been perceived internationally.

More likely is the possibility that the Suez crisis both distracted Western attention from Hungary and created a split in NATO that prevented the Western powers from taking a strong stance against Soviet intervention in Hungary. While the United States (along with a reluctant France and Britain) did request that the UN Security Council consider the situation in Hungary in late October 1956, no Western power intended to intervene on behalf of Hungary. Ultimately, France and Britain retreated

---

[67]See for example "Working Notes from the CPSU CC Presidium Session, October 28, 1956," document no. 40 in Békés, Byrne, and Rainer 2002, 262–69.

[68]The logic of this argument is suggested by Thomas M. Franck and Edward Weisband. This particular argument is, however, purely speculative and neither confirmed nor disproved by available evidence. Franck and Weisband 1971.

[69]Quoted in Kramer 1996b, 369.

from the position of condemning the Soviet intervention, as their own actions at the time were too close for comfort to Soviet actions in its satellites. Even though the Soviets probably would have invaded Hungary even without the convenience of the Suez crisis, events in the Middle East did create what Khrushchev called a "favourable moment."[70]

Although the Soviet Union does not appear to have been severely punished for the Hungarian invasion, existing global reaction was negative. In November 1956, the United Nations passed a number of resolutions regarding Hungary. These included a demand for Soviet withdrawal, a demand to be allowed to send economic and medical aid to Hungary, a call for all UN members to send aid to Hungary, a demand that the Soviet Union cease deportations of Hungarians, and finally a demand that UN observers be permitted to enter Hungary.[71] Furthermore, the Soviets appreciated that, almost alone among the great powers, the United States held the upper moral hand by virtue of its abstention from the Suez intervention.[72] Perhaps a more important cost for the Soviet Union was the observation of the Hungarian invasion as a precedent in Chinese eyes.[73] Ultimately, the most expensive independent cost of violating the norm appears to have been a temporary damage to reputation with respect to less developed countries the Soviets had been wooing prior to the invasion.[74]

The Soviets refrained from invading Poland not because it was more nationalistic but because it was more compliant. The threat of a Polish break from the Soviet bloc was minimal at most, while the possibility that the Soviet Union would lose its Hungarian buffer to the West seemed very real. Once again, the dynamics of rivalry better account for the death— or, as in this case, the survival—of states than do the anticipated costs of nationalist resistance. The Hungarian example shows that anticipated resistance was not driving Soviet decisions to intervene in one country as opposed to the other. At the same time, the comparison between Poland and Hungary in 1956 illustrates the notion that buffer states that threaten to escape indirect control are more likely to suffer negative consequences than more compliant buffers—even after 1945.[75] In the end, Soviet re-

---

[70]Kramer 1998, 192.

[71]Karpiński 1982, 70; Litván 1996, 90–98.

[72]At the same time, however, prior to the invasion, the United States prohibited NATO forces from acting to defend Hungary. Kramer 1998, 207; also see Ekiert 1996, 64.

[73]Indeed, a high-ranking Chinese delegation was visiting Moscow in October of 1956, affording them the opportunity to witness the Soviet reaction firsthand.

[74]Ekiert 1996, 213. Less importantly, the invasion also would have damaged the reputation of the Soviets in the eyes of sympathetic Western intellectuals.

[75]This logic also complements the analysis by shedding light on why the USSR did not absorb all of Eastern Europe in the way that it had annexed the Baltic states. Yugoslavia and

straint in Eastern Europe appears to have been conditioned more by the norm against conquest than by a fear of nationalist resistance.

The 1965 Intervention in the Dominican Republic: Forestalling a "Second Cuba"

One of the great ironies of the well-intentioned military reforms of the 1916 US occupation of the Dominican Republic was the emergence of Rafael Trujillo as the Republic's new dictator. The US occupation of 1916–1924 had seen the reform of the Dominican constabulary and the training of Trujillo and his cohort. Trujillo quickly rose through the ranks, gaining control of the constabulary and then of the government. For three decades, the United States supported the Trujillo regime because it adhered to Washington's Caribbean policy.[76] Thus, the Dominican Republic was a compliant neighbor for much of the postoccupation period. Then, in 1961, Trujillo was assassinated. Following a series of attempted coups and provisional governments, elections in 1962 brought Juan Bosch to the Dominican presidency.

Bosch was initially supported by US president Kennedy as the type of prodemocracy reformer needed to make the Alliance for Progress succeed.[77] Bosch's presidency, however, was short-lived. In September 1963, the Bosch government was overthrown in a military coup. The United States initially refused to recognize the military government but eventually acceded. Not quite two years later, in April 1965, the military government that had replaced Bosch was itself ousted by pro-Bosch military officers. This April 1965 coup represents the start of what has frequently been called the "Dominican crisis."

Several features of the 1965 US intervention in the Dominican Republic emerge distinctly. First, the principal motivation for the US intervention was the fear of the Dominican Republic becoming a "second Cuba." The perceived security dilemma around the Dominican Republic is underlined by the US president Johnson administration's constant concern over the influence of Communists in Santo Domingo. Second, the John-

---

Albania were on the borders of the Soviet empire, bringing geographic considerations to the fore in the consideration of expansion—or deepening—of influence. When, like Hungary in 1956, it appeared to be straying from the fold, Czechoslovakia experienced Soviet invasion a decade after the Hungarian crisis. And while Romania made early protests against the Warsaw Pact, it consistently worked within the system, advocating for changes in the alliance as opposed to withdrawal or dissolution. Variation in the means of Soviet control over Eastern Europe was primarily a function of perceived threats to that control as well as the costs of governance. D. A. Lake 1999.

[76]Atkins and Wilson 1998, 66–67, 80.
[77]Felten 1996, 1009–10.

son administration was significantly constrained by the normative environment of the time. Options like annexation or long-term occupation were never seriously considered, while concern for both domestic public opinion and the opinion of Latin American neighbors was often front and center in high-level meetings. And third, both Dominican nationalism and anticipated costs of resistance were low. Low levels of Dominican nationalism in 1965 are not predicted by the hypothesis that nationalism should increase over time; the failure of the United States to conquer the Dominican Republic under these conditions is also not predicted by this hypothesis.

WHY DID THE US INTERVENE IN THE DOMINICAN REPUBLIC IN 1965?

Johnson's foreign policy was governed by a need to prevent the spread of communism on a global—and certainly regional—basis. Although the Dominican Republic was in the United States' traditional "backyard," very little attention was paid to it during Trujillo's regime, principally because there appeared to be no threat of Communist incursion. With the "loss" of Cuba, however, and Castro's stated intentions toward the island of Hispaniola, the US foreign policy establishment slowly began to fear the possibility of a Communist takeover in the Dominican Republic.[78] It was precisely this fear, which to US policy makers was embodied in the pro-Bosch coup, that led to the US intervention of the Dominican Republic in 1965.

As Abraham Lowenthal argues, the historical US interest in the Dominican Republic was not economic or even military but "preemptive." Lowenthal notes that since the enunciation of the Monroe Doctrine, the United States' primary goal with respect to the Caribbean in general and the Dominican Republic in particular has been to prevent other powers from gaining a foothold in the region. The same was true in 1965.[79]

Indeed, even prior to the 1965 crisis, fears of a "second Cuba" in the Dominican Republic were growing. According to Lowenthal as well as Johnson, John F. Kennedy's self-imposed indicators of success in his first year as president included preventing the Dominican Republic and the Congo from turning to communism.[80] This concern was reflected both in Washington, after Kennedy's death, and in the US embassy in Santo Domingo.

During the last week of April 1965, when the crisis erupted, worries about a Communist takeover surfaced immediately. In particular, reports

[78]Lowenthal 1972, 25.
[79]Lowenthal 1972, 20.
[80]Lowenthal 1972, 26; Lyndon Baines Johnson 1971, 197.

from the US embassy fed these concerns. *New York Times* reporter Tad Szulc observed that, within twenty-four hours of the April coup, embassy officials were convinced that Bosch's return to the Dominican Republic would mean the loss of the Republic to communism.[81] US chargé d'affaires William Connett, Jr., quickly informed Washington, "We believe there is a serious threat of a communist takeover in this country and that very little time remains in which to act."[82] On April 28, US ambassador to the Dominican Republic W. Tapley "Tap" Bennett, Jr., cabled the State Department: "I regret as much as anyone that, once again, we have to rely on military solution for political crisis. . . . While leftist propaganda naturally will try to fuzz situation as fight between military and people, issue here now is fight between Castro-type elements and those who oppose it."[83] Later that same day, Bennett made the following recommendation to Washington:

> I recommend serious thought be given in Washington to armed intervention which would go beyond the mere protection of Americans and seek to establish order in this strife-ridden country. All indications point to the fact that if present efforts of forces loyal to the government fail, power will be assumed by groups clearly identified with the Communist Party. If the situation described above comes to pass, my own recommendation and that of country team is that we should intervene to prevent another Cuba from arising out of the ashes of this uncontrollable situation.[84]

Embassy concerns were echoed in the White House and State Department. Immediately following the coup, President Johnson expressed his commitment to prevent "another Cuba in this Hemisphere," although he did not take action to this end for several days.[85] An April 29 State Department telegram to the Santo Domingo embassy read: "We cannot afford permit situation deteriorate to point where Communist takeover occurs."[86] Newly sworn-in CIA director William Raborn briefed congressional leaders on the crisis he called a "Moscow-financed, Havana-

[81]Szulc 1965, 19.

[82]Cable, Santo Domingo to State Department, 4/26/65, File A-1: Incoming State Cables, April 24–May 4, 1965, document no. 40, NSF: National Security Council History—Dominican Crisis, 1965, LBJ Library. At the time of the coup, Ambassador Bennett was visiting family in Georgia. Chargé d'Affaires Connett was the next in command at the embassy.

[83]Cable, Santo Domingo to State Department, 4/28/65, in Lawler and Yee 2005, 71.

[84]Cable, Santo Domingo to National Security Agency, 4/28/65, in Lawler and Yee 2005, 85.

[85]Quoted in Lowenthal 1972, 86.

[86]Cable No. 681, State Department to Santo Domingo, 4/29/65, File A-1: Outgoing State Department Cables, April 25–May 14, 1965, document no. 30, NSF: National Security Council History: The Dominican Crisis, 1965, Box 5, LBJ Library.

directed plot to take over the Dominican Republic."[87] On April 30, Johnson told his mentor and close adviser Abe Fortas that "our troops should be prepared to take the island so that Castro doesn't take it."[88] The perceived seriousness of the "Castro threat" became increasingly clear with the rapid progression of the crisis. A few hours after his conversation with Fortas, Johnson told Undersecretary of State for Economic Affairs Thomas Mann: "We have a choice—either let Castro take over the island or, in the name of freedom and justice, somebody else will take it over."[89] These sentiments continued to be echoed throughout the intervention,[90] during the subsequent Dominican elections,[91] and in Johnson's memoir of his presidency.[92]

With the conviction that the Dominican Republic was in jeopardy of being lost to communism, US troops were landed in Hispaniola on April 28, ostensibly to protect the lives of American citizens and other foreign nationals. It was made clear to President Johnson, however, that this minimal initial contingent could not prevent the pro-Bosch rebels from winning what had by then become a civil war. According to former US ambassador to the Dominican Republic John Bartlow Martin, Johnson stated that he did not intend "to sit here with my hands tied and let Castro take that island. What can we do in Vietnam if we can't clean up the Dominican Republic? I know what the editorials will say, but it would be a hell of a lot worse if we sit here and don't do anything and the Communists take that country."[93] Similarly, Secretary of State Dean Rusk listed the United States' primary objectives in the Dominican Republic as "restoration of law and order, prevention of a possible Communist takeover, and protection of American lives."[94]

[87]Quoted in Lowenthal 1972, 105.

[88]Telephone Conversation between Lyndon B. Johnson and Abe Fortas, April 30, 1965, 10:50 a.m., Citation #7404, Recordings and Transcripts of Conversations and Meetings, LBJ Library.

[89]Telephone Conversation between Lyndon B. Johnson and Thomas Mann, April 30, 1965, 12:46 p.m., Citation #7415, Recordings and Transcripts of Conversations and Meetings, LBJ Library.

[90]See for example Telephone Conversation between Lyndon B. Johnson and Robert McNamara, May 12, 1965, 11:20 a.m., Citation #7634, Recordings and Transcripts of Conversations and Meetings, LBJ Library; Telephone Conversation between Lyndon B. Johnson and J. Edgar Hoover, May 19, 1965, 12:00 p.m., Citation #7780, Recordings and Transcripts of Conversations and Meetings, LBJ Library; and "Meeting Notes, n.d.," Papers of Bromley K. Smith, Box 33/File: Dominican republic, document no. 4: LBJ Library.

[91]Telephone Conversation between Lyndon B. Johnson and Mike Mansfield, June 26, 1965, 7:38 a.m., Citation #8196, Recordings and Transcripts of Conversations and Meetings, LBJ Library.

[92]Lyndon Baines Johnson 1971, 187–205.

[93]Quoted in Martin 1966, 661.

[94]Quoted in Brands 1995, 54.

Additional evidence that fear of a Communist takeover motivated the US intervention can be found in the text of Johnson's speeches justifying the action. Initially, on April 28, Johnson couched the intervention as motivated entirely by a desire to protect American lives.[95] Two days later, however, he suggested that "there are signs that people trained outside the Dominican Republic are seeking to gain control."[96] And by May 2, Johnson reported that "the revolutionary movement took a tragic turn. Communist leaders, many of them trained in Cuba, seeing a chance to increase disorder, to gain a foothold, joined the revolution. They took increasing control. And what began as a popular democratic revolution, committed to democracy and social justice, very shortly moved and was taken over and really seized and placed into the hands of a band of Communist conspirators. . . . The American nations cannot, must not, and will not permit the establishment of another Communist government in the Western Hemisphere."[97] Perhaps most telling, instructions to General Bruce Palmer, who commanded the action, reflected this view: "Your announced mission is to save US lives. Your unannounced mission is to prevent the Dominican Republic from going Communist. The President has stated that he will not allow another Cuba—you are to take all necessary measures to accomplish this mission."[98]

Interestingly, one of the more controversial aspects of the intervention revolves around the validity of the claim that the Dominican Republic could become "another Cuba." At the time, both Theodore Draper and Tad Szulc, for example, argued that the Communist threat was overblown. Draper contended that the evidence of a Communist role in the coup was slim, at best—although Communists supported the coup, their support was rejected by the rebels.[99] Similarly, Szulc interviewed a number of rebels during the crisis who repeatedly asked him to convey the message that they were not Communists.[100] Szulc went even further, arguing

[95]"Statement by the President Upon Ordering Troops Into the Dominican Republic," April 28, 1965, Lyndon B. Johnson 1964–1969, 1965 Book I, 461. Indeed, the administration initially felt that this was the only justification that would be palatable to the American public. This conviction was so strong that the embassy had to hint strongly to Dominicans requesting aid that their request must be framed in terms of protecting American lives, rather than protecting the Dominican Republic from communism.

[96]"Statement by the President on the Situation in the Dominican Republic," April 30, 1965, Lyndon B. Johnson 1964–1969, 1965 Book I, 465.

[97]"Radio and Television Report to the American People on the Situation in the Dominican Republic," May 2, 1965, Lyndon B. Johnson 1964–1969, 1965 Book I, 471–72.

[98]Quoted in Lawler and Yee 2005, 102.

[99]Draper 1968, 34. In fact, the theme of Draper's book is that the Dominican coup did not represent a Communist threat to US interests.

[100]Szulc 1965, 82.

that the US portrayal of the pro-Bosch forces as Communist probably drove them farther to the left than they were originally.[101]

Strong doubts continue to overlie the claim that it was necessary for the United States to intervene in the Dominican Republic in order to forestall a Communist revolution. Various analysts have argued that there was no Communist element in the coup, that there was only a very small and weak element, or that intervention to prevent a Communist revolution was unjustified. It is likely that a small group of Communists participated in the rebel movement, but it is also likely that the strength of the Communist "threat" to the Dominican Republic—and hence, the United States—was blown well out of proportion. An anxious embassy staff, an overzealous State Department,[102] and an administration generally preoccupied with international communism may have created a propitious frame for exaggeration. The salient point here, though, is that all these parties believed in a Communist threat in the Dominican Republic in April 1965 and that, for this reason, they chose to intervene to prevent a "second Cuba."

DID THE NORM AGAINST CONQUEST AFFECT US DECISION MAKING?

The history of US-Dominican relations is telling in its illustration of a trend. In 1870, the United States seriously considered annexing the Dominican Republic; in 1916, an eight-year occupation commenced; in 1965, the United States reluctantly intervened for a relatively short period of time. What accounts for this change in US behavior toward the Dominican Republic?

US behavior was increasingly conditioned by a need to respect the norm against conquest, particularly in the late twentieth century. Limited evidence of the impact of this norm can be found in the 1916 case. By 1965, however, the norm against conquest was central to the Johnson administration's decision making with respect to the Dominican Republic, and played a key role in shaping the 1965 intervention in three ways. First, from the beginning days of the crisis, Washington was very concerned about both Latin American and US domestic reaction to the intervention. Second, throughout the crisis, almost no mention was made of the 1870 or 1916 incidents—the options of annexation or prolonged occupation

---

[101]Szulc 1965, 91–92.

[102]Undersecretary of State Thomas Mann, along with the embassy in Santo Domingo, is frequently characterized as a zealot in the literature on the 1965 intervention. This general perception appears to be supported by Mann's own words. In an interview with CBS, Mann justified the intervention as preventing the Dominican Republic from falling to the Sino-Soviet bloc, which had conspired to take over the Republic. Szulc 1965, 291.

seem to have exited the US behavioral repertoire. And, finally, the United States was both reluctant to intervene in and eager to exit the Dominican Republic for reasons of reputation. Each of these behaviors reflects the power of the norm against conquest on US decision making at the time. The norm created a situation where US reputational concerns constrained both the nature and the duration of the military action. Further, the more extreme behaviors of occupation or conquest were never really considered, despite the fact that the direct material costs of such actions would have been relatively low.

Living in the Hemisphere

Immediately following the US intervention, Latin American leaders began to object to the US action. For instance, Venezuelan president Raúl Leoni sent Johnson a telegram condemning the move.[103] A May 1 CIA Intelligence Memorandum similarly described Latin American sentiment as primarily negative, condemning the US intervention.[104] World opinion was also an issue; by May 1, UN secretary-general U Thant had agreed, at the Soviet Union's request, to hold a Security Council meeting to discuss the US intervention.

What is striking about the reaction to the US intervention of the Dominican Republic is that it consisted of protest against an intervention that was always explicitly limited. Latin Americans, the USSR, and US citizens were not protesting one state's violent conquest of another but a much more discrete incursion of Dominican sovereignty. International opinions about acceptable behavior had clearly changed significantly since the nineteenth—and certainly eighteenth—centuries, when much more extreme challenges to sovereignty were common, if not expected. And in addition to the world reacting differently to US action than before, the United States reacted differently to world opinion.

Abraham Lowenthal argues that Johnson had two main goals—"to prevent a Communist takeover of the Dominican Republic and to avoid having the United States caught alone in Santo Domingo, isolated from hemispheric opinion."[105] This claim is confirmed by White House special assistant Jack Valenti's April 30 meeting notes, which report special assistant for national security affairs McGeorge Bundy as saying: "But in order to quash Castro in DR we need above all else to get hemispheric

[103]Lowenthal 1972, 116. Leoni later published an anti-intervention article in the July 1965 issue of *Foreign Affairs*. Leoni 1965.
[104]CIA Intelligence Memorandum, OCI No. 1485/65, 1 May 1965, National Security File: Country File: Latin America—Dominican Republic, Box 50/File: Situation Reports, 5/65, document no. 48, LBJ Library.
[105]Lowenthal 1972, 116. Also see Felten 1999, 103.

public opinion on our side."[106] That same morning, President Johnson told Secretary of State Dean Rusk to "find out what we have to do to make it look good. We'll get a cloak of international approval if we can get it before the baby dies."[107] Two days later, in a congressional briefing, Johnson remarked: "If I send in the Marines, I can't live in the Hemisphere— if I don't I can't live at home."[108]

The administration had already opened channels to the Organization of American States (OAS) with the intent of transforming the originally unilateral US intervention into a hemispheric action. OAS leaders quickly became involved in brokering various cease-fires, negotiating new governments, and installing Latin American troops alongside US Marines. By May 6, it was agreed that soldiers from Venezuela, Brazil, Guatemala, Costa Rica, Honduras, and Paraguay would participate in the Inter-American Peace Force (IAPF) to be stationed in the Dominican Republic. The US intent here was not difficult to discern. "We are going to have to use the OAS as a cloak for whatever we're going to do," Bundy told President Johnson on April 28.[109] The numerous telephone conversations made to and from the White House during the crisis reveal that Johnson's concern about the US reputation in Latin America permeated his thoughts at the time.[110]

[106]Notes taken during Meeting in Cabinet Room, April 30, 1965, 7:15 a.m., Office of the President File: Jack Valenti—Notes Taken at Various Meetings during 1965 and 1966, Box 13/File: Meeting Notes (Handwritten), 4/30–5/15/65, document no. 1, LBJ Library.

[107]Quoted in Felten 1999, 103.

[108]Notes taken during Congressional Briefing, May 2, 1965, 6:45 p.m., Office of the President File: Jack Valenti—Notes Taken at Various Meetings during 1965 and 1966, Box 13/ File: Meeting Notes (Handwritten), 4/30–5/15/65, document no. 5, LBJ Library. Also see Telephone Conversation between Lyndon B. Johnson and Senator Mike Mansfield, April 30, 1965, 11:51 a.m., Citation #7410, Recordings and Transcripts of Conversations and Meetings, LBJ Library; and Telephone Conversation between Lyndon B. Johnson and Dean Rusk, May 26, 1965, 3:26 p.m., Citation #7832, Recordings and Transcripts of Conversations and Meetings, LBJ Library.

[109]Quoted in Felten 1999, 104. Also see Telephone Conversation between Lyndon B. Johnson and Abe Fortas, April 30, 1965, 10:05 a.m., Citation #7402, Recordings and Transcripts of Conversations and Meetings, LBJ Library; Telephone Conversation between Lyndon B. Johnson and Abe Fortas, April 30, 1965, 11:30 a.m., Citation #7408, Recordings and Transcripts of Conversations and Meetings, LBJ Library.

[110]See for example: Telephone Conversation between Lyndon B. Johnson and Thomas Mann, April 26, 1965, 9:35 a.m., Citation #7362, Recordings and Transcripts of Conversations and Meetings, LBJ Library; Telephone Conversation between Lyndon B. Johnson and William Raborn, April 29, 1965, 8:47 a.m., Citation #7375, Recordings and Transcripts of Conversations and Meetings, LBJ Library; Telephone Conversation between Lyndon B. Johnson and Bromley Smith, April 29, 1965, 4:26 p.m., Citation #7383, Recordings and Transcripts of Conversations and Meetings, LBJ Library. Johnson even plied the shah of Iran for his view on how the US action was being viewed in Latin America, when speak-

The United States spent considerable diplomatic capital in ensuring the participation of the OAS in the Dominican intervention. The need to preserve the illusion that the region was acting as one during the crisis also constrained US military actions, for example by forcing the US Marines on the ground to behave neutrally toward both sides in the civil war,[111] as well as by having a Brazilian general command the operation. It is not clear why the United States would expend this kind of effort if not to project the impression that it were behaving as it ought; that the United States had violated Dominican sovereignty to some degree was clear, but by behaving according to certain scripts, the violation could be mitigated. One such script was the transformation of a unilateral intervention into a multilateral action.[112] The pressure of world and regional opinion, which supported the norm against conquest, constrained US behavior by shaping the nature of the 1965 intervention.

Occupy—No

The norm against conquest also influenced US decision making in that behaviors that were actively considered in the past were either not discussed or discussed only unwillingly in 1965. Indeed, the record of primary documents related to the crisis strongly reflects an inclination toward what Nina Tannenwald refers to as "taboo talk."[113] The options of occupation or conquest were barely raised, and when they were raised, they were immediately dismissed. On at least two separate occasions, for example, State Department press secretaries refused to refer to the US action as even an intervention and, similarly, refused to respond to questions that referred to the action as an occupation.[114] In laying out the United States' options at the start of the crisis, Secretary of State Dean Rusk is reported to have said: "a. International zone; b. Cordon of US forces between forces (enforce cease fire till OAS arrives); c. Occupy—*no*."[115] In public remarks on May 3, Johnson said with respect to the intervention: "We

---

ing with the shah after the Iranian head of state returned from a tour of the region. Telephone Conversation between Lyndon B. Johnson and Mohammed Reza Pahlavi, May 18, 1965, 11:01 a.m., Citation #7748, Recordings and Transcripts of Conversations and Meetings, LBJ Library.

[111] Lowenthal 1972, 127.

[112] Finnemore 2003.

[113] Tannenwald 1999, 440.

[114] "Transcript of State Department Press Conference, 5/2/65," and "Transcript of State Department Press Conference, 5/5/65," in Cables, State Department to Santo Domingo, 5/2/65 and 5/5/65, File A-2: "Outgoing State Department Cables, April 25–May 14, 1965," documents no. 102 and 122, NSF: National Security Council History: The Dominican Crisis, 1965, Box 5, LBJ Library.

[115] "Meeting Notes, n.d.," Papers of Bromley K. Smith, Box 33/File: Dominican Republic, document no. 2: LBJ Library. Emphasis added.

covet no territory. We seek no dominion over anyone."[116] Four days later, a State Department memo stated: "United States are not occupying the Dominican Republic."[117] As the crisis wore on, on May 12, a cable from the State Department to the US embassy in Santo Domingo expressed concern about US forces "giving [the] impression of being [an] occupation force."[118] And Johnson clearly stated that he did not want to be seen as having imperial designs in the region[119] and that he did not want to have his "brand" on any satellite states.[120]

Available sources do not reveal any references to the annexationism of 1870, and only brief and derogatory references to the 1916 occupation can be found. For example, Undersecretary of State George Ball recalled: "There was nothing to do but react quickly. Though none of us wanted to repeat history by stationing troops in the Dominican Republic, as America had done from 1916 to 1924, we had no option."[121] US envoy and former ambassador Martin noted that "a full-scale US military occupation" was a major danger to be avoided in the Dominican Republic.[122] Another, rare reference to the 1916 occupation surfaced in a May 6, 1965, *New York Times* editorial, which stated that, "in its development if not in its origin, the Marine intervention in the Dominican Republic was reminiscent of 1916. . . . Ours is the most powerful nation on earth, but there are things that even the United States cannot do in this period

[116]"Remarks of the President to the Building Trades Council at the Washington-Hilton Hotel, 5/3/65," NSF: National Security Council History, File: Chronology, April 29–May 3, 1965, document no. 206a: Box 9, LBJ Library.

[117]"Legal Basis for United States Actions in the Dominican Republic," May 7, 1965, NSF: Papers of Gordon Chase, File: Dominican Republic—Histories and Chronologies, document no. 9, Box 4, LBJ Library.

[118]Cable, State 996 to Santo Domingo, 5/12/65, Papers of Bromley K. Smith, File: Dominican Republic, May 16, 1965, document no. 13, Box 33, LBJ Library. Similarly, an outgoing State Department cable to Santo Domingo read: "We have report that Wessin y Wessin is doing all he can to promote idea that U.S. Government is supporting him and to associate himself with U.S. operation in Dominican Republic. In your discretion you should do what you can to convince Wessin y Wessin that it is neither in his interest nor ours for him to become over-identified with U.S. at this point. FYI. It would be particularly helpful if he could be persuaded to stop playing the 'Star Spangled Banner' over San Isidro Radio Station." Cable No. 753, State Department to Santo Domingo, 5/2/65, File A-1: Outgoing State Department Cables, April 25–May 14, 1965, document no. 87, NSF: National Security Council History: The Dominican Crisis, 1965, Box 5, LBJ Library.

[119]Telephone Conversation between Lyndon B. Johnson and Abe Fortas, May 23, 1965, 5:10 p.m., Citation #7812, Recordings and Transcripts of Conversations and Meetings, LBJ Library.

[120]Telephone Conversation between Lyndon B. Johnson and Abe Fortas, May 23, 1965, 5:10 p.m., Citation #7813, Recordings and Transcripts of Conversations and Meetings, LBJ Library.

[121]Quoted in Brands 1995, 53.

[122]Quoted in Lowenthal 1972, 119.

of history. The sooner this country extricates itself from the Dominican Republic—if at all possible with the help of the OAS—the better."[123] Thus, 1965 appears to have been barely reminiscent of 1916, and 1916 was hardly looked upon with pride. Instead, the prolonged occupation that characterized the 1916 intervention was viewed as a policy to be avoided. Johnson expressed his own view in a private conversation with McGeorge Bundy: "What I really think our role in the world is, is to avoid, to have enough power to prevent, power to prevent weak people from being gobbled up."[124]

Exit Strategy

The norm against conquest also conditioned US behavior by creating a reluctance to intervene and an eagerness to withdraw from the Dominican Republic. Two days after the coup, US chargé d'affaires Connett expressed reservations about intervening. Connett argued that intervention could have "serious implications" for the US global and regional role: "We would be cast in the role of an interventionist power opposing a popular revolution of democratic elements overthrowing an unpopular constitutional regime."[125] Similarly, Ambassador Bennett, despite his hyperbole about the Communist threat, initially resisted escalation of the intervention.[126] Johnson, in a high-level meeting on the crisis, answered a question as to how long US troops would be in the Dominican Republic by saying: "I honestly don't know—as long as necessary but I hope it's 8 o'clock tonight."[127]

Once the intervention had begun, developing an exit strategy became a priority. Indeed, the administration evaluated proposals for new Dominican governments in part based on the nature of the exit strategy for the United States, and preferred the plan proposed by former Dominican president Joaquín Balaguer precisely because it provided such a strategy.[128]

[123]The Illusion of Omnipotence 1965. Juan Bosch also expressed fears of a US occupation of the Dominican Republic. Telephone Conversation between Lyndon B. Johnson and Abe Fortas, April 29, 1965, 4:45 p.m., Citation #7388, Recordings and Transcripts of Conversations and Meetings, LBJ Library.

[124]Telephone Conversation between Lyndon B. Johnson and McGeorge Bundy, May 31, 1965, 12:45 p.m., Citation #7852, Recordings and Transcripts of Conversations and Meetings, LBJ Library.

[125]Cable No. 1071, Santo Domingo to State Department, 4/26/65, File A-1: Incoming State Department Cables, April 25–May 4, 1965, document no. 40, NSF: National Security Council History: The Dominican Crisis, 1965, Box 4 (1 of 2), LBJ Library.

[126]Lowenthal 1972, 106.

[127]Notes from Lunch meeting in 1st floor dining room, 5/21/65, 2:45 p.m., Meeting Notes (Handwritten), 5/19–5/26/65, document no. 3, Office of the President File: Jack Valenti—Notes Taken at Various Meetings during 1965 and 1966, Box 13, LBJ Library.

[128]Felten 1999, 118.

Balaguer's proposal, which included an imminent presidential election, itself led to an interesting incident with respect to the US exit strategy. Both Balaguer and Bosch—the two leading candidates for the Dominican presidency—requested that the IAPF remain in the Dominican Republic after the election, to help ensure control over the military. Their proposal was unambiguously rejected.[129] Had the United States harbored territorial ambitions toward the Dominican Republic, agreeing to this request would have provided a perfect opportunity to advance those goals.

DID DOMINICAN NATIONALISM AFFECT US DECISION MAKING?

Unlike the 1916 occupation, the 1965 intervention in the Dominican Republic does not provide confirming evidence for the argument that nationalist resistance impacted US decision making. Three questions must be asked in evaluating the argument in this case. First, could the United States have anticipated Dominican nationalism prior to the intervention? Second, did Dominican nationalism influence the decision to intervene or the nature of the intervention? And third, were the costs of the intervention low or high for the United States? Ex post, the nationalist resistance argument would suggest that the change in US behavior between 1870 and 1965 means that increased Dominican nationalism in the later years prevented US conquest or long-term occupation of the Republic in 1965. The probability of resistance—and the costs of quelling that resistance—should have become prohibitively high.

Measures of possible indicators of nationalism contradict this claim. Although some scholars have suggested that Dominican nationalism—or, at least, commitment to democracy—was in greater evidence in 1965 than in 1916, these sentiments were not expressed clearly prior to the intervention. The ethnic composition of the country was similar to what it had been in 1916 and 1870, with Dominicans of mixed descent accounting for more than 70 percent of the population. The level of industrialization also was quite low; although energy consumption was greater than in 1916 (or 1870), it was still well below the global median and mean.

Indeed, only three, weak pieces of evidence support the claim that Dominicans in 1965 were more nationalistic than in 1916. First, in Theodore Draper's estimation, the 1965 coup gave the Dominicans a cause to fight for and believe in. According to Draper, "the Dominican people will probably look back at the 1965 revolt with pride and even exaltation. They did not have much to be proud or exalted about in over a hundred years. For one of the few times in their entire history they fought for something

---

[129]Felten 1999, 125.

worth believing in."[130] Second, and similarly, Draper points to a February 1965 advertisement in a major Dominican newspaper, signed by two thousand Dominican professionals and intellectuals, deploring the lack of democracy in the country.[131] The willingness of middle-class, professional citizens to take such a political risk under a military government, argues Draper, illustrates a commitment to democracy and to country. A third piece of evidence that might demonstrate nationalism, although not a change from 1916, is popular involvement in the 1965 revolt. It is true that the pro-Bosch rebels included more civilians than the "loyalists" of the military juntas, but both groups were dominated by different sectors of the precoup military. The Dominican crisis, prior to intervention, was a civil war. It was not a fight for a separate homeland, or for freedom from foreign influence, but for political power and political change. Under these conditions, it is difficult at best to discern the level of nationalism felt by the Dominican protagonists; one could as easily argue that none or all were nationalists.

Regardless of whether the Dominicans actually were strong nationalists, an exhaustive survey of the primary documentary evidence surrounding the crisis fails to reveal serious concern about Dominican resistance in contemplating and planning the intervention. The absence of a discussion of Dominican nationalism in both primary and secondary sources is telling. US policy makers were far more concerned about the reaction of their Latin American neighbors to the intervention than they were about the reaction of the Dominicans themselves. Indeed, the United States was so confident it could tip the scales in favor of the loyalists that the primary questions driving the intervention were "when" and "how," not "whether" it would work.[132]

The United States' confidence in its ability to exercise its will in the Dominican Republic was justified. As the intervention escalated, numerous reports from the field predicted a lack of widespread opposition to the presence of US troops. On May 2, a cable from the US embassy in Santo Domingo noted: "although population has been diffident to presence of US troops here, have been few friendly overtures, but no belligerency noted."[133] The embassy similarly reported: "Some tenseness has been evident among populace but it accepting situation quietly and no danger seen in rural areas."[134] CIA reports confirmed this view, reporting little

[130]Draper 1968, 2.

[131]Draper 1968, 25–26.

[132]Lowenthal 1972, 84.

[133]Cable, Santo Domingo to State, 5/2/65, File B2, document no. 2, NSF: National Security Council History, Box 4 (1 of 2), LBJ Library.

[134]Cable, Santo Domingo to State, n.d., File A1, document no. 4: NSF: National Security Council History, Box 4 (2 of 2), LBJ Library.

or no rebel activity in the countryside.[135] Thus, it seems that Dominican nationalism did not serve as a deterrent to US action.

Not only did the Johnson administration ultimately achieve its goal of a Dominican Republic that remained in the American sphere of influence, but it did so at a very low cost. According to Peter Felten, twenty-seven US soldiers died, and the added costs of the intervention (over what the United States would have normally given the Dominican Republic in assistance) was $225 million, far short of what was and would be spent in Vietnam.[136] Once again, had the United States wished to take over the Dominican Republic, the logic of the nationalist resistance argument suggests that it should have done so in 1965, given the low costs of intervention and occupation.

Thus, the nationalist resistance argument fails on three counts with respect to the 1965 intervention in the Dominican Republic. One of the main lines of argument of this theory is that nationalism should increase over time; it is not at all clear that Dominican nationalism did increase from 1916 to 1965. Further, if worries about the resistance of nationalist populations governed US decision making, we should see evidence of such concern in telephone conversations, memos, or cables; virtually none is available. The history of US decision making regarding the 1965 intervention is as silent on the issue of nationalism as it is on the option of conquest. But while the norms argument is supported by the lack of discussion of conquest as an option, the nationalist resistance argument is challenged by US decision makers' failure to express concern about Dominican nationalism because, according to this argument, nationalism should have been at the forefront of US decision making. Finally, another line of argument germane to the nationalist resistance theory is that, when the prospects of resistance are low, states should be more likely to conquer other states. In the case of the Dominican Republic in 1965, prospects of resistance were low, but the United States sought to withdraw from the Republic as soon as its goals there were accomplished. The main cost driving the decision to intervene as opposed to conquer was not the material cost of applying direct rule but, rather, the opprobrium costs of violating the norm against conquest.

[135]"CIA Intelligence Memorandum, OCI no. 1496/65, 2 May 1965, 'Situation and Outlook in the Dominican Republic,'" and document no. 32, "CIA Intelligence Memorandum, OCI No. 1509/65, 2 May 1965—Report #75 'Summary of situation from 1–5 p.m. EDT,'" Situation Reports, 5/65, NSF: Country File: Latin America—Dominican Republic, Box 50, LBJ Library.

[136]Felten 1999, 126.

WHY DID THE UNITED STATES WITHDRAW IN 1966?

On June 28, 1966, the withdrawal of the Inter-American Peace Forces from the Dominican Republic began. By this time, US troop numbers had already declined from a high of twenty-one thousand to approximately six thousand soldiers. As noted above, the two leading candidates for the Dominican presidency requested that the IAPF troops remain, but both the United States and the OAS refused. Given that the United States was invited to stay, why did it choose to leave?

The theories explored in this chapter offer a number of explanations for the US/OAS decision to withdraw. The first is that the threat of the Dominican Republic leaving the US sphere of influence had ebbed, making (temporary) direct control of the state unnecessary. The second is that the United States had always sought a brief action in order to prevent an international backlash against violating the norm against conquest.

The nationalist resistance argument suggests a third line of reasoning. Withdrawal should be a function of nationalism. Even if the Dominicans were not sufficiently nationalistic to deter intervention, the intervention itself should have inspired nationalist revolt that increased pressure on the United States such that the intervention became too costly to continue.

As with the general nationalist resistance argument, only very limited evidence supports the claim that strong Dominican nationalist sentiment followed the US intervention. Peter Felten observed a nationalist reaction to the intervention, but with a twist: he noted Dominican graffiti in April 1966 as reading, "go home yankee y llévame contigo" [and take me with you].[137] This observation, however, seems to represent the most extreme elements of Dominican nationalist sentiment against the intervention. This is not to argue that the Dominicans welcomed the intervention, but rather that they did not, by any means, provide sufficient resistance to induce the United States to withdraw its troops.

Instead, US troops were withdrawn from the Dominican Republic because they had accomplished their goal, and because the intervention was always intended to be temporary. With Balaguer's election to the Dominican presidency in 1966, the United States once again felt it had a reliable ally. And the United States wanted to withdraw from the Dominican Republic as soon as possible in order to avoid the negative international response that would have been evoked by a long-term occupation.

[137]Felten 1999, 98.

Violating the Norm against Conquest:
The Iraqi Annexation of Kuwait

Iraq's annexation of Kuwait in 1990 represents an apparent contradiction of the claim that a norm against conquest has prevented violent state death after 1945. I conclude the empirical analysis in this book by examining this potential challenge to my argument.

The Iraqi annexation of Kuwait is the exception that proves the rule. A perceived lapse in the norm against conquest served as a key permissive cause of invasion. The norm against conquest has not become fully internalized by all states. Consider, for example, challenges to the existence of states such as Israel, Taiwan, and possibly East Timor.[138] Not all states adhere to the norm against conquest because conquest has become unthinkable for them. This approach to the norm against conquest leaves room for states that may not voluntarily subscribe to the norm. While the rarity of conquest may have the incidental effect of some degree of internalization of this norm, states that might have incentives toward conquest refrain for fear of punishment for violating the norm against conquest.[139] But if internalization is particularly weak, it may be especially easy for such a state to conclude that punishment of norm violations is unlikely. The Iraqi regime did not believe that the United States would enforce the norm against conquest.

Additional evidence further supports the norms argument. First, the norm against conquest, while not deeply internalized in Iraq, was so deeply internalized in the West that no one conceived of Iraq taking over all of Kuwait. Second, once the invasion occurred, the violation of the norm was in fact punished severely. And third, a metanorm was also enforced, in that states that failed to enforce the norm were themselves subject to punishment. In examining the existing literature[140] to understand the causes of invasion, I ask five questions meant to shed light on the best explanation for Iraq's decision to invade Kuwait: (1) What were the im-

[138]Interestingly, the legitimacy argument may hold some sway here as well, as the challengers to these states' existence have tended not to recognize them.

[139]The notion that internalization can vary across actors is undertheorized in the norms literature. It seems fairly intuitive that, as time passes, different actors may internalize the same norm to different degrees. This variation can become consequential when, for example, a strong enforcer of the norm is removed from the scene (voluntarily or not). An important next step in the literature on norms will be to investigate why some actors internalize a given norm while others do not.

[140]Unfortunately, the literature on this case is not very strong, as it occurred too recently for historians to have conducted extensive archival research, particularly in Iraq. Further, much of the available literature is fairly biased, often written from an Iraqi, Kuwaiti, or Israeli point of view.

mediate causes of the invasion? (2) Why did Iraq take over all of Kuwait?
(3) Was the norm against conquest operative in this case? (4) Was the Iraqi
leadership concerned about the prospects of Kuwaiti resistance? and (5)
How can we explain the international response to the Iraqi invasion of
Kuwait?

WHY DID IRAQ INVADE KUWAIT? THE (IL)LOGIC OF INVASION

Explanations for the Iraqi invasion of Kuwait range from vague claims
about Arab unity vis-à-vis the United States and Israel,[141] to conspiracy
theories about Kuwait prompting the Iraqi invasion,[142] to a focus on
Iraq's historical claims to Kuwait.[143] Iraqi claims to all or part of Kuwaiti
territory had been made, and even acted on, since Iraqi independence in
1932. These claims were based in part on the notion that Kuwait had been
part of the Basra province (or *vilayet*) during the heyday of the Ottoman
Empire. In truth, however, the Iraqi claim to Kuwait was motivated by
strategic need. The Kuwaiti islands of Warbah and Bubiyan blocked Iraq's
one deep-sea port, and the lucrative Rumeilah oil field was located on the
Iraqi-Kuwaiti border. Further, as Fred Lawson notes, perceived threats
from Israel (such as possible Israeli integration into the United States'
Strategic Defense Initiative) and from the United States (via the reflagging
of Kuwaiti oil tankers in the Gulf) were particularly worrying to the Iraqi
regime, creating a security dilemma–type dynamic where Iraq felt the
need to shore up its defenses through expansion.[144] Note that Iraq's
strategic need was not motivated by Kuwait's being a buffer state—
Kuwait was not a buffer state. Nonetheless, geography did create incentives for conquest.

Most of the explanations for the Iraqi invasion of Kuwait listed
above—while important—cannot account for the timing of the invasion.
The goal and principles of Arab unity, Iraqi president Saddam Hussein's
paranoia, historical claims to Kuwaiti territory, and Iraq's geostrategic
vulnerabilities had been fairly constant over the past several decades. But
Iraq in the late 1980s (and into 1990) was just emerging from a grueling
eight-year war with Iran, one that threatened Iraqi economic stability and
created a million-man army whose attention needed to be redirected in
the absence of a conflict. In essence, Saddam's regime faced threats to its
survival from many fronts—but these fronts were domestic, not interna-

[141]Hassan 1999, 8–9.
[142]Ali 1993, 85; Gause 2001, 11. Gause actually traces Saddam's perceptions of a conspiracy against him to around 1990.
[143]Rahman 1997.
[144]Lawson 2001, 10.

tional. The invasion of Kuwait was seen as the panacea that would improve Iraq's economic situation and occupy its military, at the same time providing the positive externalities of an improved geostrategic position and a supportive public.[145] As Amatzia Baram writes: "While there are indications that the Iraqi leadership had been toying with the idea of invading Kuwait since 1988, only gradually did Baghdad come to see such an invasion as the solution for all its problems."[146] In short, the Iraqi invasion of Kuwait was conducted to improve the survival prospects of the Baghdad regime.

This is not to say, however, that the Iraqi invasion of Kuwait was a pure diversionary war.[147] The conflict was meant to create a rally-round-the-flag effect, but it appears that the leadership in Baghdad viewed the annexation of Kuwaiti territory as a more permanent solution to the problems plaguing the regime. Chief among these problems was the high economic toll of the Iran-Iraq War. By the end of the war in 1988, Iraq had accumulated from $30 billion to $65 billion dollars of debt to OECD countries.[148] Generous loans (apparently $40–80 billion) from other oil-rich Arab states that had seen Iraq through the Iran-Iraq War had ended with the conflict. While certain states were willing to forgive the loans, Kuwait was not, and it was clear that Iraq would be unable to pay the interest on its debts.[149] Annual Iraqi oil revenues amounted to approximately $12 billion, about $10 billion of which was needed for debt servicing.[150] Furthermore, with Kuwait and the United Arab Emirates requesting higher oil quotas from OPEC, Iraq's already-insufficient oil revenue would only decrease. The economic price tag of arms purchases and the oil embargo alone was over $200 billion.[151] All of Iraq's oil revenue had gone toward the war, and the combination of debt servicing and military expenditures had led to inflation rates of over 40 percent.[152] At the same time, postwar market liberalization policies and a public works growth strategy (in a sector where wages had been frozen) made for a precarious economic balance.[153] Patrick Clawson notes that public works projects accounted for "$30 to 50 billion of white elephants."[154] These

---

[145]Karsh and Rautsi 1991, 26. Also see Lawson 2001.
[146]Baram 1993, 9.
[147]On diversionary wars, see J. Levy 1989b.
[148]Hassan 1999, 109.
[149]Baram 1993, 7; Rahman 1997, 293. For a contrasting view on Iraq's financial situation at the time, see Hassan 1999, 109–12.
[150]Musallam 1996, 56.
[151]Baram 1993, 6.
[152]Rahman 1997, 293.
[153]Chaudhry 1991; Rahman 1997, 293; Lawson 2001, 11.
[154]Clawson 1993, 72.

economic straits were unacceptable for a well-educated population ac-
customed to a relatively high standard of living. According to Iraqi political operative Saad al-Bazaaz, "It became necessary therefore, to find a
permanent solution to the economic predicament, with its problem of
debt, a solution which can only be geo-political which would provide new
sources for the Iraqi economy."[155] Similarly, then–foreign minister Tariq
Aziz argued:

> The economic question was a major factor in triggering the current situation.
> In addition to the forty billion dollars in Arab debts, we owe at least as much
> to the West. This year's state budget required seven billion dollars for debt ser-
> vice, which was a huge amount, leaving us with only enough for basic services
> for our country. Our budget is based on a price of eighteen dollars a barrel for
> oil, but since the Kuwaitis began flooding the world with oil, the price has gone
> down by a third. When we met again—in Jidda, at the end of the July—Kuwait
> said it was not interested in any change. We were now desperate, and could not
> pay our bills for food imports. It was a starvation war. When do you use your
> military power to preserve yourself?[156]

But economics alone cannot account for the behavior of the Iraqi
regime. A purely economic explanation fails to solve the puzzle of why
Iraq refused Kuwait's offer of a $9 billion loan in the summer of 1990.[157]
Political survival for the Ba'athist regime meant more than improving the
living conditions of the Iraqi people. It also meant keeping a million-man
army sufficiently content to avoid rebellion and social unrest.[158] Indeed,
according to Iraqi deputy prime minister Taha Yasin Ramadan, economic
and military conditions at the time demanded immediate action: "Imagine if we had waited two years, and the Gulf oil policy had continued as
it is. . . . How were we going to maintain the loyalty of the people and
their support for the leader if they saw the inability of the leadership to
provide a minimal standard of living in this rich country? In this situation, could you lead the army and the people in any battle, no matter what
its level and under any banner? I think not."[159]

To some extent, the problem of keeping the army occupied was related
to Iraq's economic difficulties. For example, the regime was reluctant to
decommission soldiers who would face bleak economic prospects and yet
possess honed fighting skills. For this reason, only about three hundred
thousand soldiers were demobilized immediately following the Iran-Iraq

[155]Quoted in Musallam 1996, 87.
[156]Quoted in Stein 1992, 158.
[157]Freedman and Karsh 1993, 60; Gause 2001, 21.
[158]Mohamedou 1998, 4.
[159]Statement at a July 24, 1991, meeting of the Revolutionary Command Council.
Quoted in Gause 2001, 11–12.

War.[160] Maintaining one million men under arms, with the attendant matériel, made for an estimated $14 billion defense budget for 1990, even without including the expected costs of the invasion of Kuwait.[161]

Another important reason for maintaining the status of the military refers to the ethnic makeup of the Iraqi state. It was expected that, if released, the large Shi'a contingent of the military could create political problems for the regime in the south.[162] At the same time, though, Iraq's ethnic makeup created opportunities for keeping the military occupied, as evidenced by the military crackdown on the Kurdish population in the late 1980s.

Invading Kuwait was seen as a convenient solution to many of Iraq's problems. Because of Iraq's limited sea access, it had to ship its oil overland via pipelines through Saudi Arabia and Turkey (there is also a usable pipeline route through Syria), neither of which had been staunch allies. Routing oil shipments through an expanded coastline would, at a minimum, provide Iraq with greater economic security. Iraq expected that Kuwait also had extensive reserves of cash and foreign currency that Saddam Hussein planned to use as temporary relief (indeed, Saddam also expected to find millions of dollars worth of gold in the Kuwaiti national bank).[163] With a sovereign Kuwait out of the picture, an important challenger to quota distributions and, critically, use of the Rumeilah oil field, would be eliminated. And of course, the military would have a long-standing—and lucrative—occupation that would be fairly easy to exploit, given Kuwait's relatively flat geography.

Ultimately, the Iraqi invasion of Kuwait may have been the right decision for the regime. Standing up to the West made Saddam Hussein a hero in Arab eyes, however ludicrous some of his accusations of the United States and Israel may have been. In Janice Stein's words, anti-Western sentiment in the region meant that Saddam Hussein could win "political victory [even in] defeat."[164] And indeed, he did win a political, if not a military, victory, surviving as the head of the Iraqi state beyond expectation.

WHY DID IRAQ ANNEX ALL OF KUWAIT?

The economic and military concerns that led to the Iraqi invasion of Kuwait did not require that Iraq take over the whole of Kuwait. Indeed, that Iraq took over all of Kuwait was a surprise to most observers at the

[160]Baram 1993, 7.
[161]Hassan 1999, 109–10.
[162]Baram 1993, 7.
[163]Baram 1993, 25.
[164]Stein 1992, 173.

time. According to then–US ambassador to Iraq April Glaspie, "Obviously I didn't think and nobody else did, that the Iraqis were going to take all of Kuwait. Every Kuwaiti and Saudi, every analyst in the Western world was wrong too."[165] Glaspie's perceptions were consistent with a US intelligence estimate that, at most, Iraq would attack Rumeilah and the Warbah and Bubiyan islands.[166] Iraqi insiders such as Tariq Aziz revealed that the decision to take over the entire country (as opposed to just the oil fields and islands) was a late one.[167] Perhaps even more surprising, once entrenched, Iraq refused to withdraw—even to withdraw such that Baghdad would still control the most valuable border territories. Kuwait, it seemed, had become a sort of indivisible property.

One potential reason that Iraq took over all of Kuwait was strategic. Given the relatively friendly relationship between Kuwait and the United States, Saddam Hussein may have feared that the United States would launch counterattacks against Iraq from Kuwaiti territory, unless that territory was occupied by Iraq. In an interview with British MP Tony Benn, Saddam Hussein suggested just this logic: "I didn't want to take over the whole of Kuwait. I just wanted the disputed areas—the 80 kilometres that he claimed the Kuwaitis had gained by moving the frontier north, and the Rumayla oil field, and access to the sea. But if I had just done that, the Americans would have come into Kuwait and attacked me from there."[168]

This logic, however, is so flawed as to be suspicious. As a tactical move, annexing the entire country was hardly practical. Politically speaking, withdrawing to the disputed territories would have undermined the coalition against Iraq.[169] And militarily speaking, all Iraq's armies needed to do was to take Kuwait City—which housed the only airport where the United States could have conducted major landings—to prevent the United States from using Kuwait as an air base.[170]

Another reason behind the decision to annex Kuwait may have been related to Iraq's bargaining position. By taking more than it wanted, Iraq could return Kuwaiti sovereignty and most Kuwaiti territory with few costs. This logic was suggested by Jordan's King Hussein. "He [King Hussein] reports that Saddam told him that he did not intend to stay but 'that he believed he would be in a stronger position . . . if he eventually with-

---

[165]Bulloch and Morris 1991, 14.

[166]Missed Signals in the Middle East 1991.

[167]Baram 1993, 23; Also see Mohamedou 1998, 132.

[168]Interview with Tony Benn in the London-based Arabic magazine *al-Ghad,* February 22/23, 1992. Quoted in Hassan 1999, 29, note 12; also see Stein 1992, 167–68.

[169]de la Billiere, quoted in Rahman 1997, 319.

[170]Stein 1992, 168.

drew to a point that left Iraq with the disputed territories only.'"[171] The clear problem with this explanation, though, is that, despite the fact that he was given many opportunities to do so, Saddam Hussein did not withdraw to the disputed territories. While it is possible that his intentions changed, it does not appear that Iraq annexed all of Kuwait for the purpose of increasing its bargaining leverage later.

A third explanation for the Iraqi annexation of Kuwait in its entirety was that, insofar as the war was started to pacify various domestic constituencies, the war also had to be justified to these constituencies. Saddam Hussein repeatedly referred to Kuwait as Iraq's nineteenth province. This rhetorical justification for the war required that Kuwait be taken in toto.[172] As Saddam told former Turkish prime minister Ecevit, "We would not have been able to ask our people and the armed forces to fight to the last drop of blood if we had not said that Kuwait was now part of Iraq."[173] Similarly, in response to UN secretary-general Javier Perez de Cuellar's proposal for an Iraqi withdrawal, Saddam insisted that "Kuwait is the nineteenth province of Iraq. There can be no compromise on that."[174]

DID THE NORM AGAINST CONQUEST FACTOR INTO IRAQI DECISION MAKING?

The presence and strengthening of a norm against conquest provides a compelling explanation for the post-1945 trend away from conquest and annexation. This is not to say, however, that all states have internalized the norm to the degree that they would never conceive of undertaking such actions. Given the relatively short tenure of the norm in the scope of international history, coupled with the fact that it is essentially enforced from on high (in the sense that the United States is the key normative entrepreneur in this case), it seems sensible to expect that different states will view the norm differently. Some states—particularly those that face no incentives to take over other states—may have in fact internalized the norm so deeply that conquest and annexation are unthinkable to them. But for other states, such as Iraq, the threat of punishment for violating the norm may be essential to its enforcement. For these states, when there is no threat of punishment, there is no reason to abstain from conquest.

[171]Stein 1992, 169.

[172]One could still question the extent of the Iraqi claim, though. Why not simply state that Warbah, Bubiyan, and the Rumeilah oil field were historically part of Iraq? In part, such a justification may have been *too* transparent. Further, the Iraqi regime in 1990 was able to draw on earlier claims to the entire state of Kuwait to justify the invasion.

[173]Bulloch and Morris 1991, 23.

[174]Quoted in Rahman 1997, 310.

That poor signaling by the United States led to a failure of deterrence of the Iraqi invasion of Kuwait is an important point of consensus for most scholars of this conflict. With hindsight, it is not difficult to find multiple examples of poor diplomatic communication that most likely led Saddam Hussein to believe that he could conduct the invasion with impunity. The most prominent of these weak signals emerges from Ambassador April Glaspie's July 25, 1990, conversation with the Iraqi president. In response to Saddam's list of Iraqi grievances and an assertion that the United States "is a society which cannot accept 10,000 dead in one battle," Glaspie, while emphasizing the US desire for peace in the region, remarked that "we [the US administration] have no opinion on the Arab-Arab conflicts, like your border disagreement with Kuwait."[175] In Omar Ali's estimation, Glaspie made five critical mistakes in this meeting: (1) She failed to warn Saddam Hussein that the United States knew about Iraqi troop deployments on the Kuwait border. (2) She was obsequious in her meeting with Saddam Hussein, apologizing for anti-Iraqi statements in the US media, and suggesting that American interests supported the preferred Iraqi oil price of $25 a barrel. (3) She did not warn Saddam Hussein that the use of force against Kuwait would be unacceptable. (4) She informed Saddam that the United States "had no opinion" on the Iraq-Kuwait border dispute (see above). And (5) she told Saddam that the United States did not have defense treaties with any Gulf states.[176]

While the July 25 meeting between Ambassador Glaspie and the Iraqi president is the most well-known example of poor signaling, it was both preceded and followed by similar instances. In mid-July, in response to Secretary of Defense Dick Cheney's comment that "those commitments [to come to Kuwait's defense if threatened] haven't changed," a Pentagon spokesman remarked that the secretary had been quoted "with some degree of liberty."[177] Similar remarks—and a similar reversal—were made by the navy secretary (and a Pentagon spokesperson) a few days later.[178] Just before Glaspie's meeting with Saddam Hussein, State Department spokesperson Margaret Tutwiler made a statement underlining the US commitment to support its friends in the Gulf, but then stated: "We do not have any defense treaties with Kuwait and there are no special defense or security commitments to Kuwait."[179] And six days after the Glaspie-Saddam meeting, Assistant Secretary of State John Kelly reaffirmed in public—and widely reported—remarks to Congress: "We have no de-

---

[175]*New York Times*, September 23, 1990, section 1, 19.
[176]Ali 1993, 88–89.
[177]Quoted in Stein 1992, 150–51.
[178]Stein 1992, 151.
[179]Rahman 1997, 298; Missed Signals in the Middle East 1991.

fence treaty relationship with any Gulf country. That is clear. We support the security and independence of friendly states in the region. . . . We have historically avoided taking a position on border disputes or on internal OPEC deliberations, but we have certainly, as have all administrations, resoundingly called for the peaceful settlement of disputes and difference in the area."[180]

Even if the US diplomatic corps had been more effective in conveying a consistent message that the United States would punish any invasion of Kuwait, Iraq still would have questioned US credibility. In this case, deterrence required more than words. Saddam Hussein firmly believed that US domestic politics—and specifically, casualty aversion—would keep American troops away from the Gulf. The Bush administration was unwilling or unable to take action to tie its hands and enhance the credibility of any signals. In then–secretary of state James Baker's words: "I continue to believe that if the President had said prior to August 1990 that we were willing to go to war to protect Kuwait, many members of Congress would have been muttering impeachment."[181] In general, it appears that the Iraqi regime was convinced that the United States would not use force to liberate Kuwait and that, even if the United States did attack, Iraq could wait out the assault as American casualties mounted, eroding support for any war.[182] The image of the United States as a paper tiger could only have been enforced by the absence of a strong American response to Iraq's use of chemical weapons on its Kurdish population and to Iraqi threats to Israel.[183]

Interestingly, a comparison case suggests that a stronger deterrent may have, in fact, been much more effective in preventing the Iraqi invasion of Kuwait. Days after Kuwait's independence in 1961, Iraqi president General Abdel Karim Qassem laid claim to the new state. Qassem and Saddam Hussein used very similar rhetoric, with Qassem describing Kuwait as an "integral and indivisible part" of Iraq.[184] The British immediately responded by sending troops to Kuwait, and Qassem stood down (indeed, Iraqi troops had not yet been sent to Kuwait). Further, after British troops were replaced by troops from the Arab League, the British were very clear in reaffirming their promise to come to Kuwait's aid in the event of attack. While Qassem never relinquished Iraq's claim to Kuwait, he also never threatened to attack again. The British military attaché described British signals and actions as "a major factor" in deterring Qassem from attack-

[180]Quoted in Bulloch and Morris 1991, 2; also see Cooley 1991, 128.
[181]Baker 1995, 273.
[182]Gause 2001, 14.
[183]Rubin 1993, 263.
[184]Rahman 1997, 241; also see Bulloch and Morris 1991, 122.

ing Kuwait.[185] In contrast to US behavior in the summer of 1990, the British were extremely clear about their defense obligations to Kuwait, and relied on more than words—by sending troops to Kuwait—to bolster their efforts at deterrence.

Why did the United States fail to implement an effective strategy of deterrence? One explanation for US inaction was that no one expected such dramatic action from the Iraqis. This finding is consistent with the notion that the norm against conquest was probably more deeply internalized in the West than in the Middle East (or, at least, than within the Iraqi leadership). In the words of one US administration official, "the idea that a country would march up to the border, put 100,000 troops there, go in and do what they've done; I don't think anyone here thought they'd do it."[186] Western (or US) complacency with regard to the norm against conquest may well have inhibited the ability to see the need for enforcement.

Because of poor signaling by the United States, the norm against conquest was an ineffective deterrent in the summer of 1990. Deep internalization of the norm in the West may have undermined the probability of its efficacy. Interestingly, one can also make the argument that the norm against conquest *encouraged* the Iraqi annexation of Kuwait. The public Iraqi justification for the war (and the attendant explanation for taking over all of Kuwait)—that Kuwait was the nineteenth Iraqi province—is very much related to the principles of self-determination and nationalism, if in a somewhat perverted fashion. By using the rhetorical device of nationalism, Saddam Hussein was paying lip service to one version of this principle. Of course, it is transparently clear that his remarks were made out of political expediency rather than any actual conviction. While the claim that Kuwait is part of Iraq is by no means a new one, it was never nurtured by the Ba'athist regime prior to the invasion.[187] Nonetheless, the Iraqi propaganda machine was launched into action to justify the invasion on these grounds; and this particular justification required that Iraq take over all of Kuwait.

Iraqi rhetoric in the summer of 1990 helps reveal some of the potential contradictions—or, at least, unintended consequences—of the norm against conquest. The norm grew out of the principle of self-determination, and it strengthened in an era of colonial delegitimation. As shown earlier, state resurrection—including the resurrection of some precolonial states—increased as violent state death decreased. By labeling Kuwait as a colonial vestige that

[185]Rahman 1997, 271.
[186]Quoted in Missed Signals in the Middle East 1991.
[187]Hassan 1999, 75.

rightly belonged to a historical Iraqi state, the Hussein regime could manipulate the underpinnings of the norm against conquest.[188]

DID KUWAITI NATIONALISM FACTOR INTO IRAQI DECISION MAKING?

A second, plausible explanation both for the general trend away from conquest and occupation and for the Iraqi invasion of Kuwait is the argument that nationalism has been increasing over the past century. Would-be conquerors today refrain from taking over highly nationalistic states that will, ultimately, cost more to occupy than they will yield in profits. As mentioned before, one important problem with this argument is that it ignores the possibility that highly nationalistic (educated and industrialized) societies also may possess the type of infrastructure—or, more relevant to this case, natural resources—that makes revenue extraction easier. Thus, while the costs of occupation may go up, the benefits may also increase.[189]

What predictions would this argument make with respect to a potential Iraqi invasion of Kuwait? The answer to this question depends on the measures used to predict nationalism and, by extension, resistance. Most scholars who argue that nationalism has increased over time rely on the well-known claim that industrialization has led to centralized education and higher literacy rates, which in turn lead to nationalism. While Kuwait is not highly industrialized, it does have a centralized education system and literacy rates of over 70 percent.[190] Because the logic of this argument ultimately hinges on the level of education of the population, we can say (despite relatively low levels of Kuwaiti industrialization) that the prediction here would be one of high levels of nationalism and, therefore, resistance. This variant of the nationalist resistance argument suggests that Iraq should not have invaded Kuwait.

A second logic that claims to predict nationalism refers to the ethnic composition of a state. While the native Kuwaiti population itself was fairly homogeneous, an extremely high proportion of the people living in Kuwait were foreign workers, who would not have been expected to fight for Kuwait. It is not entirely clear, then, how Kuwait's ethnic makeup would have translated into the generation of nationalist resistance.

With hindsight, available evidence both supports and challenges differ-

---

[188]In so doing, Hussein was questioning Kuwait's legitimacy as a member of the international system, lending some additional support to the claim that more legitimate states are more likely to survive.

[189]Liberman 1996.

[190]Ward 1990.

ent parts of the nationalist resistance argument. Immediately following the occupation, community networks sprang up to provide basic services and to organize resistance to the Iraqis. Limited militarized resistance followed. However, at least in part because the Kuwaitis were truly surprised by the Iraqi invasion, the army essentially did not fight at the border, and many of the air force's planes were flown to Saudi Arabia as soon as possible. Iraq quickly began targeting opposition fighters and was successful in encouraging many Kuwaitis to leave the country.[191] In total, the fighting lasted about seven hours, with the Kuwaiti leadership on planes to exile almost immediately.[192]

The Iraqis anticipated little resistance to the invasion, and their prediction was correct. While the Kuwaiti population clearly did not support the Iraqi action, it also did not put up much of a fight. Ultimately, what was probably more important than the prospect of nationalist resistance in this case was the impact of Kuwaiti oil on Iraq's cost-benefit calculation. Even if the probability of resistance was relatively high—and here the data send somewhat mixed signals—Kuwaiti oil was an extremely exploitable resource. By taking over Kuwait's oil infrastructure, Iraq could derive great net economic benefit at very little cost, especially given high levels of Iraqi surplus labor coupled with low levels of Kuwaiti nationalist resistance.

EXPLAINING THE INTERNATIONAL RESPONSE

The norms hypothesis makes two predictions about the nature of the international response to any attempt at conquest such as the Iraqi invasion of Kuwait: first, that the norm violator (Iraq) will be punished; and second, that states that fail to punish the violator will themselves be punished as well (enforcement of the metanorm).[193] That Iraq was punished for its invasion and annexation of Kuwait is transparently clear (although interestingly, it is not as clear that Iraq would have been punished for the lesser infraction of taking only over Warbah and Bubiyan and the Rumeilah oil field).[194] The UN Security Council met on August 2 to condemn the invasion. Although sanctions—a nonmilitary tool—were the first form of punishment, it was always clear that a military option was in the offing, unless Iraq withdrew. It is also interesting to note that, once Iraq claimed Kuwait in its entirety, the West (like Iraq) treated Kuwait as an indivisible entity, insisting on "[nothing] less than a total and uncon-

---

[191]Crystal 1992, 157–58.
[192]Bulloch and Morris 1991, 106–7.
[193]Axelrod 1986.
[194]Bulloch and Morris 1991, 5. Compare for example the international reaction to the Iraqi annexation of Kuwait with the UN response to the Turkish invasion of Cyprus.

ditional Iraqi withdrawal from the Emirate."[195] British prime minister
John Major insisted, "There can be no question of negotiations, concessions, partial solutions or linkage of other issues."[196] These remarks were
made partly in response to Soviet envoy Yevgeny Primakov's attempt to
negotiate a partial Iraqi withdrawal from Kuwait.[197] The issue at hand
was about more than territory—it was also about the outlawry of taking
over an entire state.

The size, speed, and commitment of the US-led coalition against Iraq is
testament to the degree of opposition to the invasion of Kuwait. In the
diplomatic pregame to the war, Iraq was given multiple opportunities to
withdraw without having to pay the costs of war. But once the January
15 ultimatum deadline passed, the coalition could and did use the force
at its disposal to defeat Iraq soundly.

While the coalition was indeed quite broad, a few states were notably
not members. These included Jordan, Yemen, and Cuba. Jordan's King
Hussein faced a staunchly anti-West population that leaned strongly toward supporting Iraq. The West, keenly aware that Jordan might violate
the embargo on Iraq, put King Hussein on notice of the punishment for
supporting the Iraqi regime.[198] Similarly, as the Security Council was voting on the resolution that would issue an ultimatum to Iraq, the Yemeni
representative was warned that a no vote on the resolution would mean
a withdrawal of US aid.[199] While Cuba also nominally supported Iraq, it
was difficult to punish Cuba beyond the extant US embargo. What is important to note here, though, is that a metanorm was indeed active. Key
states—particularly key Arab states—that attempted neutrality or appeared to stand with Iraq were punished.

One should not attribute purely altruistic motives to the coalition member states, however, as altruism may well have been a mask for greed. The
importance of oil here is undeniable. In 1990, the United States imported
over 50 percent of its oil, with the Gulf region supplying more than 10
percent of US oil imports.[200] The United States did not feel that it could
allow one state—and especially a state like Iraq in 1990—to control 20
percent of global oil reserves.

Although it might not be possible to disentangle the different motivations for the coalition's military response, there are at least three relevant
counterfactuals to consider. These brief thought experiments are meant to
help tease out the extent to which the norm against conquest affected the

[195]Rahman 1997, 309.
[196]Rahman 1997, 309.
[197]Rahman 1997, 305.
[198]Freedman and Karsh 1993, 189.
[199]Freedman and Karsh 1993, 233.
[200]Bulloch and Morris 1991, 101.

international response to the annexation of Kuwait. The first counterfactual asks, What if Iraq had annexed Kuwait in a world *without* a norm
against conquest? Would states like those in the coalition have opposed
the annexation? Given the importance of oil, the answer is probably yes.
The second counterfactual is, what if Kuwait had not possessed oil? While
there is no true comparison case, we can certainly point to events like
North Korea's invasion of the South in 1950—and the subsequent reaction—as consistent with a general commitment to support this norm. Similarly, if Indonesia were to take over East Timor today, the likelihood that
the collective security mechanism of the United Nations would be invoked
is high. While the level of effort and funding might vary with the presence
or absence of strategic interests in a challenged area, such incursions have
been met with force and punishment in the post-1945 era. The third counterfactual is, what if Iraq had taken over only part of Kuwait, rather than
annexed the entire country? Here is where the argument that the norm
against conquest played an important role in determining the international response to the annexation may be most compelling, as it is not
clear that the Persian Gulf War would have occurred had Iraqi war aims
been more limited.[201]

Other factors—that relate both to US interests and to the norm against
conquest—were at work as well. Hegemons (such as the United States),
for example, seek to promote international order. Challenges to state sovereignty can upset this order. Similarly, the United States and its allies
wanted to avoid setting a precedent that could imply that such behavior
was acceptable. Margaret Thatcher, in a late summer speech to the Aspen
Institute, contended: "If we let [the Iraqi invasion of Kuwait] succeed
no small country can ever feel safe again. The law of the jungle takes
over."[202] The objective of international stability was particularly salient
in a world just emerging from the Cold War, where the United States faced
critical windows of opportunity in terms of setting—and clarifying—the
"rules of the game" in international relations. "'Let no nation think it can
devour another nation and the United States will somehow turn a blind
eye. Let no dictator believe that we are deaf to the tolling of the bell as
our fundamental principles are attacked. And let no one believe that because the Cold War is over, the United States is somehow going to abdicate its international leadership,'" proclaimed Secretary of State James
Baker.[203]

What of Iraq's brother Arab states? Following the logic of "there but
for the grace of God go I," the smaller Gulf states in particular were quick

---

[201]Bulloch and Morris 1991, 5.
[202]Quoted in Bulloch and Morris 1991, 111.
[203]Quoted in Rubin 1993, 267.

to support efforts of the US-led coalition. Hassan argues that, given the alien relationship between the Arab world and the concept of sovereignty, Arab states that supported the coalition did not necessarily oppose Iraq because they had internalized the norm against conquest. Initially, they characterized the Iraqi action as wrong in Koranic terms;[204] in part, this rhetoric must have been used as a counterbalance to the request for help from Western infidels. But leaders of these states also followed the self-interested logic of wanting to preserve their own sovereignty. Again, we see how misinterpretation and miscalculations as to how and why other states would respond to violation of the norm against conquest may have fueled Iraqi policy. It appears that Saddam Hussein never believed that fellow Gulf states—and Saudi Arabia in particular—could or would support Western efforts and Western troops in a policy against Iraq.[205] This is not to say that these states had deeply internalized the norm against conquest, but rather to point out that they saw sufficient benefit from the norm to support punishing a violator (particularly a nearby violator).[206]

The coalition's behavior in terms of war aims is also consistent with the norm against conquest. In past eras, such conflicts would have led to the destruction—and state death—of the initial offender. Consider, for example, British imperialism in response to the possibility of any would-be colony slipping away, or even the Allied powers' reaction to German conquests during World War II. In 1991, however, the idea of taking over Iraq was anathema. In James Baker's words: "We believed, moreover, that marching on Baghdad was ridiculous from a practical standpoint. . . . Suddenly, a coalition war to liberate Kuwait from a universally condemned invasion could have been portrayed as a US war of conquest."[207] Once the norm against conquest had been violated, the violation was reversed and the offender punished, but Iraq retained its sovereignty.

To what degree did the norm against conquest affect the international response to Iraq's invasion of Kuwait? Given the multiplicity of factors arguing for the coalition's response to the invasion, it is admittedly difficult to isolate the causal power of the norm. The analysis of this case is, however, consistent with the claim that one of the reasons that conquest is rare today is because the probability of punishment is known to be high. When punishment appears to be less certain—as in the case of the Iraqi invasion of Kuwait—the likelihood of norm violation may increase.

---

[204]Hassan 1999, 147.

[205]Hassan 1999, 4. Another miscalculation refers to Saddam's plan to attack Israel if Iraq were attacked by the West. Saddam's expectation was that Israel would retaliate against Iraq, which would then lead to a united Arab front against Israel (ideally, under Iraqi leadership).

[206]Note that this reasoning for supporting the norm against conquest conforms with Wendt's second degree of internalization.

[207]Baker 1995, 437.

Conclusion

The goal of this chapter is fourfold: to test corollary hypotheses derived from the norms argument; to provide additional evidence for the argument that the dynamics of rivalry create incentives to take over buffer states; to continue to test the claim that nationalist resistance forestalls conquest and intervention; and to illustrate how the norm against conquest has functioned as an intervening variable that generated a shift from conquest to intervention after 1945. Each of the corollaries derived from the normative argument is supported by available data. Further, where tests were conducted to control for variables suggested by alternative explanations, these explanations fared poorly. Because no other explanation for the post-1945 turn away from violent state death predicts the shift from conquest to intervention, a significant (but lesser) decline in forcible territorial change, an increase in state failure, a rise in state resurrections after 1920, *and* the use of occupation as an intermediary form of control between conquest and intervention, the empirical support for these hypotheses translates into support for the claim that the rise of a norm against conquest has in fact been an important cause of the decline in violent state death.

Evidence from the case studies is similarly telling. Poland and Hungary in 1956 and the Dominican Republic in 1965 are all cases of states that suffered the threat of intervention. In none of these cases—nor in the case of Kuwait in 1990—do calculations about nationalist resistance appear to have strongly conditioned the behavior of would-be conquerors. By contrast, the norm against conquest appears to have limited Soviet and US action in 1956 and 1965 respectively (although the evidence in 1956 is admittedly slim) and to have helped shape the international community's response to Iraq's invasion of Kuwait.

More than any other general explanation, the emergence and strengthening of the norm against conquest accounts for the virtual cessation of violent state death after 1945. The argument that an increased likelihood of nationalist resistance could explain the shift away from conquest is plausible, but by and large fails when examined in individual cases, and especially when tested against the argument that a norm against conquest explains this change. At the same time, current US policy may challenge the tenure of this norm. The international response to the US occupation of Iraq in 2003 was very different from the world community's reaction to the Iraqi invasion of Kuwait in 1990. To the degree that the norm against conquest can be eroded by unchallenged incursions of sovereignty, the norm may be as short-lived as many states prior to 1945.

Chapter 8 _____

Conclusion

THIS BOOK asks and answers three questions: What is the historical record of state death? Under what conditions do states die? And, how can we explain the dramatic decline in violent state death after 1945?

The answers to these questions challenge a number of conventional wisdoms. State death has been considerably more widespread than most international relations scholarship has suggested—over the past two hundred years, more than a quarter of all states have died. The causes of state death are similarly surprising. It is not a state's strength, alliance portfolio, or even its level of nationalism that determines survival, but rather its geography. States engaged in enduring rivalries form security dilemmas around the states that lie between them—buffer states. And it seems that these buffer states are born to lose. Each rival fears the possibility that its opponent will take over the buffer. This fear produces a strategic imperative that leads to a fatal outcome: buffer state death.

Buffer states are likely to die because surrounding rivals are typically unable to make credible commitments *not* to take them over. But in certain, atypical situations, the security dilemma can be resolved such that buffer states survive. If rivals' resources are simultaneously constrained, they *cannot* take over buffer states. If rivals must become temporary allies in another theater, they prefer not to sap each other's resources by fighting over buffer states. And if a more powerful third party intervenes to protect the buffer state, rivals will refrain from conquest because costs will exceed benefits.

The US sponsorship of a norm against conquest following World War II is akin to this type of intervention, and explains the relative lack of violent state death after 1945. With its roots in Wilsonian idealism and American antiwar sentiment, this norm entered the international system after World War I but received strong great-power sponsorship only following the Second World War. The norm against conquest has served as an intervening mechanism since 1945, causing would-be conquerors to revise their territorial ambitions in a world where conquest is prohibited but intervention is permitted.

In the remainder of this concluding chapter, I assess the findings of this book first by considering the theoretical implications that emerge from its analysis. I next turn to policy implications—dos and don'ts of state death—suggested by the theoretical argument and empirical findings. Third, I discuss questions raised but unanswered here that open avenues for future research. Finally, I consider the normative implications of the analysis, asking whether state death is necessarily undesirable and, conversely, whether the norm against conquest should be altered or maintained today.

Theoretical Implications

In addition to the claim that states tend not to die, the prevailing view in international relations scholarship is that states that fail to balance against power will be particularly likely to die. This argument suggests that a process of state selection governs international relations. Although selection could take many forms, testing this argument on state death and survival constitutes a plausible and important first step in testing the broader claim.

This book generates two fairly pessimistic conclusions for the balancing argument. First, the quantitative analysis fails to reveal a relationship between balancing behavior and state survival or death. Even when restricted to cases of only threatened states—specifically, buffer states—balancing vis-à-vis surrounding rivals is unrelated to survival. In the cases as well as in the quantitative analysis, there is little correlation between balancing behavior and state survival. States that chose not to balance, as in the case of the Dominican Republic in 1870, survived, while states that succeeded in finding allies and strengthening their militaries often died.

Second, evidence from the case studies also suggests a slightly different, but no less discouraging, conclusion. Almost universally, buffer states that attempted to balance were typically unsuccessful in their efforts to build up their military power and form alliances *because they were buffer states.* When probed, the balancing argument reveals a catch-22. States—especially threatened states—must balance to survive. But threatened states are unlikely to be able to balance precisely because they *are* threatened. If this is the case, the utility of prescriptions from the balancing argument must be reconsidered.

Another claim that is often made but rarely tested is that would-be conquerors will be deterred from taking over highly nationalistic states. Like the balancing argument, this claim is not supported by the evidence. The quantitative indicators suggested by proponents of the nationalist resistance argument bear no relationship to the probability of state death or survival.[1] Furthermore, as illustrated in the eighteenth-century Polish

---

[1] Even if better predictors of nationalism were available, nationalism itself might not be the best predictor of resistance. The current "Iraqi" insurgency, for example, has attracted members from many countries.

case, conquerors may be more likely to be spurred on by the threat of nationalism than to be deterred by these costs. Poland's partitioners were disgusted by Polish nationalism in part because it threatened their ability to indirectly control the Polish buffer. Repeatedly, they made reference to eradicating all vestiges of Polish nationalism. And consistently, they responded to nationalist uprisings—both before and after partition—with repression instead of retreat.

This is not to say that nationalism is irrelevant, or that nationalists cannot inflict costs on conquerors. The analysis of state resurrection presented in chapter 6 suggests a positive relationship between more nationalistic conquerered states and the probability of resurrection. One explanation for the important role of nationalism in state resurrection—but not in state death—is that conquerors may not be able to assess accurately the level of resistance they will face until conquest has actually occurred.

The negative findings discussed above are extremely important. They cast doubt on a number of key international relations theories and suggest new areas for study. For instance, geography should play a more central role in international relations scholarship. If strategic location is a crucial factor in determining whether states live or die, what else might political geography explain? One finding in this book is that rough terrain is positively related to state survival. James Fearon and David Laitin have found a relationship between mountainous terrain and ethnic insurgency.[2] Monica Toft effectively argues that geographic concentration of ethnic groups is an important permissive cause for civil war.[3] Finally, the finding that buffer states are particularly likely to die also could be folded into the broader literature on territorial conflict to refine claims about the relationship between rivalry, contiguity, and war.[4]

The argument about buffer states advanced here could also be applied to a deeper understanding of colonization. While there is no doubt that the pursuit of material gain drove European colonialism, the imperial powers had effectively extracted gains from their future colonies for years. Given the cost of direct versus indirect control, why colonize when trade alone was meeting their needs? Colonization became more likely when imperial rivals arrived on the scene—when precolonial states and polities became buffers.[5]

The norm against conquest that emerged in the early twentieth century saved the lives of states under threat of conquest and, arguably, helped resurrect a number of colonized states. The process by which this norm—

[2]Fearon and Laitin 2003.
[3]Toft 2003.
[4]Vasquez 1993.
[5]Gallagher and Robinson 1953.

indeed, any norm—became internalized raises fascinating questions. The literature on international norms has come a long way in a short time, and we now have important tools that help us identify stages of norm internalization. What we are missing, however, is an explanation for how we get from here to there—we lack the causal mechanisms behind internalization.

A prominent mode of norm emergence is the imposition of a new behavioral rule by a powerful actor. But how does the transition from adhering to the rule for fear of punishment to adhering to the rule because of a belief that it dictates proper behavior occur? One hypothesis looks to the role of repetitive behavior in moral learning. Repeating a behavior, coupled with being told that that behavior is correct, may lead to internalization. Of course, levels of internalization may differ among actors; even when repetition is constant, we should expect that internalization can vary with actors' *ex ante* interests. This logic offers a causal mechanism for the relationship between time and norm internalization.

Considering the history of the norm against conquest suggests additional behavioral implications. It may help explain cases of state dissolution and unification, as well as state failure, regime change, and resurrection. To the extent that multiethnic states like the Soviet Union and coethnic states like North and South Korea have emerged as the result of conquest, a strengthening of the norm against conquest might lend support to conquered peoples seeking secession, and to divided peoples hoping for reunification. Thus, the norm against conquest might help explain the recent rise of state dissolutions and voluntary unifications, just as it explains the decline in violent state death.

To conclude that geography matters more than balancing in determining state death and survival is at once freeing and constraining. Making geography more central to the field opens new avenues for scholarship. But geography is difficult to change. Certainly, buffer states are unable to move to alternative locations. Had this analysis found support for the balancing argument, the news would have been more encouraging, as states would be able to do more to promote their own survival. So what, in fact, can be done? I consider this question as well as others in the next section.

Policy Implications

The question of why some states survive while others die has become increasingly relevant over the past few years. Recent shifts in US policy—especially the occupation of Iraq in 2003—suggest a possible return to a world of conquest. This potential change in behavior contains implications for states at the greatest risk of attack—buffer states—as well as for the international community as a whole.

The first policy implication applies to *non*buffer states. This implication stems from the predictive power of buffer status in models of state death, coupled with the absence of a relationship between balancing and state death and survival. If it is geography, not balancing, that leads to state survival, then states in relatively safe neighborhoods face a low risk of being conquered. Especially for poorer states in this situation, the trade-off between guns and butter may not be a particularly severe one. Of course, states fund their militaries and seek alliances for a number of reasons, including the maintenance of internal security. But for nonbuffer states, survival against conquest should not be one of those reasons. Demilitarization, while sure to be controversial, may well be a viable option, particularly for relatively isolated states.

Advising buffer states seeking to promote their own survival is a more difficult—but not impossible—task. If we look at the map of the world today, we see a number of buffer states that could be in danger—especially if the norm against conquest were to weaken. Caught between two rising powers, Nepal is in a particularly difficult spot. Likewise for Paraguay, Uruguay, Mongolia, and the two Koreas. What, if anything, can these states do to preserve their sovereignty?

First, buffer states should seek international recognition. The quantitative analysis in chapter 4 reveals a strong relationship between levels of international legitimacy and the probability of state survival. Although all these states have been accorded some measure of international recognition, regimes like the one governing the Democratic People's Republic of Korea are generally considered less "legitimate" than others. This suggests a tension between regime survival and state survival for buffer states. Less legitimate governing regimes must weigh the consequences of policy change against their state's survival. Citizens of buffer states face a similar dilemma. To the extent that populations of buffer states value the survival of their state over the survival of the governing regime, they should distinguish their loyalties to both. This holds especially true for buffer states that receive relatively lower levels of international recognition. While not a conventional buffer state, Taiwan has done well to seek international recognition. And states like Tajikistan are less likely to be conquered, because they have received such recognition.

Second, buffer states should support the norm against conquest. Particularly in international organizations or other forums where their votes or ability to persuade may carry some weight, they should be vigilant about the preservation of this norm if they themselves wish to survive. Buffer states should strongly support punishment of violations of this norm, lending aid wherever possible. And they should keep a keen eye out for violations at the edges of the norm; in addition to opposing conquest, they also should stand firm against any case of forcible territorial aggression.

Third, should a buffer state (indeed, any state) suffer conquest, leaders of that state should mobilize their population such that a strong resistance can be mounted. Although the prospect of nationalist resistance appears to be ineffective in deterring conquest, the evidence suggests that resistance is a useful tool in reversing conquest. Conquered populations that can inflict costs on their occupiers via resistance have a greater chance of regaining their sovereignty than populations unable or unwilling to resist conquest.

The policy implications stemming from this book apply to great as well as small powers. The most important implications for great powers refer to the consequences and tenure of the norm against conquest. Chapter 7 outlines a number of corollary hypotheses derived from the argument that a norm against conquest accounts for the post-1945 decline in violent state death. These corollaries can be thought of as unintended consequences of the norm. Increases in resurrections and decreases in forcible territorial change are fairly uncontroversial. But the possibility that the norm against conquest is causally related to an increase in state failure is cause for concern. The human consequences of state failure can be severe and terrible. Insofar as states fail in part because other states are prohibited from taking them over, it is important to reconsider the utility of the norm against conquest in such cases. As recent scholarship has suggested, the increase in state failure should encourage policy makers to at least discuss options for prevention and redress of failure that, while violating state sovereignty, may relieve human suffering.[6]

At the same time, policy makers should not take lightly the prospect of even seemingly minor violations of territorial sovereignty. Even if they harbor ambivalence regarding the utility of the norm, it remains important to understand the conditions under which its strength might decline, for such a decline would most likely be followed by a return to a world of frequent conquest.

The health of the norm against conquest is very much related to US power and preferences. While US power shows no sign of decline, decisions taken by the George W. Bush administration raise the question of whether preferences have changed. On the one hand, the United States has been very vocal about *not* having territorial ambitions in recently occupied states like Iraq. On the other hand, US behavior in recent years has

[6]For example, Jeffrey Herbst has argued for decertification of failed states, while Jim Fearon, David Laitin, and Stephen Krasner have urged policy makers to consider options like neotrusteeship. Herbst 1996–1997; Fearon and Laitin 2004; Krasner 2004.

been such that it is difficult to imagine that other states do not see new precedents being set.

It may be that the 2003 invasion and occupation of Iraq echo a logic for the US surprise over Iraq's invasion of Kuwait. Just as the norm against conquest may have been sufficiently internalized in US policy-making circles to hinder decision makers in anticipating Iraqi behavior, US policy makers today may assume that other states will view American actions as benign. Observing states, however, may instead see US actions as license for conquest.

Available evidence does suggest that the Bush administration may have believed it acted in accordance with the norm against conquest, in that regime (and leader) replacement was the explicit goal of the 2003 Iraq War and, moreover, postwar plans shied away from the notion of occupation. Indeed, the goal of overthrowing Saddam Hussein went back at least as far as the Iraq Liberation Act, passed under the second Clinton administration.[7] Very soon after George W. Bush's first inauguration, a national security meeting addressed the issue of toppling Saddam.[8] The goal of replacing the Iraqi regime and leader certainly remained important to the administration following the attacks of September 11, 2001; the CIA was asked to report on the possibility of covert actions that could topple the Iraqi regime. When covert actions were judged insufficient, the agency was directed to develop strategies that would further a military effort to this end.[9] With characteristic directness, President Bush made his intention to "take Saddam out" clear to National Security Adviser Condoleeza Rice and several senators in a March 2002 meeting; less than a year later, he expressed the same intention to a group of Iraqi exiles during a White House meeting.[10] Regime change remained the administration's explicit goal in Iraq through the summer of 2002, when United States Central Command (CENTCOM) commander general Tommy Franks briefed his major commanders on the war plan for Iraq, informing them that "the end state for this operation is regime change."[11] At around the same time, an internal White House document outlined the major goals in a war with Iraq, which were to overthrow Saddam Hussein, democratize the country, and eliminate any Iraqi capability to build or use weapons of mass destruction.[12] Reports of these internal documents and meetings, which explicitly focused on replacing the Iraqi leader and regime, agree

[7]Packer 2005, 24.
[8]Packer 2005, 39.
[9]Woodward 2004, 72, 108.
[10]Packer 2005, 45; Woodward 2004, 258.
[11]Gordon and Trainor 2006, 73.
[12]Gordon and Trainor 2006, 73.

with a multitude of public statements that emerged from the administration during the lead-up to the war.

The internally and externally stated limited goal of regime and leader change carried over to a series of efforts to avoid the rhetoric and appearance of occupation, an intention to withdraw from Iraq as quickly as possible, and extremely poor postwar planning. Indeed, not even the Iraqi military leadership believed that the United States would take over the entire country.[13] In a striking resemblance to the rhetoric employed by the Johnson administration during the 1965 Dominican crisis, US policy makers and military officials made every effort *not* to appear as occupiers both before and during combat operations.[14] Vice President Dick Cheney, in an interview with Tim Russert of *Meet the Press,* asserted repeatedly that US forces would be "greeted as liberators, not occupiers."[15] Representatives of nongovernmental organizations meeting with USAID in preparation for the fall of Iraq were told that the international law of occupation would not apply to postwar Iraq, because "the American troops would be 'liberators' rather than occupiers, so the obligations did not apply."[16] The desire to avoid the impression of occupation also was reflected in an order to troops not to display the American flag in Iraq—even when it might protect US forces from friendly fire.[17] A postwar report by the Army's Third Infantry Division actually concluded that the failure to declare a US occupation at the outset contributed to the general anarchy across Iraq following the fall of Baghdad.[18]

The bungling of the occupation was not only due to the administration's commitment to the "liberators, not occupiers" line; it reflected a genuine desire on the part of the Bush White House to avoid a long-term stay in Iraq. Like the Johnson administration almost forty years earlier, the Bush administration fully expected a quick and easy withdrawal from the war. Among other members of the administration, both Secretary of Defense Donald Rumsfeld and President Bush sought to avoid the kind of prolonged nation-building efforts undertaken during the Clinton administration.[19] In line with this goal, early military estimates suggested withdrawal around the eighteen-month mark.[20] When army chief of staff Gen-

[13]Gordon and Trainor 2006, 121.

[14]Woodward 2004, 155–56, 260, 297; Gordon and Trainor 2006, 73, 106, 155, 163, 433; Packer 2005, 142, 185, 227.

[15]Cheney 2003.

[16]Fallows 2004.

[17]Gordon and Trainor 2006, 137, 337, 428.

[18]Lumpkin and Linzer 2003.

[19]Gordon and Trainor 2006, 103, 142, 151, 169, 457. Also see Woodward 2004, 308.

[20]Gordon and Trainor 2006, 68, 74; Woodward 2004, 148; Packer 2005, 132–33, 142, 225; Fallows 2004.

eral Shinseki offered Congress a much higher troop estimate (and, by implication, a longer timeline) for postwar operations than the administration was suggesting, this effective contradiction of the party line generated a host of upset phone calls and conversations at the highest levels of government.[21]

The commitment to a brief postwar stay in Iraq also was reflected in the poverty of planning for "Phase IV," or postcombat, operations. Indeed, the weakness of Phase IV planning went back to the Clinton administration's Iraq war plan, although the Clinton plan acknowledged the need for large numbers of troops for Phase IV operations.[22] Key observers of US war planning, such as the director of Britain's MI6, concluded early in the process that postwar planning was insufficient at best.[23] Similarly, Secretary of State Colin Powell made strong efforts to impress on President Bush that Bush would "own" Iraq after the war, but to little avail.[24] As Nora Bensahel argues, "the prewar planning process for postwar Iraq was plagued by myriad problems, including a dysfunctional interagency process, overly optimistic assumptions, and a lack of contingency planning for alternative outcomes."[25]

The placement of blame for the ensuing "fiasco"[26] in Iraq aside, the lack of focus on postwar Iraq, the desire to exit quickly, and the desire to avoid the appearance of occupation are all consistent with the notion that the United States did not intend a long-term occupation. Instead, the Bush administration held the more limited goal of replacing the Iraqi regime and leadership. Thus, the intentions of the administration were to some degree in line with the proscriptions of the norm against conquest. That said, the fact of occupation is undeniable. From the disbanding of the Iraqi army[27] to the establishment of the Coalition Provisional Authority (CPA)—and the United Nations' effective recognition of the CPA as the governing authority in Iraq[28]—it is clear that the United States ended up as an occupier even if that was not its original intention.

Even an unintentional norm violation can be consequential, particularly insofar as it sets a precedent. In evaluating the consequences of the US violation of the norm against conquest in this case, it is important to ask whether a precedent has been set both for future US actions and/or for other states that might seek to engage in occupations or occupation-

[21] Gordon and Trainor 2006, 102.
[22] Gordon and Trainor 2006, 27, 53.
[23] Gordon and Trainor 2006, 54.
[24] Gordon and Trainor 2006, 71; Woodward 2004, 150, 152, 270.
[25] Bensahel 2006, 454.
[26] Ricks 2006.
[27] Packer 2005, 195.
[28] *United Nations Security Council Resolution 1483* 2003.

like behavior. On the first question, both US public opinion and military constraints make the possibility of near-term future occupations unlikely. The Iraq War drove President Bush's job approval downward significantly, and extensive deployments of US forces in Iraq and elsewhere constrained the military such that another occupation would be exceedingly difficult.

The extent to which the US occupation of Iraq might set a precedent for other would-be occupiers is a murkier issue. This possibility raises the question of how international norms may be "de-internalized." If, in Wendt's terms, the norm against conquest is at the first degree of internalization, the removal of the United States as the key normative entrepreneur or "coercer" could signal a reversal in norm internalization. But even if the norm against conquest is fairly deeply internalized on a global level today, internalization is no guarantee of permanence. One question to ask is whether challenging a norm head-on would be a more effective means of "de-internalization" than chipping away at the norm in a more subtle manner. Interestingly, the Iraqi invasion of Kuwait may be viewed as an example of the first type of challenge; in this case, a direct challenge to the norm may have strengthened, rather than undermined, the norm. The 2003 US-led invasion of Iraq, on the other hand, may be more damaging to the future of the norm by creating ambiguity as to what kinds of occupation and conquest might be permissible in the international system, rather than maintaining a bright-line rule against these types of actions. Likewise, the interventions to replace regimes and leaders that have substituted for conquest after 1945 might be viewed as relatively minor violations of the norm, suggesting that the norm could even contain the seeds of its own demise. In more concrete terms, it is not too difficult to imagine observers of US behavior appropriating US rhetoric—particularly rhetoric against terrorism—to justify interventions that turn into occupations that turn into conquests.

G. John Ikenberry has suggested that a victorious hegemon should behave with restraint, lest would-be friends begin to perceive the hegemon as a danger and start to balance against it.[29] While legitimate security concerns may underlie current US policy, the nature of the recent increase in military operations has raised eyebrows worldwide. To the degree that conquest and annexation are undesirable behaviors, international relations may soon take a turn for the worse, particularly if the US ability to enforce the norm against conquest is viewed as constrained because of a decline in US power as well as a lessened commitment to the norm. It may be that this price is worth the putative security benefit, but it is essential

[29]Ikenberry 2001.

to approach this potential change in policy—and in the norm against conquest—with open eyes. When the critical enforcer of a norm that is not deeply internalized on a global scale begins to chip away—even unintentionally—at the edges of the norm, the norm itself may not survive. US policy may generate a return to a world of violent state death, in which case the norm against conquest may go the way of the states it was designed to protect.

Future Research

This book contributes to IR scholarship in challenging the conventional wisdom about state death, and also derives important theoretical and policy implications about the likelihood and nature of violent state death. The primary contribution here, though, is in providing an answer to the question, under what conditions do states die?

This question itself raises further questions and issues. For example, my current analysis is restricted to the dichotomous dependent variable of violent state death, which is defined in terms of foreign policy control. As discussed in chapter 2, however, foreign policy control is not a dichotomous variable. How would this analysis change if control over foreign policy were considered over a continuum? Are buffer states more likely to suffer all types of incursions of sovereignty, or are the rivals surrounding buffer states concerned only about some kinds of control over their buffers but not others? How would a continuum of foreign policy control even be constructed?[30] Violent state death, as defined here, is an extreme loss of foreign policy control, but how could we compare other infringements of sovereignty?

A second set of questions raised by this analysis refers specifically to the normative argument made here. It is inherently difficult to test normative arguments, because norms are invisible features of international relations. I have tried to address this problem in part by deriving and then testing corollary hypotheses of the norms argument as well as alternative explanations for the post-1945 trend away from violent state death. More scholarship, however, is needed on the general problem of testing for the role of specific norms in international politics.

Related to research on norms, the findings here suggests additional research on the role of state—or possibly regime—recognition in international relations. States that receive greater levels of recognition do appear to be more likely to survive. But as the number of states in the international system has proliferated since the 1960s, recognition—or legiti-

[30]Lake 2003.

macy—may be as important for individual regimes and leaders as it has been for states. Just as the norm against conquest might have prevented violent state death and promoted interventions after 1945, changes in the way that legitimacy and recognition are accorded today may mean that "less-recognized" (often "rogue") regimes and leaders are particularly likely targets for intervention and replacement.

Another question not answered in this book is, under what conditions do states die *non*violently? I chose to focus on violent state death here for three reasons. First, most state deaths are violent. Second, current international relations theories are best suited to predict violent state death. And third, there appeared to be no a priori reason to expect that the causes of violent and nonviolent state death would be the same or even similar.

Having concluded this portion of an analysis of state death, however, I suspect that my argument may in fact bear on nonviolent state death. In examining variation in buffer state death, for instance, I find that many buffer states die nonviolently. Two prime examples of this phenomenon are the German city-states of Bavaria and Württemburg, which voluntarily joined the Prussian confederation. The fate of Bavaria and Württemburg contrasts sharply with that of Hanover and Saxony, which fought and lost wars against the advancing Prussians. Faced with their imminent end, the German city-states had at least one choice to make: they could stand and fight—and probably lose—or they could negotiate themselves out of existence. The second choice might appear to be the obvious one, but it contains an inherent conundrum in that the would-be conquering state would have to convince the buffer that it would keep promises made to the buffer. Understanding the choices made and bargains struck by buffer states under these conditions would enhance our ability to account for the variation in outcomes of state death. As discussed above, the norm against conquest also may explain the increase of state dissolutions and voluntary unifications, just as it explains the decrease of violent state death.

Finally, while buffer states account for an impressive proportion—40 percent—of state deaths, a great deal of unexplained variance remains. Improved measures of some of the variables employed here may come with time and may help reduce this variance, but there is surely more theoretical work to be done as well. Avenues for additional research on state death abound.

Conclusion

I began this book by noting the prevailing view that states both do not and should not die. It is clear that states do die—but should they? It is difficult to know which metric to use in addressing this question; perhaps the best candidate is the quality of life for individuals whose states are at risk of death. In this context, Woodrow Wilson may have gotten it right; war waged for the purpose of territorial gain should be avoided, especially if the human costs of conflict outweigh the victor's gain. But there are other state deaths—even violent ones—that might be more humane in consequence if not in cause. During the 1916 US occupation of the Dominican Republic, for example, roads and schools were built, a constabulary force was trained, and attempts were made to improve the Republic's fiscal situation. Citizens in states formerly part of the Austro-Hungarian Empire probably prefer independence to domination. And popular opinion in recently unified states like Germany does not support a return to partition. This is not to say that good intentions make a good state death. Such a statement could be tantamount to justifying all (neo)colonialism and occupation. Rather, I want to point out that state death is not a normatively black-and-white issue.

The good and bad in state death is paralleled in the norm against conquest. The unintended consequences of the norm outlined above suggest serious reconsideration of its utility. Is intervention to replace domestic political structures normatively better than straight-out conquest? Should state sovereignty be preserved even when the state is unable to provide basic services to its people? How can policy makers balance these issues against the possibility that minor norm violations may undermine the power of the norm more than major infractions? Clarity seems to be the best rule here. As illustrated in the discussion of the Iraqi invasion of Kuwait, it is important for would-be conquerors to understand exactly what type of punishment they will suffer if they violate the norm against conquest. If the norm is to be refined, it should be refined publicly, and the justification for the refinement should be very clearly stated. International organizations such as the United Nations would likely be critical to these efforts, further underlining the point that the United States should continue to work through such institutions.

The normative questions surrounding the issue of state death are compelling, but will likely remain unresolved for some time. For the most part, this book has addressed a narrower question: under what conditions do states die, or exit the international system? I have argued that we must look to the conquerors as well as the conquered if we are to comprehend the phenomenon of state death. My argument upsets basic notions in international relations theory about balancing against power, and about the impact of norms in constraining great-power behavior. The argument also generates important policy implications regarding the future stability of the international system and the current viability of various regimes and leaders. Henry Kissinger once wrote that a lack of historical memory was a root cause of the failure of European statesmen to keep the peace before the First World War: "For in the long interval of peace the sense of the tragic was lost; it was forgotten that states could die."[31] This first step in understanding state death should also serve as a reminder that no state— be it weak, powerful, highly nationalistic, or even surrounded by water— is guaranteed a permanent spot on the map of the world.

[31]Kissinger 1957, 6.

Appendix A _____

Revising the Correlates of War
List of Members of the Interstate System

THIS APPENDIX expands on the brief discussion of problems with the Correlates of War (COW) list of members of the interstate system and my proposed solution to these problems presented in chapter 2. The list of members of the interstate system comprises the universe of cases for this study as well as many others. Understanding and correcting any biases that may characterize this list is therefore essential to producing unbiased, generalizable scholarship in international relations.

Critique of COW

To be included in the COW list for the years prior to 1920, a polity must meet two criteria: a population of 500,000; and international recognition from Britain and France. Singer and Small measure international recognition exclusively by the establishment of diplomatic missions from Britain and France. The logic of relying on only these two states is not contested here; as they note, as Britain and France went, "so went the majority."[1] I do, however, object to the practice of relying *exclusively* on the establishment of diplomatic missions as a measurement of international legitimacy from 1816 to 1920.

---

[1] Small and Singer 1982, 40. Given that I do not amend the use of Britain and France as the system's "legitimizers," I am also vulnerable to criticisms of Eurocentrism. Two responses to this criticism can be made. The first is an acknowledgment of the validity of this criticism; however, it is important to note that the revised data set I propose is significantly less Eurocentric than the original data set. Second, it is also essential to consider the feasibility of alternative approaches to revising the COW list. In order to completely avoid, or almost eliminate, Eurocentrism in the data set, one would have to either eliminate the use of legitimizers or select a number of legitimizers from inside and outside Europe. The nature of the issue suggests the usefulness of legitimizers in constructing the list; relying on non-European legitimizers would be a very useful approach to take but would also require linguistic skills beyond the scope of this book.

Debates over the procedures, purposes, and import of diplomatic recognition remain alive among international legal scholars today. These scholars agree, however, on the basic purposes and modes of recognition. They hold that the primary intent of recognition is to identify a state's capacity to engage in international legal activities. Further, they agree that a number of acts can constitute either de jure or de facto recognition.[2]

Singer and Small use the establishment of diplomatic missions "at or above the rank of chargé d'affaires" as their measure of pre-1920 state legitimacy.[3] While the sending of diplomatic representatives—a necessary condition for inclusion in the pre-1920 COW list—is a strong signal to the recipient and other states, it nonetheless falls into the category of implied recognition. This is a relatively uncontroversial form of recognition,[4] but its use as the exclusive measure of pre-1920 legitimacy is problematic for a number of reasons.

First, the practice of sending permanent envoys to foreign courts was a relatively new one in the nineteenth century, especially when compared to other long-standing diplomatic practices.[5] Second, it is difficult to ascertain when and where diplomatic missions were established. Many European and precolonial states did receive permanent envoys from Britain and/or France prior to their appearance on the COW list. For example, an 1801 treaty between France and Algeria permitted the return of the French chargé d'affaires and stated that an Algerian ambassador would be sent to France.[6] Missions such as this one, however, are absent from

[2]Brownlie 1998; Chen 1951; J. Crawford 1979; Lauterpacht 1947.

[3]Small and Singer 1982, 40. The Vienna Convention on Diplomatic Relations states: "Heads of mission are divided into three classes, namely: (a) that of ambassadors or nuncios [representatives of the Holy See] accredited to Heads of State, and other heads of mission of equivalent rank; (b) that of envoys, ministers and internuncios, accredited to Heads of State; (c) that of *chargés d'affaires* accredited to Ministers for Foreign Affairs. Except as concerns precedence and etiquette, there shall be no difference between heads of mission by reason of their class." Quoted in Brownlie 1998, 353.

[4]Chen 1951, 196–98; Lauterpacht 1947, 381–82.

[5]A Mantuan diplomatic agent sent to the Bavarian court in 1341 was reportedly the first permanent diplomatic resident sent from one state to another. Permanent diplomatic agents were not used with any frequency for another century. Further, the practice of establishing permanent diplomatic missions was limited to the Italian peninsula until the late sixteenth century. Alexandrowicz 1967, 185–86; Mattingly 1955, esp. ch. 7.

[6]de Clercq and de Clercq 1864–1917, 1:476–78. The diplomatic missions data set used to construct the COW list of members of the interstate system lists data only for states that are counted as members by COW. While Algeria certainly met COW's population criterion in 1816, it is possible that it did not meet the legitimacy criterion if it did not receive an appropriate British mission at that time. The way in which the diplomatic missions data are presented, however, makes it difficult to verify which states met COW's legitimacy criterion. The diplomatic missions data set, in other words, cannot be used to determine which states might have come close to membership in the interstate system, because it includes only states that meet COW's criterion.

the list of diplomatic missions used to construct the COW list of members of the interstate system.[7]

Third, the establishment of permanent diplomatic missions may have held different meanings for Europeans and non-Europeans, particularly Asians. J. C. Hurewitz asserts that, in Ottoman culture, permanent diplomatic missions were established only in "inferior" or subject states.[8] States subscribing to this belief system might then refuse a permanent diplomatic residence in their state, as the receiving state would be seen as inferior to the state sending the mission. In this instance, important cultural differences may undermine the validity of the Correlates of War coding system.

Fourth, Singer and Small require that members of the interstate system receive diplomatic missions from Britain *and* France. They chose Britain and France as their "legitimizers" because those two states were the major powers of the day and engaged in the most international relations. At the same time, though, not all of their international relations overlapped. Particularly with respect to polities in Asia and Africa, their attentions were divided. Sole French or British recognition of a polity, however, should not exclude it from the roster of nineteenth-century states. Particularly given the limitations of the transportation technology of the times, the criterion should be amended to include states that were recognized by Britain *or* France. It is important to recognize the freedom Britain and France enjoyed by virtue of their power; they did not have to accord recognition to states too weak to withstand the European colonial onslaught. That they did so in many cases—despite the perceived barbarism of these polities— is telling. It indicates that these polities were formidable powers, and potential allies or enemies.

Although this adjustment to the recognition criterion could be challenged on the basis that recognition by two states is better—and stronger—than recognition by only one of the two legitimizers, this new coding creates an opportunity to test claims about the effects of varying levels of recognition. More specifically, it allows more refined evaluation of claims (as discussed in chapters 3 and 4) regarding the relationship between inter-

---

[7]An additional implementation problem undermines the value of the Correlates of War list. Of sixty-nine states that are identified from 1816 to 1919, thirty-one do not appear to meet the requirement of receiving missions from both Britain and France. A number of these states received missions prior to 1816, received missions prior to meeting the population criterion, or shared missions with neighboring states. Several states (particularly those entering the system in the 1910s), however, did not meet even these amended criteria for membership in the system. For the original diplomatic missions data, see Singer and Small 1991. Additional information about the sources of these discrepancies was obtained through personal correspondence with the principal investigators.

[8]Hurewitz 1961.

national legitimacy and state death. For the purposes of this study, the legitimacy measure allows comparison of the survival prospects of states that conclude treaties with one legitimizer, states that conclude treaties with both legitimizers, and states that receive missions from both legitimizers. This more nuanced coding of international legitimacy also could be useful for analyses of the conditions under which states are accorded—or deprived of—international recognition.

The problems with the construction of COW's list of members of the interstate system combine to generate an artificially low number of states, as listed in the Correlates of War. The highest number of state entries (twenty-three) occurs in 1816, when the data set begins. Other high-entry years include 1960 (eighteen), as decolonization occurred; 1991 (eighteen), following the collapse of the Soviet Union; and 1920 (ten). While 1920 is close to the end of the First World War, most of the actual postwar state entries took place from 1917 to 1919. The spike in state entries in 1920 is not due to an actual increase in the number of states but, instead, to the switching of measurement techniques starting with 1920.

These data suggest that the COW list of members of the interstate system is artificially low for the pre-1920 period. This is not surprising, given that it is much easier to meet the criteria for membership in the interstate system after 1920 than before. The data suggest the need for another measure of legitimacy—one that maintains a commitment to finding legally capable states that interacted with like states, but that more accurately reflects the composition of nineteenth-century international relations.

Using Treaties as an Alternative Mode of Recognition

Interstate treaties long predate the use of diplomatic missions in international relations. Furthermore, the conclusion of a bilateral treaty—and especially a treaty of commerce, alliance, or navigation—has historically been taken to be a signal of legitimacy and recognition. It therefore seems advisable to add the conclusion of a treaty of commerce, navigation, or alliance with Britain *or* France to the Correlates of War criteria for membership in the interstate system prior to 1920.[9]

One might argue, though, that there are treaties and there are treaties. As Lauterpacht points out, not all treaties with all parties should be taken to imply recognition. Prudence suggests careful development of criteria to

---

[9]Although it might seem that Britain and France would be disinclined to recognize states they were about to take over, the history of colonization indicates that most of the polities colonized by these imperial powers—even those on the scale of villages, rather than states—had previously received some sort of diplomatic recognition from them.

distinguish among substantive treaties between international actors and conditions imposed on weaker parties through pro forma treaties. This advice is particularly important with regard to treaty relations between colonial powers and precolonial states. Does the conclusion of the Treaty of Amritsar (which settled the boundaries between British and Sikh territory) confer legitimacy on the Sikh state in the same way that the Treaty of Lunéville (in which Spain ceded Louisiana to France) indicates the membership of Spain or France in the interstate system? How seriously can we take treaties concluded between major European powers and polities conquered soon after by them?

This question can be answered in two parts. First, we can examine the content of treaties between European powers and precolonial states. Were these treaties grossly unfair? Were they imposed on leaders of precolonial polities? Second, we can ask whether the Europeans signing these treaties took them seriously. Did they consider the African and Asian leaders who were party to the treaties to be heads of state, or lackeys signing worthless pieces of paper? If treaties and treatment seem equal, then we must include precolonial states (that also meet the population criterion) left out of the original COW list.

Histories of the colonization of Asia and Africa reveal that conquest was often preceded by bargaining, concession, and even vassalage on the part of Europeans. British envoys to the Mughal Empire were required to become vassals to establish trade relations.[10] Similarly, French representatives paid tribute to African states for the protection of commerce. This type of European treatment of and by native princes was reflected in treaties between European powers and precolonial states. For instance, the 1832 treaty between the East India Company and the Rajah of the Punjab explicitly refers to the Punjab as a state, requires British merchants to respect the rajah's authority, and recognizes both the rajah and the British government as having the right to issue passports.[11] Similarly, an 1856 French treaty with Siam, signed prior to Siamese reception of French diplomatic missions, recognizes Siam as a state, grants equal rights of protection to French and Siamese subjects in each other's countries, and states that France and Siam will aid each other's ships in times of distress.[12] As Hedley Bull argues, assumptions that these treaties were universally invalid are suspect; in fact, conclusion of a treaty with a major European power often benefited individual leaders even if it eventually undermined the sovereignty of their polity.[13]

[10]Alexandrowicz 1967, 93–94.
[11]Aitchison 1929–1933, 1:36–38.
[12]de Clercq and de Clercq 1864–1917, 7:138–49.
[13]Bull 1984, 111–12.

It is also useful to examine historical perceptions of these polities and treaties. The nineteenth-century European view of the constitution of the "family of nations" was, in fact, a Eurocentric one. While the existence of other states was acknowledged, they were not originally admitted to the club of civilized nations. Primarily, the distinction between civilized (member) and uncivilized (nonmember) states was drawn along religious lines. Non-Christian states were not considered to be part of the society of nations. "States not so accepted were not (at least in theory) bound by international law, nor were the 'Civilized Nations' bound by it in their behaviour towards them."[14] The Spanish, in particular, seized on religious justification for their conquests in the Americas.[15]

This doctrine, however, met resistance when the constraints imposed by Christian international law met the exigencies of commerce. As far back as the fifteenth century, the question of the validity of treaties between Christian and non-Christian powers had been considered in Rome. Popes and scholars alike agreed that commercial treaties with non-Christian states were valid, as the extension of commerce was the will of God. Opinions on the validity of alliances with non-Christian states were more mixed. Alliances directed against non-Christian powers that did not augment the powers of those non-Christian states were uncontested. But alliances directed against other Christian states were highly controversial.[16]

Certainly with regard to commercial treaties (the vast majority of treaties signed with precolonial states), validity was not questioned. In fact, House of Commons impeachment proceedings against Marquess Wellesley included, among others, accusations of breaking treaties with East Indian states.[17] More recently, in 1960 the International Court of Justice (ICJ) ruled that the 1779 Treaty of Poona, wherein the Maratha ruler granted rights of passage to the Portuguese, was valid, over Indian objections. The court's view was:

> It is sufficient to state that the validity of a treaty concluded as long ago as the last quarter of the eighteenth century, in the conditions then prevailing in the Indian Peninsula, should not be judged upon the basis of practices and procedures which have since developed only gradually. The Marathas themselves regarded the Treaty of 1779 as valid and binding upon them, and gave effect to its provisions. The Treaty is frequently referred to as such in subsequent formal Maratha documents, including the two sanads of 1783 and 1785 which purport to have been issued in pursuance of the Treaty. The Marathas did not at any time cast any doubt upon the validity or binding character of the treaty.[18]

[14]J. Crawford 1979, 13.
[15]Donelan 1984.
[16]Alexandrowicz 1967, 83–90.
[17]James 1998, 66.
[18]Quoted in Alexandrowicz 1967, 5.

The rendering of the ICJ decision strongly suggests that the treaty was, and in fact continued to be, as binding on the Portuguese as it was on the Marathas.[19]

Both the content and the contemporary treatment of French and British treaties with precolonial states in Asia and Africa testify to the import and validity of these treaties. It is also important to remember that European treatment of precolonial African and Asian polities did not necessarily differ substantially from treatment of small European states.[20] International law supports the use of treaties of commerce, alliance, and navigation as a form of recognition. Because the Correlates of War measure of nineteenth-century international recognition relies on a relatively new practice and generates a biased list, the use of treaties as an alternative measure of recognition is justified.

To restate from chapter 2, the alternative criteria for membership in the international system from 1816 to 1919 proposed here are

  (a) population of 500,000 or more, and
  (b) *either* receipt of diplomatic missions from both Britain and France
       or conclusion of a treaty of commerce, alliance, or navigation with
       Britain *or* France

Given the critique just leveled at Singer and Small's coding process, it may seem surprising that the revised criteria include the original coding rules. Despite my objections to the exclusivity of the legitimacy measure used by COW, it is important to remember that states receiving diplomatic missions are also receiving international recognition. If a state receives a diplomatic mission but does not conclude an appropriate treaty with Britain or France, I do not exclude it from the list of members of the interstate system.

This coding scheme yields sixteen additions and twenty-two revisions of dates of entry or exit to the COW list (see tables A.1 and A.2).[21] Any state whose first incarnation is omitted from COW is included in the "added states" list; states included in the "revised states" list have either had a continuous existence from the date of entry to the end date of the

---

[19]Nonetheless, it is important to note that many treaties signed by Britain and France and precolonial states were patently unequal. International lawyers voice mixed opinions on the validity of unequal treaties. As explained below, however, such treaties were generally excluded from the process of identifying "new" states.

[20]Gillard 1984, 90–91.

[21]Data on treaties were collected from Aitchison 1929–1933; Parry 1969; Parry et al. 1970; and de Clercq and de Clercq 1864–1917. Data on population were collected from McEvedy and Jones 1978; Chandler 1987; *Encyclopaedia Britannica* (4th through 12th editions); and primary and archival sources at the Centre d'Archives d'Outre-Mer (Aix-en-Provence, France) and the Oriental & India Office Reading Room of the British Library (London, UK).

TABLE A.1
States Added to the Correlates of War

State	Date of entry	Date of exit
Afghanistan (Cabul)[a]	1816	1879
Algeria (Algiers)[a]	1816	1830
Annam	1875	1884
Bolivia[b]	1836	1836
Burma	1826	1885
Dahomey	1851	1895
Eastern Turkistan	1874	1877
Fouta Toro	1841	1888
Indore[a]	1816	1818
Madagascar	1865	1885
Nagpur[a]	1816	1818
Peru-Bolivia Confederation	1837	1839
Peshwa[a]	1816	1817
Punjab[a]	1816	1846
Sind[a]	1816	1839
Soudan	1886	1886

[a]Denotes that recognition was accorded prior to 1816.
[b]Treaty concluded in 1834 but ratified in 1836.

data set or, if they die at a later time, that death is recorded in the COW list. The results markedly change the face of the Correlates of War list of members of the interstate system from 1816 to 1920.[22]

Between added and revised states, twelve additional states enter the interstate system in 1816. This change raises the original Correlates of War estimate (twenty-three) by 50 percent. Three states—Liberia, Nepal, and

[22]Interestingly, a number of the added states—including Afghanistan, Burma, and Madagascar—exit the interstate system and are later resurrected. This phenomenon suggests a strong sense of boundaries and nationality that preceded and outlasted colonization. This is not to undermine the statehood of those members of the interstate system not reborn. In fact, relations with states like the Peshwa (also known as the Maratha) occupied a good deal of European attention.

TABLE A.2
Revised Entry Dates for States Already in the Correlates
of War

State	New entry date	COW entry date
Bolivia	1840	1848
Bulgaria	1898	1908
China	1842	1860
Colombia	1825	1831
Ecuador	1844	1854
Egypt	1840	1855
El Salvador	1859	1875
Guatemala	1849	1888
Haiti	1838	1859
Hanover[a]	1816	1838
Iran (Persia)[a]	1816	1855
Japan	1855	1860
Korea	1884	1888
Liberia	1869	1920
Mexico	1826	1831
Morocco[a]	1816	1847
Nepal[a]	1816	1920
South Africa	1885	1920
Thailand	1827	1887
Tunis (Tunisia)[a]	1816	1825
Uruguay	1880	1882
Venezuela	1834	1841

[a]Denotes that recognition was accorded prior to 1816.

South Africa—that COW codes as entering the system in 1920 treated
with Britain or France prior to that time. Thus, the 1920 spike in state entries becomes less glaring. Furthermore, the nineteenth-century composition of the system now reflects more accurately the wide array of states
conducting international relations at that time.

A number of the added states seem to have had very short lives. In fact, these states were not short-lived. Censoring in terms of the starting date of the data set (1816) generates the illusion that they were members of the interstate system only very briefly. Algeria, for example, signed its first treaty with a major European power in 1662 and did not exit the system until 1830. Similarly, the first Anglo-Peshwa treaty was concluded in 1789. The impression given of short lives is an artifact of the starting date of the data set. In other cases, states appear to be short-lived because of the recognition criterion. Bolivia, for example, met all the qualifications for statehood except recognition around 1825. Note that because Bolivia and Soudan enter and exit the system in the same year (1836 and 1886, respectively), they were not included in the data analysis in this book.

Added and Revised States

Figures A.1 and A.2 map the location of most of the states added to the COW list of members of the interstate system. The majority of these new entries were located in Asia—particularly South and Southeast Asia—and in Africa.

While some of these states (like Afghanistan and Algeria) were eventually resurrected and will therefore be familiar to most readers, others (like Peshwa and Dahomey) are less well known. It may therefore be useful to discuss briefly the lives and deaths of a few of the states added to the COW list.

The international context surrounding Britain's colonization of South Asia was a complex one. The fall of the Mughal Empire, coupled with perceived threats from Napoleonic France,[23] made negotiations with India's princes quite tricky. Negotiations were also complicated by the fact that the British were entering a fairly institutionalized realm, having to adapt to well-established local modes of trade as well as ceremonies of statehood.[24]

The vacuum left by the Mughals was filled in part by the Marathas.[25] In 1720, Baji Rao I became the Maratha *peshwa* (loosely translated, the prime minister). Under his leadership, Maratha territory expanded considerably, opening up several new opportunities in the north.[26] But following Baji Rao's reign, the Maratha state broke up into several new en-

[23]James 1998, 68–69.
[24]Ray 1995.
[25]For a discussion of the transition from Mughal to Maratha rule, see Gordon 1977.
[26]Cooper 2003, 34–42.

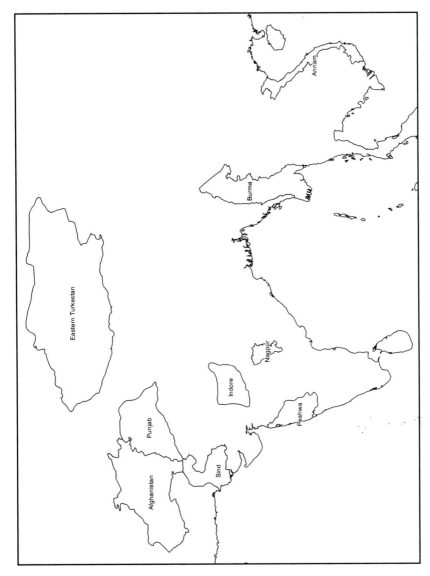

Figure A1. Precolonial States in Asia

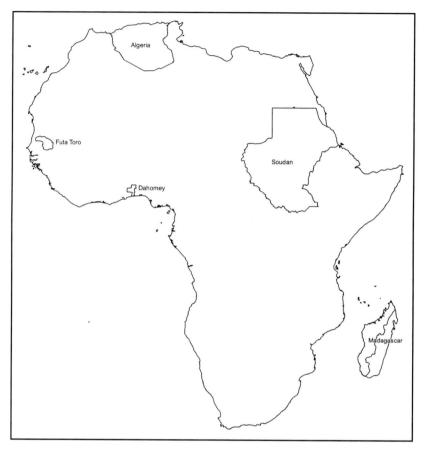

Figure A2. Precolonial States in Africa

tities, including Maratha, Gwalior, Indore, Nagpur, and Baroda. Maratha
was also known as Peshwa, in honor of its ruling family.[27]

Peshwa/Maratha included what is today Mumbai (Bombay), and its
reach covered the west-central coastline of current India. Not surprisingly,
Peshwa as a state was hardly democratic but, rather, "very much a war-
lord state with fortified strongholds and revenue sources well beyond the
depleted heartland."[28] Its leader around the turn of the nineteenth century, Baji Rao II, suffered a serious defeat at the hands of Indore at the

[27]James 1998, 69–70. Similarly, Gwalior is sometimes referred to as "Scindia," Indore as
"Holkar," etc.
[28]Cooper 2003, 86.

Battle of Poona. With British assistance, Baji Rao II was restored during the Second Maratha War of 1803, but once gained, British assistance—and attention—was difficult to lose. Indeed, defeat at the hands of the British weakened not only the Peshwa's enemies but also Peshwa itself; all these states resented the British incursion.[29] It is not clear whether the Pindari,[30] who began to organize attacks against British forces, became troublesome intentionally (because the leaders of Peshwa, Indore, Nagpur, etc. saw use of the Pindari as a means to challenge the British) or simply because the states from which they came were weakening in their ability to control their militaries. Marquess Hastings's response to the Pindari attacks, however, was unequivocal.[31] The Third Maratha War led to the demise of Peshwa as well as nearby states (such as Indore and Nagpur).[32]

Early European relationships with precolonial states in South Asia were governed by trade. The treaties of alliance, commerce, and navigation signed with these states were meant to secure trading rights, and often to secure these rights against European rivals. That these trading relationships dominated South Asia for a very long time preceding formal imperialism is somewhat puzzling for those who argue that colonialism was motivated entirely by the desire to gain raw materials. If these materials could be gained through trade, why pay the costs of governance by imposing colonial rule?[33] As suggested in chapter 3, when imperial rivals arrived on the scene, securing goods through trade meant securing the states that generated these goods. In different parts of South and Southeast Asia, British and French rivalry often led to colonization. For instance, the British in India feared French encroachments from the east and west—as well as the Russians in the north—while the French worried about the British extending their empire east.

Concerns about European rivals were equally lively in Africa, where trading relationships with precolonial states took on a slightly different—but no less consequential—character.[34] In addition to trading for raw materials, the slave trade was particularly active in Africa. A number of precolonial African states that participated in this trade, such as Fouta Toro and Dahomey, could trace their origins to at least the late eighteenth century.[35]

---

[29]James 1998, 70–71; Dupuy and Dupuy 1986, 860–61.

[30]Mercenaries, mostly former soldiers, from the former Maratha states.

[31]Although the British had earlier seriously underestimated these forces, especially those of Indore. Bennell 1965.

[32]James 1998, 71–73; Dupuy and Dupuy 1986, 861–62.

[33]On governance costs, see D. A. Lake 1999; on the transition from informal to formal imperialism, see Gallagher and Robinson 1953.

[34]Ade Ajayi and Oloruntimehin 1976, 208–9.

[35]Flint 1976, 4; Robinson 1975, 185.

The farmers of Fouta Toro supplied the region with grain. Access to the sea and fertile land combined to make the state an influential trading port and agricultural exporter. Fouta Toro was governed by the almamy of Fouta, who was in turn elected by tribal leaders. Accounts describe the almamy's frequent late-eighteenth-century disputes with the French (over trade agreements) at the same time that he waged campaigns to Islamize nearby areas. Fouta Toro was powerful both economically and military, challenging European traders while proselytizing in surrounding regions. But by the turn of the century, the strong state the almamy had governed weakened significantly and was instead ruled by a council of tribal rulers.[36]

Similarly to Fouta, Dahomey was governed by a traditional monarchy, where the king's power was undergirded by chieftains. Dahomian warrior culture and available ports made it a particularly useful partner for Europeans engaged in the slave trade. King Gezo of Dahomey ruled from 1818 to 1858, developing his country's trading prospects and military strength in tandem. When his second son, Gelele, inherited the throne, the British were in the throes of abolitionism. While one could argue that the abolition of the slave trade was as beneficial to British merchants vis-à-vis their European rivals as to would-be slaves, the consequences of British policy were profound for African states like Dahomey.[37]

Forced to develop an agricultural alternative—specifically, the production of palm oil—to its slave-trading foundation, the Dahomian state was undermined. While it is unclear whether the Dahomians ever fully converted from a slave-trading to an agricultural economy, historians agree that there was a significant shift in production and practice.[38] By 1889, when Gelele's son Behanzin had taken over as king, tensions between traditionalists and merchants were becoming acute.[39]

Behanzin took a hard line on Dahomian sovereignty, stating: "The King of Dahomey gives his country to no-one. God has given the white men their share; when God gave everyone his share, it was Dahomey which had this place. The man who comes to take the country of Dahomey without the King's permission will die."[40] In an attempt to shore up his military defenses, he funded purchases of weapons with increased slave trading, giving the French—in whose tacit sphere of influence Behanzin operated—a convenient excuse for conquest in 1892.[41] The death of the

[36]Robinson 1975.
[37]Atmore 1985, 46–47.
[38]Law 1997.
[39]Hargreaves 1985, 264–65.
[40]Quoted in Hargreaves 1985, 264–65.
[41]Hargreaves 1985, 269.

Dahomian state was preceded by Behanzin's surrender in 1894, and cemented by an 1895 treaty of protection.

Discussion of Revisions to COW

The precolonial states in Asia and Africa discussed above possessed long histories, clear governmental structures, and, frequently, strong militaries that were often successful against European foes. The fact that relatively few "new" states are listed in these regions is not necessarily indicative of a general absence of states—or of state deaths. To some extent, this result is an artifact of when the data set begins. British colonization of South Asia, for example, long preceded the Napoleonic Wars; were figure A.1 to be redrawn beginning in 1750, we might see many more states in what is today India. For instance, the British spent a great deal of toil and treasure to subdue Tipu Sultan's Mysore, located in what is today southern India. Beginning in 1767, the British fought four wars with Mysore, the first of which concluded with a treaty of alliance, and the second of which ended in a clear British loss. During this time, Mysore and its "tiger prince" expanded its territory and military might. By the late eighteenth century, the British were able to reverse the balance of power with Mysore. But because Mysore was taken over by the British in 1799, seventeen years prior to the start of the data set used here, it is not included as a new state.

The low number of precolonial states in Africa, on the other hand, may accurately depict historical states in the region. The state as an institution may not have been (or may not be) particularly well suited to Africa, where land has historically been plenty while people have been scarce. Given these conditions, territorially bounded states may be a less efficient form of political organization than one that delineates rights over specific populations.[42] Not surprisingly, most precolonial African states appeared along coastlines, where European explorers were most likely to transplant their native institutions, or where these institutions were likely to emerge in order to facilitate contact with and defense against Europeans.

That almost all the precolonial states listed in tables A.1 and A.2 appear in Asia and Africa also may be misleading. Again, this result is at least partly an artifact of timing. Spain's hold on Latin America was long-standing—indeed, was eroding—by 1816. While I have not conducted a study of the polities that governed Latin America prior to colonization, it is possible that some of them would have qualified as states that would have later died. North of the Spanish Empire, Native American tribes

[42]Herbst 2000.

would likely not be considered states, because of their approach to ownership of territory.[43] But it is important to note that the British and French—as well as the US government—did sign many treaties with these tribes, affording them at least some type of recognition.[44] A data set that went back further in time and relied on a more liberal definition of "state," then, would produce many more precolonial states and revisions to the Correlates of War list all around the globe. My point is that a less conservative coding of states could generate a more extensive list—both geographically and temporally—than what is presented here.

The Correlates of War list of members of the interstate system has served as a foundation for most quantitative international relations scholarship. The founders of COW rendered the discipline an invaluable service. But sound scholarship requires looking backward as well as forward, and by examining the COW list of states, we find serious bias in the construction of the list. The revisions discussed above constitute one among many steps in correcting that bias. Hopefully, the data collected on the states added to COW will allow more generalizable quantitative analysis in the field.

[43]Ronda 1999.
[44]Prucha 1997; Parry 1969; Parry et al. 1970.

Appendix B

Variable Coding

TABLE B.1
Buffer States Based on Diehl & Goertz List of Enduring Rivalries, 1816–1992

Buffer state	Years as buffer	Associated rivalries
Albania	1914–1939	France-Turkey
	1944–1956	Italy-Yugoslavia
		Italy-Turkey
Austria	1919–1938	UK-USSR
	1955–1985	UK-Iraq
		UK-Russia
		UK-Turkey
		France-Germany
		France-Turkey
		Germany-Italy
Austria-Hungary	1876–1918	UK-Russia
		UK-Turkey
		France-Germany
		France-Turkey
		France-China
		Germany-Italy
		Italy-Turkey
		Russia-Turkey
Baden	1830–1870	France-Germany
Bavaria	1830–1871	France-Germany
Belgium	1830–1940	UK-Germany
	1945–1985	UK-Russia (USSR)
		UK-Turkey
		UK-Iraq
		France-Germany
Bhutan	1971–1987	China-India
Bulgaria	1908–1938	UK-Turkey

(*continued*)

TABLE B.1
Continued

Buffer state	Years as buffer	Associated rivalries
	1958–1992	UK-Iraq
		France-Turkey
		Italy-Turkey
		Russia-Turkey
Cambodia	1975–1989	Thailand–North Vietnam (Vietnam)
China	1895–1984	USSR-Japan
Czechoslovakia	1918–1939	UK-Russia (USSR)
	1945–1992	UK-Turkey
		UK-Iraq
		Germany-Italy
Denmark	1887–1934	UK-Germany
	1939–1940	UK-Russia (USSR)
	1945–1985	UK-Turkey
Djibouti	1977–1985	Somalia-Ethiopia
Estonia	1918–1923	UK-USSR
	1939–1940	
Finland	1917–1923	UK-USSR
	1939–1987	
France	1887–1934	UK-Germany
German Democratic Republic	1954–1990	UK-USSR
		UK-Iraq
German Federal Republic	1955–1990	UK-USSR
		UK-Iraq
Germany	1876–1945	UK-Russia (USSR)
	1990–1992	UK-Turkey
		UK-Iraq
		France-Turkey
		France-China

(*continued*)

TABLE B.1
Continued

Buffer state	Years as buffer	Associated rivalries
Greece	1880–1938	France-Turkey
		Italy-Turkey
Hanover	1830–1866	France-Germany
Hesse Electoral	1830–1866	France-Germany
Hesse Grand Ducal	1830–1867	France-Germany
Hungary	1919–1992	UK-Russia (USSR)
		UK-Turkey
		UK-Iraq
		France-Turkey
Italy	1830–1945	France-Germany
		France-Turkey
		France-China
Jordan	1957–1991	Iraq-Israel
		Israel–Saudi Arabia
Korea	1884–1905	Russia-Japan
		China-Japan
Korea, North	1948–1987	USSR-Japan
		China–South Korea
		China-Japan
Korea, South	1948–1984	USSR-Japan
		China-Japan
Laos	1961–1989	Thailand–North Vietnam (Vietnam)
Latvia	1918–1923	UK-Russia (USSR)
	1939–1940	
Lebanon	1948–1986	Syria-Israel
Lithuania	1918–1923	UK-USSR
	1939–1940	UK-Turkey
Luxembourg	1920–1940	UK-USSR

(*continued*)

TABLE B.1
Continued

Buffer state	Years as buffer	Associated rivalries
	1944–1992	UK-Iraq
		France-Germany
		UK-Germany
		UK-Turkey
		Belgium-Germany
Mecklenburg Schwerin	1843–1867	France-Germany
Mongolia	1921–1986	USSR-China
		USSR-Japan
Nepal	1950–1987	China-India
Netherlands	1887–1940	UK-Germany
	1945–1985	UK-Russia (USSR)
		UK-Turkey
		UK-Iraq
		Belgium-Germany
		France-Germany
Norway	1905–1923	UK-Russia (USSR)
	1939–1940	UK-Germany
	1945–1985	
Parma	1851–1860	France-Germany
Poland	1919–1934	UK-USSR
	1945–1992	UK-Turkey
		UK-Iraq
Romania	1878–1985	UK-Russia (USSR)
		UK-Turkey
		France-Turkey
		France-China
		Russia-Turkey
		UK-Iraq

(*continued*)

TABLE B.1
Continued

Buffer state	Years as buffer	Associated rivalries
Russia	1870–1900	France-China
Saudi Arabia	1967–1991	Iraq-Israel
Saxony	1830–1867	France-Germany
Sweden	1876–1923	UK-Russia (USSR)
	1939–1987	USSR-Norway
Switzerland	1830–1945	UK-Turkey
		France-Germany
		France-Turkey
		France-China
		Germany-Italy
Syria	1957–1958	UK-Iraq
	1961–1992	Iraq-Israel
		Israel–Saudi Arabia
Turkey	1958–1992	UK-Iraq
Württemberg	1830–1870	France-Germany
Yugoslavia	1878–1938	UK-Turkey
	1958–1992	UK-Iraq
		France-Turkey
		France-China
		Italy-Turkey

Sources: Compiled from the Correlates of War list of members of the interstate system; Diehl and Goertz 2000; Bartholemew 1955–1959; Bartholemew and Son 1998; Cussans 1998; Muir, Treharne, and Fullard 1965; Palmer 1957; Shepherd 1956; National Geographic Society, 1999.

TABLE B.2
Buffer States Based on Bennett List of Enduring Rivalries, 1816–1992

Buffer state	Years as buffer	Associated rivalries
Albania	1914–1923	Italy–Ottoman Empire (Turkey)
Austria	1919–1938	France-Prussia
	1955–1970	Germany-Russia
Austria-Hungary	1833–1918	Russia-UK
		France-Prussia
		Germany-Russia
		Ottoman Empire–Russia
Baden	1850–1870	France-Prussia
Bavaria	1833–1871	Russia-UK
		France-Prussia
Belgium	1833–1940	Russia-UK
	1945–1955	France-Prussia
		Germany-UK
Bhutan	1971–1992	China-India
Bulgaria	1908–1923	Ottoman Empire–Russia
		Italy–Ottoman Empire
China	1853–1992	Japan-Russia
Czechoslovakia	1918–1939	Germany-Russia
	1945–1970	
Denmark	1833–1940	Russia-UK
	1945–1970	Germany-UK
		Germany-Russia
Djibouti	1977–1992	Ethiopia-Somalia
Estonia	1918–1940	Germany-Russia
Finland	1917–1970	Germany-Russia
France	1899–1942	Germany-UK
	1944–1945	

(continued)

TABLE B.2
Continued

Buffer state	Years as buffer	Associated rivalries
German Democratic Republic	1954–1970	Germany (FRG)-Russia
Germany (Prussia)	1816–1923	Russia-UK
		Ottoman Empire–Russia
Greece	1880–1923	Italy–Ottoman Empire
Hanover	1838–1866	Russia-UK
		France-Prussia
Hesse Electoral	1833–1866	Russia-UK
		France-Prussia
Hesse Grand Ducal	1833–1867	Russia-UK
		France-Prussia
Hungary	1919–1970	Germany-Russia
Italy/Sardinia	1850–1955	France-Prussia
Korea	1884–1905	Japan-Russia
		China-Japan
Korea, North	1948–1992	Japan-Russia
		China-Japan
Korea, South	1949–1992	Japan-Russia
		China-Japan
Latvia	1918–1940	Germany-Russia
Lebanon	1948–1992	Israel-Syria
Lithuania	1918–1940	Germany-Russia
Luxembourg	1920–1940	Germany-UK
	1944–1955	France-Germany
Mecklenburg Schwerin	1843–1867	Russia-UK
		France-Prussia
Modena	1843–1860	Austria-Hungary–Italy
Mongolia	1921–1992	China-Russia
Nepal	1950–1992	China-India

(*continued*)

TABLE B.2
Continued

Buffer state	Years as buffer	Associated rivalries
Netherlands	1833–1940	Russia-UK
	1945–1955	France-Prussia
		Germany-UK
Norway	1905–1907	Russia-UK
Papal States	1843–1860	Austria-Hungary–Italy
Parma	1851–1860	Austria-Hungary–Italy
Poland	1919–1939	Germany-Russia
	1945–1970	
Romania	1878–1970	Germany-Russia
		Ottoman Empire–Russia
		Russia-UK
Saxony	1833–1867	Russia-UK
		France-Prussia
Sweden	1833–1907	Russia-UK
Switzerland	1843–1955	Austria-Hungary–Italy
		France-Prussia
Tuscany	1843–1860	Austria-Hungary–Italy
Württemberg	1850–1870	France-Prussia
Yugoslavia/Serbia	1880–1923	Italy–Ottoman Empire

Sources: Compiled from the Correlates of War list of members of the interstate system; Bartholemew 1955–1959; Bartholemew and Son 1998; Cussans 1998; Muir, Treharne, and Fullard 1965; Palmer 1957; Shepherd 1956; National Geographic Society 1999; Bennett 1996.

TABLE B.3
Imperial Buffer States

Buffer state	Years as buffer	Associated rivalries
Afghanistan	1867–1879	British India–Imperial Russia
Burma	1884–1885	British India–French Empire
Dahomey	1880–1895	British Empire–French Empire
Eastern Turkistan	1874–1877	British India–Imperial Russia
Persia/Iran	1843–1914	British India–Imperial Russia
Siam/Thailand	1885–1904	British India–French Empire

TABLE B.4
Externally Caused Regime and Leader Changes, 1816–1998

State	Year	Notes
Two Sicilies	1821	Austrians intervened to restore Ferdinand IV
Sardinia	1821	Charles Felix's throne secured by Austria
Spain	1823	Spanish monarchy restored by French
Portugal	1833	Quadruple alliance restored Dom Pedro
Baden	1849	Prussians restored Leopold following revolution
Mexico	1864	Juárez overthrown by French in favor of Maximilian
Spain	1870	Prim y Prats assassinated as a result of Franco-Prussian War
France	1870	Empire toppled after loss in Franco-Prussian War
Honduras	1908	Nicaraguan intervention after Honduras lost war
Nicaragua	1909	US intervention to assure free elections
Belgium	1914	Charles, baron de Broqueville, exiled to France
Greece	1915	Entente allies ousted King Constantine
Belgium	1918	Von Falkenhausen's rule ended with German war loss
Germany/Prussia	1918	Wilhelm II abdicated after World War I

(continued)

TABLE B.4
Continued

State	Year	Notes
Bulgaria	1918	Tsar Ferdinand abdicated after World War I
China	1937	Chiang Kai-shek retreated from Japanese
Iran	1941	Reza Shah abdicated after Anglo-Soviet invasion
Iraq	1941	Rashid Ali resigned after British intervention
Hungary	1944	Horthy overthrown by Gestapo
Romania	1944	Antonescu overthrown; new regime in support of Allies
Finland	1944	Ryti resigned in favor of Mannerheim after Soviet invasion
Romania	1947	Soviet-backed regime installed
Nepal	1951	Rebels from India restored Nepali monarchy
Guatemala	1954	US intervention to overthrow Arbenz
Hungary	1956	Rakosi replaced with Gërö by USSR
Hungary	1956	Nagy ousted by USSR
Dominican Republic	1965	US intervention to prevent Bosch's return to power
Czechoslovakia	1968	Dubçek arrested by USSR and taken to Moscow
Czechoslovakia	1968	Svoboda forced to ratify new USSR-installed government
Uganda	1979	Amin removed by Tanzanian invasion, exiled to Libya
Cambodia	1979	Vietnamese intervention installed puppet government
Grenada	1983	US intervention to "protect medical students"
Panama	1990	Noriega deposed by US invasion
Haiti	1994	Cedras resigned under pressure from US/OAS
Sierra Leone	1998	Koroma junta ousted by ECOMOG

Note: there are three post-1875 cases not in the Archigos data set that I include here: Romania 1947, Dominican Republic 1965, and Grenada 1983.

TABLE B.5
State Collapses, 1800–2000

State	Collapse began	Collapse ended
United Province Central America	1838	1838
Colombia	1860	1861
Dominican Republic	1861	1865
Iran	1906	1921
Mexico	1911	1917
Albania	1915	1925
Turkey	1922	1923
Bulgaria	1943	1944
Italy	1945	1945
China	1949	1949
Cuba	1959	1960
Congo Kinshasa	1960	1965
Laos	1961	1973
Cyprus	1963	1968
Dominican Republic	1964	1965
Pakistan	1971	1971
Ethiopia	1974	1975
Cambodia	1975	1976
Lebanon	1975	1990
Afghanistan	1978	1979
Chad	1979	1984
Iran	1979	1979
Nicaragua	1979	1981
Uganda	1985	1986
Liberia	1990	1996
Ethiopia	1991	1991
Somalia	1991	1999

(continued)

TABLE B.5
Continued

State	Collapse began	Collapse ended
USSR	1991	1991
Yugoslavia	1991	1991
Afghanistan	1992	1996
Angola	1992	1993
Bosnia	1992	1995
Congo Kinshasa	1992	1999
Burundi	1993	1996
Rwanda	1993	1994
Comoros	1995	1996
Sierra Leone	1997	1999
Guinea-Bissau	1998	1999
Lesotho	1998	1999

Source: From Polity IV, excluding World War II cases, as noted in chapter 7.

Bibliography

Abente, Diego. 1987. The War of the Triple Alliance: Three Explanatory Models. *Latin American Research Review* 22 (2): 47–69.

Adams, Karen Ruth. 2000. State Survival and State Death: International and Technological Contexts. Ph.D. Dissertation, Department of Political Science, University of California–Berkeley.

———. 2003/4. Attack and Conquer? International Anarchy and the Offense-Defense-Deterrence Balance. *International Security* 28 (3): 45–83.

Ade Ajayi, J. F., and B. O. Oloruntimehin. 1976. West Africa in the Anti-Slave Trade Era. In *The Cambridge History of Africa*, edited by John E. Flint. Cambridge: Cambridge University Press.

Aitchison, C. U. 1929–1933. *A Collection of Treaties, Engagements and Sanads Relating to India and Neighbouring Countries*. 14 vols. Calcutta: Government of India Central Publication Branch.

Alexandrowicz, Charles Henry. 1967. *An Introduction to the History of the Law of Nations in the East Indies: 16th, 17th, and 18th Centuries*. Oxford: Clarendon.

Ali, Omar. 1993. *Crisis in the Arabian Gulf: An Independent Iraqi View*. Westport, CT: Praeger.

Atkins, G. Pope, and Larman C. Wilson. 1998. *The Dominican Republic and the United States: From Imperialism to Transnationalism*. Athens: University of Georgia Press.

Atmore, A. E. 1985. Africa on the Eve of Partition. In *The Cambridge History of Africa*, edited by Roland Oliver and G. N. Sanderson. Cambridge: Cambridge University Press.

Axelrod, Robert. 1984. *The Evolution of Cooperation*. New York: Basic Books.

———. 1986. An Evolutionary Approach to Norms. *American Political Science Review* 80 (4): 1095–1111.

Axelrod, Robert, and Robert O. Keohane. 1993. Achieving Cooperation under Anarchy: Strategies and Institutions. In *Neorealism and Neoliberalism: The Contemporary Debate*, edited by David A. Baldwin. New York: Columbia University Press.

Baker, James A. 1995. *The Politics of Diplomacy*. New York: G. P. Putnam's Sons.

Baram, Amatzia. 1993. The Iraqi Invasion of Kuwait: Decision-Making in Baghdad. In *Iraq's Road to War*, edited by Amatzia Baram and Barry Rubin. New York: St. Martin's Press.

Barbieri, Katherine. 2002. *The Liberal Illusion: Does Trade Promote Peace?* Ann Arbor: University of Michigan Press.

Barbieri, Katherine, and R. A. Peters. 2003. Measure for Mis-measure: A Response to Gartzke and Li. *Journal of Peace Research* 40 (6): 713–19.

Bartholemew, John, ed. 1955–1959. *The Times Atlas of the World*. Vol. 3. London: Times Publishing Company.

Bartholemew, John, and Son, eds. 1998. *The Times Atlas of the World, Eighth Comprehensive Edition.* New York: Times Books.

Beck, Nathaniel, Jonathan Katz, and Richard Tucker. 1998. Taking Time Seriously: Time-Series-Cross-Section Analysis with a Binary Dependent Variable. *American Journal of Political Science* 42 (4): 1260–88.

Békés, Csaba, Malcolm Byrne, and János M. Rainer, eds. 2002. *The 1956 Hungarian Revolution: A History in Documents, a National Security Archive Cold War Reader.* New York: Central European University Press.

Bennell, A. S. 1965. Factors in the Marquis Wellesley's Failure against Holkar, 1804. *Bulletin of the School of Oriental and African Studies, University of London* 28 (3): 553–81.

Bennett, D. Scott. 1996. Security, Bargaining, and the End of Interstate Rivalry. *International Studies Quarterly* 40 (2): 157–84.

———. 1998. Integrating and Testing Models of Rivalry Duration. *American Journal of Political Science* 42 (4): 1200–1232.

Bennett, D. Scott, and Allan Stam. 2000. EUGene: A Conceptual Manual. *International Interactions* 26:179–204.

Bennett, Robert William, and Joseph Zitomersky. 1982. The Delimitation of International Diplomatic Systems, 1816–1970: The Correlates of War Project's Systems Reconsidered. In *On Making Use of History: Research and Reflections from Lund,* edited by Joseph Zitomersky. Lund: Scandinavian University Books.

Bensahel, Nora. 2006. Mission Not Accomplished: What Went Wrong with Iraqi Reconstruction. *Journal of Strategic Studies* 29 (3): 453–73.

Biddle, Stephen. 1999. Testing Offense-Defense Theory: The Second Battle of the Somme, March 21 to April 9, 1918. Paper read at the 1999 meeting of the American Political Science Association.

———. 2004. *Military Power: Explaining Victory and Defeat in Modern Battle.* Princeton, NJ: Princeton University Press.

Black, Jan Knippers. 1986. *The Dominican Republic: Politics and Development in an Unsovereign State.* Boston: Allen & Unwin.

Blainey, Geoffrey. 1988. *The Causes of War.* 3rd ed. London: MacMillan Press.

Borgwardt, Elizabeth. 2005. *A New Deal for the World: America's Vision for Human Rights.* Cambridge, MA: The Belknap Press of Harvard University Press.

Box-Steffensmeier, Janet M., and Bradford S. Jones. 2004. *Event History Model: A Guide for Social Scientists.* New York: Cambridge University Press.

Brands, H. W. 1995. *The Wages of Globalism: Lyndon Johnson and the Limits of American Power.* New York: Oxford University Press.

Bremer, Stuart A., and Faten Ghosn. 2003. Defining States: Reconsiderations and Recommendations. *Conflict Management and Peace Science* 20 (1): 21–41.

Brooks, Stephen G. 1999. The Globalization of Production and the Changing Benefits of Conquest. *Journal of Conflict Resolution* 43 (5): 646–70.

———. 2005. *Producing Security: Multinational Corporations, Globalization, and the Changing Calculus of Conflict.* Princeton, NJ: Princeton University Press.

Brownlie, Ian. 1998. *Principles of Public International Law.* 5th ed. Oxford: Clarendon Press.

Bueno de Mesquita, Bruce. 1978. Systemic Polarization and the Occurrence and Duration of War. *Journal of Conflict Resolution* 22 (2): 241–68.

Bueno de Mesquita, Bruce, and David Lalman. 1992. *War and Reason: Domestic and International Imperatives.* New Haven, CT: Yale University Press.

Bueno de Mesquita, Bruce, James D. Morrow, Randolph M. Siverson, and Alastair Smith. 1999. An Institutional Explanation of the Democratic Peace. *American Political Science Review* 93 (4): 791–807.

Bueno de Mesquita, Bruce, Alastair Smith, Randall M. Siverson, and James D. Morrow. 2003. *The Logic of Political Survival.* Cambridge, MA: MIT Press.

Bull, Hedley and Adam Watson. 1984. *The Expansion of International Society.* New York: Oxford University Press.

Bulloch, John, and Harvey Morris. 1991. *Saddam's War: The Origins of the Kuwait Conflict and the International Response.* London: Farber and Farber.

Burr, Robert N. 1955. The Balance of Power in Nineteenth-Century South America: An Exploratory Essay. *Hispanic American Historical Review* 35 (1): 37–60.

Calder, Bruce J. 1984. *The Impact of Intervention: The Dominican Republic during the U.S. Occupation of 1916–1924.* Austin: University of Texas Press.

Carr, William. 1991. *The Origins of the Wars of German Unification.* London: Longman.

Carrere d'Encausse, Helene. 1994. Systematic Conquest, 1865–1884. In *Central Asia: 130 Years of Russian Dominance, a Historical Overview,* edited by Edward Allworth. Durham, NC: Duke University Press.

Casey, William M., and Roger B. Burton. 1982. Training Children to Be Consistently Honest through Verbal Self-Instructions. *Child Development* 53 (4): 911–19.

Central Intelligence Agency. 2006. *World Factbook 2006.* Washington, DC: Supt. of Docs., U.S. GPO.

Chandler, Tertius. 1987. *Four Thousand Years of Urban Growth.* Lewiston/Queenston: St. David's University Press.

Chaudhry, Kiren Aziz. 1991. On the Way to Market: Economic Liberalization and Iraq's Invasion of Kuwait. *Middle East Report* (170): 14–23.

Chay, John, and Thomas E. Ross, eds. 1986. *Buffer States in World Politics.* Boulder, CO: Westview Press.

Chen, Ti-Chiang. 1951. *The International Law of Recognition.* London: Stevens & Sons.

Chiozza, Giacomo, and Hein Goemans. 2004. International Conflict and the Tenure of Leaders: Is War Still *Ex Post* Inefficient? *American Journal of Political Science* 48 (3): 604–19.

Cioffi-Revilla, Claudia. 1998. The Political Uncertainty of Interstate Rivalries: A Punctuated Equilibrium Model. In *The Dynamics of Enduring Rivalries,* edited by Paul F. Diehl. Urbana: University of Illinois Press.

Clapham, Christopher. 1996. *Africa and the International System: The Politics of State Survival.* Cambridge: Cambridge University Press.

Clawson, Patrick. 1993. Iraq's Economy and International Sanctions. In *Iraq's Road to War,* edited by Amatzia Baram and Barry Rubin. New York: St. Martin's Press.

Cobban, Alfred. 1969. *The Nation-State and National Self-Determination.* London: Collins.

Cooley, John K. 1991. Pre-war Gulf Diplomacy. *Survival* 33 (2): 125–39.

Cooper, John Milton. 2001. *Breaking the Heart of the World: Woodrow Wilson and the Fight for the League of Nations.* New York: Cambridge University Press.

Cooper, Randolph G. S. 2003. *The Anglo-Maratha Campaigns and the Contest for India: The Struggle for Control of the South Asian Military Economy.* Cambridge and New York: Cambridge University Press.

Copeland, Dale C. 1996. Neorealism and the Myth of Bipolar Stability: Toward a New Dynamic Realist Theory of Major War. *Security Studies* 5 (3): 29–89.

———. 2000. *The Origins of Major War.* Ithaca, NY: Cornell University Press.

Crawford, James. 1979. *The Creation of States in International Law.* Oxford: Clarendon Press.

Crawford, Neta. 1993. Decolonization as an International Norm. In *Emerging Norms of Justified Intervention: A Collection of Essays from the American Academy of Arts and Sciences,* edited by Laura W. Reed and Carl Kaysen. Cambridge, MA: Committee on International Security Studies, American Academy of Arts and Sciences.

Crystal, Jill. 1992. *Kuwait: The Transformation of an Oil State.* Boulder, CO: Westview Press.

Curzon, George N. 1892. *Persia and the Persian Question.* 2 vols. New York: Barnes & Noble.

Cussans, Thomas, et al., eds. 1998. *The Times Atlas of European History.* 2nd ed. London: Times Books.

Dallek, Robert. 1995. *Franklin D. Roosevelt and American Foreign Policy, 1932–1945.* New York: Oxford University Press.

Davies, Norman. 1982. *God's Playground, a History of Poland.* New York: Columbia University Press.

de Clercq, Alexandre, and Jules de Clercq. 1864–1917. *Recueil de Traités de la France.* 23 vols. Paris: Ministre des Affaires Étrangères.

Diamond, Jared. 1997. *Guns, Germs and, Steel: The Fates of Human Societies.* New York: W. W. Norton.

Diehl, Paul, and Gary Goertz. 2000. *War and Peace in International Rivalry.* Ann Arbor: University of Michigan Press.

Donelan, Michael. 1984. Spain and the Indies. In *The Expansion of International Society,* edited by Hedley Bull and Adam Watson. Oxford: Clarendon Press.

Draper, Theodore. 1968. *The Dominican Revolt: A Case Study in American Policy.* New York: Commentary.

Dupuy, R. Ernest, and Trevor N. Dupuy. 1986. *The Encyclopedia of Military History: From 3500 B.C. to the Present.* 2nd revised ed. New York: Harper & Row.

Edelstein, David M. 2004. Occupational Hazards: Why Military Occupations Succeed or Fail. *International Security* 29 (1): 49–91.

Ekiert, Grzegorz. 1996. *The State against Society: Political Crises and Their Aftermath in East Central Europe*. Princeton, NJ: Princeton University Press.

Emerson, Rupert. 1967. *From Empire to Nation: The Rise to Self-Assertion of Asian and African Peoples*. Cambridge, MA: Harvard University Press.

Esty, Daniel C., Jack A. Goldstone, Ted Robert Gurr, Pamela T. Surko, and Alan N. Unger. 1995. State Failure Task Force Report. Working paper, University of Maryland.

Eversley, G. Shaw-Lefevre. 1915. *The Partitions of Poland*. London: T. F. Unwin.

Fabry, Mikulas. 2005. International Society and the Establishment of New States: The Practice of State Recognition in the Era of National Self-Determination. Ph.D. Dissertation, Department of Political Science, University of British Columbia, Vancouver.

Fallows, James. 2004. Blind into Baghdad. *Atlantic Monthly,* Jan./Feb.

Fazal, Tanisha M. 2006. The Informalization of Interstate War. Paper read at the annual meeting of the Midwest Political Science Association, Chicago.

Fearon, James D. 1994. Signaling versus the Balance of Power and Interests: An Empirical Test of a Crisis Bargaining Model. *Journal of Conflict Resolution* 38 (2): 236–69.

———. 1995. Rationalist Explanations for War. *International Organization* 49 (3): 379–414.

———. 1997. Signaling Foreign Policy Interests: Tying Hands versus Sinking Costs. *Journal of Conflict Resolution* 41 (3): 68–90.

———. 1998. Bargaining, Enforcement, and International Cooperation. *International Organization* 52 (2): 269–305.

Fearon, James D., and David D. Laitin. 2003. Ethnicity, Insurgency, and Civil War. *American Political Science Review* 97 (1): 75–90.

———. 2004. Neotrusteeship and the Problem of Weak States. *International Security* 28 (4): 5–43.

Feis, Herbert. 1967. *Churchill-Roosevelt-Stalin: The War They Waged and the Peace They Sought*. Princeton, NJ: Princeton University Press.

Felten, Peter G. 1996. The Path to Dissent: Johnson, Fulbright, and the 1965 Intervention in the Dominican Republic. *Presidential Studies Quarterly* 26 (4): 1009–18.

———. 1999. Yankee, Go Home and Take Me with You: Lyndon Johnson and the Dominican Republic. In *The Foreign Policies of Lyndon Johnson: Beyond Vietnam,* edited by H. W. Brands. College Station: Texas A&M University Press.

Filkins, Dexter. 2004. US Transfers Power to Iraq 2 Days Early. *New York Times,* June 29, A1.

Fineman, Mark. 1989. Trade Dispute with India Brings Economic Crisis: Nepalese Bracing for a "Grim Year." *Los Angeles Times,* April 14, 18.

Finnemore, Martha. 2003. *The Purpose of Intervention: Changing Beliefs about the Use of Force*. Ithaca, NY: Cornell University Press.

Finnemore, Martha, and Kathryn Sikkink. 1998. International Norm Dynamics and Political Change. *International Organization* 52 (4): 887–917.

Flint, John E. 1976. Introduction. In *The Cambridge History of Africa,* edited by John E. Flint. Cambridge: Cambridge University Press.

Florini, Ann. 1996. The Evolution of International Norms. *International Studies Quarterly* 40 (3): 363–89.

Fortna, Virginia Page. 2004. Where Have All the Victories Gone? War Outcomes in Historical Perspective. Paper read at Conference on Order and Violence, Yale University.

Franck, Thomas M., and Edward Weisband. 1971. *Word Politics: Verbal Strategy among the Superpowers.* New York UniversityCenter for International Studies, Studies in Peaceful Change. New York: Oxford University Press.

Fravel, M. Taylor. 2005. Regime Insecurity and International Cooperation: Explaining China's Compromise in Territorial Disputes. *International Security* 30 (2): 46–83.

Freedman, Lawrence, and Efraim Karsh. 1993. *The Gulf Conflict, 1990–1: Diplomacy and War in the New World Order.* Princeton, NJ: Princeton University Press.

Fuller, Stephen M., and Graham A. Cosmas. 1974. *Marines in the Dominican Republic, 1916–1924.* Washington, DC: History and Museums Division Headquarters, US Marine Corps.

Gallagher, John, and Ronald Robinson. 1953. The Imperialism of Free Trade. *Economic History Review* 6 (1): 1–15.

Gartzke, Erik, and Quan Li. 2003a. All's Well That Ends Well: A Reply to Oneal, Barbieri & Peters. *Journal of Peace Research* 40 (6): 727–32.

———. 2003b. Measure for Measure: Concept Operationalization and the Trade-Interdependence-Conflict Debate. *Journal of Peace Research* 40 (5): 553–71.

Gartzke, Erik, and Michael Simon. 1999. "Hot Hands": A Critical Analysis of Enduring Rivalries. *Journal of Politics* 61 (3): 777–98.

Gause, F. Gregory, III. 2001. Iraq and the Gulf War: Decision-Making in Baghdad. CIAO-net. New York (online articles and working papers).

Gellner, Ernest. 1983. *Nations and Nationalism.* Ithaca, NY: Cornell University Press.

Gibler, Douglas M., and Meredith Sarkees. 2004. Measuring Alliances: The Correlates of War Formal Interstate Alliance Data Set, 1816–2000. *Journal of Peace Research* 41 (2): 211–22.

Gifford, Prosser, and William Roger Louis, eds. 1971. *France and Britain in Africa: Imperial Rivalry and Colonial Rule.* New Haven, CT: Yale University Press.

Gilderhus, Mark T. 1986. *Pan American Visions: Woodrow Wilson in the Western Hemisphere, 1913–1921.* Tucson: University of Arizona Press.

Gillard, David. 1984. British and Russian Relations with Asian Governments in the Nineteenth Century. In *The Expansion of International Society,* edited by Hedley Bull and Adam Watson. Oxford: Clarendon Press.

Gilpin, Robert. 1981. *War and Change in World Politics.* New York: Cambridge University Press.

Glaser, Charles L., and Chaim Kaufmann. 1998. What Is the Offense-Defense Balance and Can We Measure It? *International Security* 22 (4): 44–82.

Gleditsch, Kristian S., and Michael D. Ward. 1999. A Revised List of Independent States since the Congress of Vienna. *International Interactions* 25 (4): 393–413.

Glennon, John P., ed. 1990. *Foreign Relations of the United States, 1955–1957.* Vol. XXV: Eastern Europe. Washington, DC: US Government Printing Office.

Gluchowski, L. W. 1995. Khrushchev, Gomulka, and the "Polish October." *Cold War International History Project Bulletin* 5:1, 38–49.

Goemans, H. E. 2000. *War and Punishment: The Causes of War Termination and the First World War.* Princeton, NJ: Princeton University Press.

———. 2003. Four Rivers, Gaul, Natural Frontiers or the Hexagon: What and Where Is France. Typescript, Duke University.

Goemans, H. E., Kristian Skrede Gleditsch, Giacomo Chiozza, and Jinhee L Choung. 2004. Archigos: A Database on Political Leaders. Typescript, University of Rochester and University of California San Diego.

Goertz, Gary, and Paul F. Diehl. 1993. Enduring Rivalries: Theoretical Constructs and Empirical Patterns. *International Studies Quarterly* 37:147–91.

———. 1995. The Initiation and Termination of Enduring Rivalries: The Impact of Political Shocks. *American Journal of Political Science* 39 (1): 30–52.

Gordon, Michael R., and General Bernard E. Trainor. 2006. *Cobra II: The Inside Story of the Invasion and Occupation of Iraq.* New York: Pantheon Books.

Gordon, Stewart N. 1977. The Slow Conquest: Administrative Integration of Malwa into the Maratha Empire, 1720–1760. *Modern Asian Studies* 11 (1): 1–40.

Granville, Johanna C. 2004. *The First Domino: International Decision Making during the Hungarian Crisis of 1956.* College Station: Texas A&M Press.

Greaves, Rose Louise. 1959. *Persia and the Defence of India, 1884–1892: A Study in the Foreign Policy of the Third Marquis of Salisbury.* London: Athlone Press.

———. 1965a. British Policy in Persia, 1892–1893—II. *Bulletin of the School of Oriental and African Studies, University of London* 28 (2): 284–307.

———. 1965b. British Policy in Persia, 1892–1903—I. *Bulletin of the School of Oriental and African Studies, University of London* 38 (1): 34–60.

———. 1968a. Some Aspects of the Anglo-Russian Convention and Its Working in Persia, 1907–1914—II. *Bulletin of the School of Oriental and African Studies, University of London* 31 (2): 290–308.

———. 1968b. Some Aspects of the Anglo-Russian Convention and Its Working in Persia, 1907–1914—I. *Bulletin of the School of Oriental and African Studies, University of London* 31 (1): 69–91.

———. 1986c. Sistan in British Indian Frontier Policy. *Bulletin of the School of Oriental and African Studies, University of London* 49 (1): 90–102.

Grimes, Barbara F. 1996–1999. *Ethnologue: Languages of the World.* 13th. SIL International. Available from http://www.sil.org/ethnologue/.

Gurr, Ted Robert. 1990. Polity II: Political Structures and Regime Change, 1800–1986. Inter-university Consortium for Political and Social Research (ICPSR).

Gurr, Ted Robert, Monty Marshall, and Keith Jaggers. Polity IV Data Set. Available from http://www.bsos.umd.edu/cidcm/inscr/polity/index.htm.

Hale, Henry E. 2004. Divided We Stand: Institutional Sources of Ethnofederal State Survival and Collapse. *World Politics* 56 (2): 165–93.

Hargreaves, J. D. 1985. Western Africa, 1886–1905. In *The Cambridge History of Africa,* edited by Roland Oliver and G. N. Sanderson. Cambridge: Cambridge University Press.

Hassan, Hamdi A. 1999. *The Iraqi Invasion of Kuwait: Religion, Identity and Otherness in the Analysis of War and Conflict.* London: Pluto Press.

Heard-Bay, Frauke. 1982. *From Trucial States to United Arab Emirates: A Society in Transition.* London and New York: Longman.

Herbst, Jeffrey. 1989. The Creation and Maintenance of National Boundaries in Africa. *International Organization* 43 (4): 673–92.

———. 1990. War and the State in Africa. *International Security* 14 (4): 117–39.

———. 1996–1997. Responding to State Failure in Africa. *International Security* 21 (3): 120–44.

———. 2000. *States and Power in Africa: Comparative Lessons in Authority and Control.* Edited by Jack L. Snyder, Mark Trachtenberg, and Fareed Zacharia. Princeton Studies in International History and Politics. Princeton, NJ: Princeton University Press.

Hertslet, Lewis, and Edward Hertslet. 1840–1925. *Hertslet's Commercial Treaties.* 31 vols. London: Butterworths.

Hoopes, Townsend, and Douglas B. Brinkley. 1997. *FDR and the Creation of the UN.* New Haven, CT: Yale University Press.

Hopf, Ted. 1991. Polarity, the Offense-Defense Balance, and War. *American Political Science Review* 85 (2): 475–93.

Howes, Dustin Ellis. 2003. When States Choose to Die: Reassessing Assumptions about What States Want. *International Studies Quarterly* 47 (4): 669–92.

Hui, Victoria Tin-Bor. 2005. *War and State Formation in Ancient China and Early Modern Europe.* New York: Cambridge University Press.

Hurewitz, J. C. 1961. Ottoman Diplomacy and the European State System. *Middle East Journal* 15 (2): 141–52.

Huth, Paul, and Bruce Russett. 1984. What Makes Deterrence Work: Cases from 1900 to 1980. *World Politics* 36 (4): 496–526.

———. 1988. Deterrence Failure and Crisis Escalation. *International Studies Quarterly* 32 (1): 29–46.

Ikenberry, G. John. 2001. *After Victory: Institutions, Strategic Restraint, and the Rebuilding of Order after Major Wars.* Princeton, NJ: Princeton University Press.

The Illusion of Omnipotence. 1965. Editorial, *New York Times,* May 6, 38.

Ingram, Edward. 1973. An Aspiring Buffer State: Anglo-Persian Relations in the Third Coalition, 1804–1807. *Historical Journal* 16 (3): 509–33.

Israel, Fred, ed. 1967–1980. *Major Peace Treaties of Modern History, 1648–1967.* New York: Chelsea House Publishers.

Jackson, Robert H. 1990. *Quasi-States: Sovereignty, International Relations, and the Third World.* Cambridge: Cambridge University Press.

Jaggers, Keith, and Ted Robert Gurr. Polity III: Regime Change and Political Authority, 1800–1994. 2nd ICPSR version. Ann Arbor, MI: Inter-university Consortium for Political and Social Research.

James, Lawrence. 1998. *Raj: The Making and Unmaking of British India.* New York: St. Martin's Press.

Jenkins, David B. 1986. The History of Afghanistan as a Buffer State. In *Buffer States in World Politics*, edited by John Chay and Thomas E. Ross. Boulder, CO: Westview.

Jervis, Robert. 1978. Cooperation under the Security Dilemma. *World Politics* 30 (2): 167–214.

Johnson, Lyndon Baines. 1964–1969. *Public Papers of the Presidents: Lyndon B. Johnson.* Washington, DC: US Government Printing Office.

———. 1971. *The Vantage Point: Perspectives of the Presidency, 1963–1969.* New York: Holt, Rinehart and Winston.

Jones, Robert A. 1990. *The Soviet Concept of "Limited Sovereignty" from Lenin to Gorbachev: The Brezhnev Doctrine.* London: Macmillan.

Kaplan, Herbert H. 1962. *The First Partition of Poland.* New York: Columbia University Press.

Karpiński, Jakub. 1982. *Countdown, the Polish Upheavals of 1956, 1968, 1970, 1976, 1980.* New York: Karz Publishers.

Karsh, Efraim, and Inari Rautsi. 1991. Why Saddam Hussein Invaded Kuwait. *Survival* 33 (1): 18–30.

Karski, Jan. 1985. *The Great Powers & Poland, 1919–1945: From Versailles to Yalta.* New York: University Press of America.

Kashani-Sabet, Firoozeh. 1999. *Frontier Fictions: Shaping the Iranian Nation, 1804–1946.* Princeton, NJ: Princeton University Press.

Katz, Friedrich. 1981. *The Secret War in Mexico: Europe, the United States, and the Mexican Revolution.* Chicago: University of Chicago Press.

Kaysen, Carl. 1990. Is War Obsolete? A Review Essay. *International Security* 14 (4): 42–64.

Kazemzadeh, Firuz. 1968. *Russia and Britain in Persia, 1864–1914: A Study in Imperialism.* New Haven, CT: Yale University Press.

Kelsey, Carl. 1922. The American Intervention in Haiti and the Dominican Republic. *Annals of the American Academy of Political and Social Science* C (189): 113–202.

Kemp-Welch, Tony. 1996. Khrushchev's "Secret Speech" and Polish Politics: The Spring of 1956. *Europe-Asia Studies* 48 (2): 181–206.

Keohane, Robert O. 1984. *After Hegemony: Cooperation and Discord in the World Political Economy.* Princeton, NJ: Princeton University Press.

Khrushchev, Nikita Sergeevich. 1974. *Khrushchev Remembers: The Last Testament.* Translated by Strobe Talbott. 1st ed. Boston: Little Brown.

King, Gary, and Langche Zeng. 2001a. Improving Forecasts of State Failure. *World Politics,* 53(4): 623–58.

———. 2001b. Logistic Regression in Rare Events Data. *Political Analysis* 9 (2): 137–63.

Kissinger, Henry. 1957. *A World Restored: Metternich, Castlereagh and the Problems of Peace, 1812–22.* Boston: Houghton Mifflin.

Klein, Ira. 1971. The Anglo-Russian Convention and the Problem of Central Asia, 1907–1914. *Journal of British Studies* 11 (1): 126–47.

———. 1972. British Intervention in the Persian Revolution, 1905–1909. *Historical Journal* 15 (4): 731–52.

Knock, Thomas J. 1992. *To End All Wars: Woodrow Wilson and the Quest for a New World Order.* New York: Oxford University Press.

Korman, Sharon. 1996. *The Right of Conquest: The Acquisition of Territory by Force in International Law and Practice.* Oxford: Clarendon Press.

Kramer, Mark. 1996a. The "Malin Notes" on the Crises in Hungary and Poland, 1956. *Cold War International History Project Bulletin* 8/9:385–410.

———. 1996b. New Evidence on Soviet Decision-Making and the 1956 Polish and Hungarian Crises. *Cold War International History Project Bulletin* 8/9: 358–84.

———. 1998. The Soviet Union and the 1956 Crises in Hungary and Poland: Reassessments and New Findings. *Journal of Contemporary History* 33 (2): 163–214.

Krasner, Stephen D. 1976. State Power and the Structure of International Trade. *World Politics* 28 (3): 317–47.

———. 1999. *Sovereignty: Organized Hypocrisy.* Princeton, NJ: Princeton University Press.

———. 2004. Sharing Sovereignty: New Institutions for Collapsed and Failing States. *International Security* 29 (2): 85–120.

Lake, David A. 1992. Powerful Pacifists: Democratic States and War. *American Political Science Review* 86 (1): 24–37.

———. 1999. *Entangling Relations: American Foreign Policy in Its Century.* Princeton, NJ: Princeton University Press.

———. 2003. The New Sovereignty in International Relations. *International Studies Review* 5 (3): 303–23.

Lauterpacht, H. 1947. *Recognition in International Law.* Cambridge: Cambridge University Press.

Law, Robin. 1997. The Politics of Commercial Transition: Factional Conflict in Dahomey in the Context of the Ending of the Atlantic Slave Trade. *Journal of African History* 38 (2): 213–33.

Lawler, Daniel, and Carolyn Yee, eds. 2005. *Foreign Relations of the United States, 1964–1968: Dominican Republic; Cuba; Haiti; Guyana.* Edited by Edward C. Keefer. Vol. XXXII, *Foreign Relations of the United States.* Washington, DC: US Government Printing Office.

Lawson, Fred H. 2001. Rethinking the Iraqi Invasion of Kuwait. *Review of International Affairs* 1 (1): 1–20.

Leeds, Brett Ashley. 2003. Do Alliances Deter Aggression? The Influence of Military Alliances on the Initiation of Militarized Interstate Disputes. *American Journal of Political Science* 47 (3): 427–39.

Leeds, Brett Ashley, Andrew G. Long, and Sarah McLaughlin Mitchell. 2000. Reevaluating Alliance Reliability: Specific Threats, Specific Promises. *Journal of Conflict Resolution* 44 (5): 686–99.

Leffler, Melvyn P. 1992. *A Preponderance of Power: National Security, the Truman Administration, and the Cold War.* Stanford, CA: Stanford University Press.

Legro, Jeffrey W. 2000. Whence American Internationalism. *International Organization* 54 (2): 253–89.

Lemke, Douglas. 2006. Power Politics and the Violent Creation of Order. Typescript, Pennsylvania State University.

Leoni, Raúl. 1965. View from Caracas. *Foreign Affairs* 43 (4): 639–46.

Levy, Jack S. 1984. The Offensive/Defensive Balance of Military Technology: A Theoretical and Historical Analysis. *International Studies Quarterly* 28 (2): 219–38.

————. 1989a. The Causes of War: A Review of Theories and Evidence. In *Behavior, Society, and Nuclear War,* edited by Philip Tetlock, Jo L. Husbands, Robert Jervis, Paul C. Stern, and Charles Tilly. New York: Oxford University Press.

————. 1989b. The Diversionary Theory of War: A Critique. In *Handbook of War Studies,* edited by Manus I. Midlarsky. London: Unwin-Hyman.

Liberman, Peter. 1996. *Does Conquest Pay? The Exploitation of Occupied Industrial Societies.* Princeton, NJ: Princeton University Press.

Link, Arthur Stanley, ed. 1966. *The Papers of Woodrow Wilson.* Princeton, NJ: Princeton University Press.

Litván, György. 1996. *The Hungarian Revolution of 1956: Reform, Revolt, and Repression, 1953–1963.* New York: Longman.

Lord, Robert H. 1925. The Third Partition of Poland. *The Slavonic Review* 3 (9): 481–98.

Love, Eric T. 2004. *Race over Empire: Racism and US Imperialism, 1865–1900.* Chapel Hill: University of North Carolina Press.

Lowenthal, Abraham F. 1972. *The Dominican Intervention.* Cambridge, MA: Harvard University Press.

Luard, Evan. 1982. *A History of the United Nations.* Vol. I, *The Years of Western Domination, 1945–1955.* London: Macmillan Press.

Lukowski, Jerzy. 1999. *The Partitions of Poland: 1772, 1793, 1795.* London and New York: Longman.

Lumpkin, John J., and Dafna Linzer. 2003. U.S. Officials Were Reluctant to Call Troops Occupiers. *Associated Press,* Nov. 28.

MacDonald, Paul K. 2006. Hierarchic Realism and Imperial Rule in International Politics. Ph.D. Dissertation, Department of Political Science, Columbia University, New York.

Machcewicz, Pawel. 1997. Intellectuals and Mass Movements: The Study of Political Dissent in Poland in 1956. *Contemporary European History* 6 (3): 361–82.

Mackinder, Halford J. 1962. *Democratic Ideals and Reality.* New York: W. W. Norton.

Malia, Joseph. 1986. Buffer States: The Issue of Sovereignty. In *Buffer States in World Politics,* edited by John Chay and Thomas E. Ross. Boulder, CO: Westview.

Marshall, Monty, Keith Jaggers, and Ted Robert Gurr. 2002. Polity IV Project: Political Regime Characteristics and Transitions, 1800–2000. Center for International Development and Conflict Management, University of Maryland.

Martin, John Bartlow. 1966. *Overtaken by Events: The Dominican Crisis from the Fall of Trujillo to the Civil War.* Garden City, NY: Doubleday & Co.

Martínez-Fernandez, Luis. 1993. Caudillos, Annexationism, and the Rivalry between Empires in the Dominican Republic, 1844–1874. *Diplomatic History* 17 (4): 571–97.

Matthews, Chris. 2004. Interview with Zell Miller. *Hardball with Chris Matthews*. MSNBC, September 1.

Mattingly, Garrett. 1955. *Renaissance Diplomacy*. London: Jonathan Cape.

McEvedy, Colin, and Richard Jones. 1978. *Atlas of World Population History*. New York: Penguin Books.

McLean, David. 1979. *Britain and Her Buffer State: The Collapse of the Persian Empire, 1890–1914*. London: Royal Historical Society.

Mearsheimer, John J. 1994. The False Promise of International Institutions. *International Security* 19 (3): 5–49.

Missed Signals in the Middle East. 1991. *Washington Post Magazine*, Mar. 17.

Mitchell, B. R., ed. 1982. *International Historical Statistics: Africa and Asia*. New York: New York University Press.

———, ed. 1993. *International Historical Statistics: The Americas, 1750–1988*. New York: Stockton Press.

———, ed. 1998. *International Historical Statistics: Europe, 1750–1993*. New York: Stockton Press.

Mitchell, Nancy. 1999. *The Danger of Dreams: German and American Imperialism in Latin America*. Chapel Hill: University of North Carolina Press.

Mohamedou, Mohammad-Mahmoud. 1998. *Iraq and the Second Gulf War: State Building and Regime Security*. San Francisco: Austin & Winfield.

Morrow, James D. 2001. The Institutional Features of Prisoners of War Treaties. *International Organization* 55 (4): 971–92.

Mueller, John. 1988. *Retreat from Doomsday: The Obsolescence of Major War*. New York: Basic Books.

Muir, Ramsey, R. F. Treharne, and Harold Fullard, eds. 1965. *Muir's Historical Atlas: Ancient, Medieval and Modern*. London: George Philip and Son.

Musallam, Musallam Ali. 1996. *The Iraqi Invasion of Kuwait: Saddam Hussein, His State and International Power Politics*. London: British Academic Press.

National Geographic Society, 1999. *National Geographic Maps*. Washington, DC, CD-ROM.

Nelson, William Javier. 1990. *Almost a Territory: America's Attempt to Annex the Dominican Republic*. Newark: University of Delaware Press.

Nettl, J. P. 1968. The State as a Conceptual Variable. *World Politics* 20 (4): 559–92.

Newbury, C. W., and A. S. Kanya-Forstner. 1969. French Policy and the Origins of the Scramble for Africa. *Journal of African History* 10 (2): 253–76.

Ninkovich, Frank A. 1999. *The Wilsonian Century: U.S. Foreign Policy since 1900*. Chicago: University of Chicago Press.

Oneal, John. 2003. Measuring Interdependence and Its Pacific Benefits: A Reply to Gartzke and Li. *Journal of Peace Research* 40 (6): 721–25.

Oneal, John, and Bruce Russett. 1997. The Classical Liberals Were Right: Democracy, Interdependence, and Conflict, 1950–1985. *International Studies Quarterly* 42 (1): 267–93.

―――. 2001. Clear and Clean: The Fixed Effects of the Liberal Peace. *International Organization* 55 (2): 469–86.

Organski, A.F.K., and Jacek Kugler. 1980. *The War Ledger*. Chicago: University of Chicago Press.

Oulette, Judith A., and Wendy Wood. 1998. Habit and Intention in Everyday Life: The Multiple Processes by Which Past Behavior Predicts Future Behavior. *Psychological Bulletin* 124 (1): 54–74.

Packer, George. 2005. *The Assassins' Gate: America in Iraq*. New York: Farrar, Straus and Giroux.

Palmer, R. R., ed. 1957. *Rand McNally and Company Atlas of World History*. Chicago: Rand McNally and Company.

Parry, Clive, ed. 1969. *The Consolidated Treaty Series, 1648–1919*. Dobbs Ferry, NY: Oceana.

Parry, Clive, Charity Hopkins, International Law Fund, British Institute of International and Comparative Law, and Great Britain. 1970. *An Index of British Treaties, 1101–1968*. London: H.M.S.O.

Partem, Michael Greenfield. 1983. The Buffer System in International Relations. *Journal of Conflict Resolution* 27 (1): 3–26.

Pierce, Edward Lillie. 1893. *Memoir and Letters of Charles Sumner*. Boston: Roberts Brothers.

Posen, Barry R. 1993. Nationalism, the Mass Army, and Military Power. *International Security* 18 (2): 80–124.

Prucha, Francis Paul. 1997. *American Indian Treaties: The History of a Political Anomaly*. Berkeley: University of California Press.

Rahman, H. 1997. *The Making of the Gulf War: Origins of Kuwait's Long-Standing Territorial Dispute with Iraq*. Reading, UK: Ithaca Press.

Ray, Rajat Kanta. 1995. Asian Capital in the Age of European Domination: The Rise of the Bazaar, 1800–1914. *Modern Asian Studies* 29 (3): 449–554.

Rector, Chad. 2003. Federations in International Politics. Ph.D. Dissertation, Department of Political Science, University of California—San Diego, La Jolla, CA.

Reiter, Dan, and Allan C. Stam. 2002. *Democracies at War*. Princeton, NJ: Princeton University Press.

Richardson, James D., ed. 1911. *Compilation of the Messages and Papers of the Presidents*. New York: Bureau of National Literature.

Ricks, Thomas E. 2006. *Fiasco: The American Military Adventure in Iraq*. New York: Penguin Press.

Risen, James. 2000. Secrets of History: The CIA in Iran. *New York Times,* April 16, A1.

Roberts, Michael. 1964. Great Britain and the Swedish Revolution, 1772–73. *Historical Journal* 7 (1): 1–46.

Robinson, David. 1975. The Islamic Revolution of Futa Toro. *International Journal of African Historical Studies* 8 (2): 185–221.

Ronda, James P. 1999. "We Have a Country": Race, Geography, and the Invention of Indian Territory. *Journal of the Early Republic* 19 (4): 739–55.

Rosecrance, Richard. 1986. *The Rise of the Trading State: Commerce and Conquest in the Modern World*. New York: Basic Books.

Ross, Thomas E. 1986. Buffer States: A Geographer's Perspective. In *Buffer States in World Politics,* edited by John Chay and Thomas E. Ross. Boulder, CO: Westview Press.

Rotberg, Robert I. 2003. Failed States, Collapsed States, Weak States: Causes and Indicators. In *State Failure and State Weakness in a Time of Terror,* edited by Robert I. Rotberg. Washington, DC: Brookings Institution.

Rousseau, Jean-Jacques. 1985. *The Government of Poland.* Translated by Willmoore Kendall. Indianapolis: Hackett Pub. Co.

Rubin, Barry. 1993. The United States and Iraq: From Appeasement to War. In *Iraq's Road to War,* edited by Amatzia Baram and Barry Rubin. New York: St. Martin's Press.

Russell, Ruth B. 1958. *A History of the United Nations Charter: The Role of the United States, 1940–1945.* Washington, DC: Brookings Institution.

Russert, Tim. 2003. Interview with Vice-President Dick Cheney. *Meet the Press.* NBC News, March 16.

Sahabi, Houshang. 1990. *British Policy in Persia, 1918–1925.* London: Frank Cass.

Schroeder, Paul W. 1994. *The Transformation of European Politics, 1763–1848.* Oxford: Oxford University Press.

Schultz, Kenneth A., and Barry R. Weingast. 2003. The Democratic Advantage: The Institutional Sources of State Power in International Competition. *International Organization* 57 (1): 1–40.

Setear, John K. 2004. Taking Both Biology and International Law Seriously. Typescript, University of Virginia Law School.

Shepherd, William R., ed. 1956. *Historical Atlas (with Supplement by C. S. Hammond & Company).* 8th ed. Pikesville, MD: Colonial Offset Company.

Sicker, Martin. 1988. *The Bear and the Lion: Soviet Imperialism in Iran.* New York: Praeger.

Siegel, Jennifer. 2002. *Endgame: Britain, Russia, and the Final Struggle for Central Asia.* New York: I. B. Tauris Publishers.

Signorino, Curtis S., and Ahmed Tarar. 2006. A Unified Theory and Test of Extended Immediate Deterrence. *American Journal of Political Science* 50 (3): 586–605.

Simon, John Y., ed. 1995. *The Papers of Ulysses S. Grant.* 26 vols. Carbondale and Edwardsville: Southern Illinois University Press.

Singer, J. David, Stuart Bremer, and John Stuckey. 1972. Capability Distribution, Uncertainty, and Major Power War, 1820–1965. In *Peace, War, and Numbers,* edited by Bruce M. Russett. Beverly Hills, CA: Sage Publications.

Singer, J. David, and Melvin Small. 1966. Formal Alliances, 1815–1939: A Quantitative Description. *Journal of Peace Research* 1:1–32.

———. 1991. Diplomatic Missions Received by Each International System Member, 1817–1970. Ann Arbor, MI: ICPSR.

———. 1993. National Material Capabilities Data, 1816–1985. Ann Arbor, MI: ICPSR.

Small, Melvin, and J. David Singer. 1969. Formal Alliances, 1816–1965: An Extension of the Basic Data. *Journal of Peace Research* 3 (1): 257–82.

———. 1982. *Resort to Arms: International and Civil Wars, 1816–1980*. Beverly Hills, CA: Sage Publications.

Smith, Alastair. 1995. Alliance Formation and War. *International Studies Quarterly* 39 (4): 405–25.

Smith, Anthony D. 1988. *The Ethnic Origins of Nations*. Oxford, UK: Blackwell Publishers.

Smith, Joseph. 1979. *Illusions of Conflict: Anglo-American Diplomacy toward Latin America, 1865–1896*. Pittsburgh: University of Pittsburgh Press.

Smith, Theodore Clarke. 1901. Expansion after the Civil War, 1865–71. *Political Science Quarterly* 16 (3): 412–36.

Sotomayor, Arturo. 2004. The Peace Soldier from the South: From Praetorianism to Peacekeeping? Ph.D. Dissertation, Department of Political Science, Columbia University, New York.

Spykman, Nicholas J., and Abbie A. Rollins. 1939. Geographic Objectives in Foreign Policy, I. *American Political Science Review* 33 (3): 391–410.

Stein, Janice Gross. 1992. Deterrence and Compellance in the Gulf, 1990–1991: A Failed or Impossible Task? *International Security* 17 (2):147–79.

Stone, Randall. 1995. *Satellites and Commissars: Strategy and Conflict in the Politics of Soviet-Bloc Trade*. Princeton, NJ: Princeton University Press.

Strang, David. 1991. Anomaly and Commonplace in European Political Expansion: Realist and Institutional Accounts. *International Organization* 45 (2): 143–62.

Strange, Susan. 1996. *The Retreat of the State: The Diffusion of Power in the World Economy*. New York: Cambridge University Press.

Suri, Jeremi. 2003. *Power and Protest: Global Revolution and the Rise of Detente*. Cambridge, MA: Harvard University Press.

Syrop, Konrad. 1957. *Spring in October: The Polish Revolution of 1956*. London: Weidenfeld and Nicolson.

Szulc, Tad. 1965. *Dominican Diary*. New York: Delacorte Press.

Tannenwald, Nina. 1999. The Nuclear Taboo: The United States and the Normative Basis of Nuclear Non-use. *International Organization* 53 (3): 433–68.

Taras, Ray. 1997. The Making of Post-bipolar Buffer States: Mongolia and Nepal. *International Politics* 34 (4): 449–76.

Temperley, Harold William Vazeille, Institute of International Affairs, and Royal Institute of International Affairs. 1920. *A History of the Peace Conference of Paris*. London: H. Frowde and Hodder & Stoughton.

Thomas, Ward. 2000. Norms and Security: The Case of International Assassination. *International Security* 25 (1): 105–33.

Thornton, A. P. 1954. British Policy in Persia, 1858–1890, I. *English Historical Review* 69 (273): 554–79.

———. 1955. British Policy in Persia, 1858–1890, III. *English Historical Review* 70 (274): 55–71.

Tilly, Charles. 1990. *Coercion, Capital, and European States*. Cambridge, MA, and Oxford, UK: Blackwell.

Tir, Jaroslav, Philip Schafer, Paul Diehl, and Gary Goertz. 1998. Territorial Changes, 1816–1996: Procedures and Data. *Conflict Management and Peace Science* 16 (1): 89–97.

Toft, Monica Duffy. 2003. *The Geography of Ethnic Violence: Identity, Interests, and the Indivisibility of Territory.* Princeton, NJ: Princeton University Press.

United Nations Security Council Resolution 1483. 2003. May 22.

Van Evera, Stephen. 1999. *Causes of War: Power and the Roots of Conflict.* Ithaca, NY: Cornell University Press.

Vasquez, John A. 1993. *The War Puzzle.* Cambridge and New York: Cambridge University Press.

Walt, Stephen M. 1987. *The Origins of Alliances.* Ithaca, NY: Cornell University Press.

Walter, Barbara. 2001. *Committing to Peace: The Successful Settlement of Civil Wars.* Princeton, NJ: Princeton University Press.

Walters, F. P. 1952. *A History of the League of Nations.* London: Oxford University Press.

Waltz, Kenneth N. 1979. *Theory of International Politics.* New York: McGraw-Hill.

Wandycz, Piotr Stefan. 1974. *The Lands of Partitioned Poland, 1795–1918.* Seattle: University of Washington Press.

Ward, Olivia. 1990. Iraqis Roll Dangerous Dice but Experts Say Their Stay in Kuwait Will Be Short. *Toronto Star,* Aug. 3, A17.

Weber, Max. 1946. Politics as a Vocation. In *From Max Weber: Essays in Sociology,* edited by H. H. Gerth and Wright Mills. New York: Oxford University Press.

Weinberg, Gerhard L. 1994. *A World at Arms: A Global History of World War II.* Cambridge and New York: Cambridge University Press.

Welles, Sumner. 1928. *Naboth's Vineyard: The Dominican Republic, 1844–1924.* 2 vols. New York: Payson & Clarke.

Wendt, Alexander. 1999. *Social Theory of International Politics.* Cambridge: Cambridge University Press.

White, Gifford, ed. 1966. *The 1840 Census of the Republic of Texas.* Austin: Pemberton Press.

Williams, Beryl J. 1966. The Strategic Background to the Anglo-Russian Entente of August 1907. *Historical Journal* 9 (3): 360–73.

Wohlforth, William C. 1991. The Stability of a Unipolar World. *International Security* 24 (1): 5–41.

Woodward, Bob. 2004. *Plan of Attack.* New York: Simon & Schuster.

Yamaguchi, Kazuo. 1991. *Event History Analysis.* Newbury Park, CA: Sage.

Yapp, M. A. 1987. British Perceptions of the Russian Threat to India. *Modern Asian Studies* 21 (4): 647–65.

Zacher, Mark W. 2001. The Territorial Integrity Norm: International Boundaries and the Use of Force. *International Organization* 55 (2): 215–50.

Zahlan, Rosemarie Said. 1978. *The Origins of the United Arab Emirates: A Political and Social History of the Trucial States.* London: MacMillan.

Zamoyski, Adam. 1992. *The Last King of Poland.* London: J. Cape.

Zartman, I. William, ed. 1995. *Collapsed States: The Disintegration and Restoration of Legitimate Authority.* Boulder, CO: Lynne Rienner Publishers.

Ziblatt, Daniel. 2004. Rethinking the Origins of Federalism: Puzzle, Theory, and Evidence from Nineteenth Century Europe. *World Politics* 57 (1): 70–98.

Zielinski, Jakub. 1999. Transitions from Authoritarian Rule and the Problem of Violence. *Journal of Conflict Resolution* 43 (2): 213–28.

Zinner, Paul E. 1956. *National Communism and Popular Revolt in Eastern Europe: A Selection of Documents on Events in Poland and Hungary, February–November, 1956.* New York: Columbia University Press.

Index

Page numbers in italics refer to tables.